THE INCREDIBLE DISCOVERY OF NOAH'S ARK

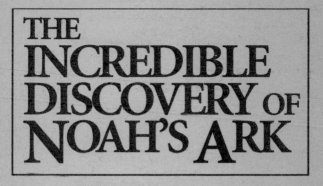

CHARLES E. SELLIER &
DAVID W. BALSIGER

A Book That Is the Basis of a CBS-TV Network Special

A DELL BOOK

Published by
Dell Publishing
a division of
Bantam Doubleday Dell Publishing Group, Inc.
1540 Broadway
New York, New York 10036

ISBN: 0-440-21799-7

Printed in the United States of America

Published simultaneously in Canada

April 1995

10 9 8 7 6 5 4 3 2 1

OPM

ACKNOWLEDGMENTS

The authors wish to express their appreciation to Regina Spencer Sipple for her editorial assistance on this book and to the numerous experts quoted herein who granted interviews for this book and the related television special.

EXPERT INTERVIEWS

Experts who granted interviews for this book and the television special are usually not footnoted. All interviews were conducted in 1992.

SCRIPTURE USAGE

TABLE OF CONTENTS

DEDICATION

This book is dedicated to the brave twentieth-century explorers and expeditioners who have advanced the search for Noah's ark on Mount Ararat in eastern Turkey. Those who stand above all others for their contributions and are most deserving of this appreciative dedication include Eryl Cummings, Fernand Navarra, Dr. John Morris, Dr. Elfred Lee, Don Shockey, Col. James Irwin, Carl Baugh, Dr. Charles Willis, Bill Crouse, John McIntosh, Dick Bright, Mary Irwin, Scott Van Dyke, Chuck Aaron, A. J. Smith, John Libi, Gunnar Smars, Dr. Ahmet Ali Arslan, Ray Anderson, John Bradley, and Orhan Baser.

Significance of
Finding Noah's Ark

If the Ark exists at about the 15,500-foot elevation, and its details match those described in Genesis, we would all be descended from Noah and his family, who lived about 5,000 years ago. This would mean that we were all cousins. What would the world be like if most people understood that?

Walter Brown, Ph.D., Mathematician/Physicist

The discovery of Noah's Ark, in my estimation, would prove conclusively the authenticity of the Genesis account of a worldwide Flood. It constitutes the one remaining link to the pre-Flood world.

Roger Oakland, Author/Science Educator

The finding of the 450-foot-long remains of an ancient boat near the top of the 17,000-foot Mt. Ararat would be one of the most important events in all of history. It would shatter a century of skeptical opposition to the Bible.

Brad Sparks, Author/Archaeological Researcher

Imagine having an artifact to study from before the Flood. We know very little about that period, and it might shed much new light on the interpretation of the early chapters of Genesis. These chapters are among the most attacked by liberal scholars who maintain the flood account is largely myth.

Bill Crouse, Publisher, *Ararat Report*

Evolution inevitably, although to varying degrees, rests on the assumption of uniformity, that "the present is the key to the past." There is no room in this view for a mountain-covering global flood. To find the Ark at a high elevation would destroy the very concept of uniformity, the basic assumption upon which evolution rests. It would probably ring the death knell of evolutionism.

John D. Morris, Ph.D., Professor of Geology

The only common denominator of the three major Western religions that we know of is Noah's Ark. Islam, Christianity, and Judaism all say that there was in fact an Ark. If it were found in this time of crisis in the Middle East, would it not have a tendency to unite the people . . . Can it be wrong to look for it under this circumstance?

Jack Donohue, International Government
Relations Consultant

No event in Scripture is doubted as much as Noah's Ark and the accompanying global Flood. To find the Ark would silence the detractors and increase the faith of many.

Carl Baugh, Ph.D., Author/Museum Curator

1

ANCIENT MYSTERY IMPACTS WORLD

The process of scientific discovery is, in effect, a continual flight from wonder.

Albert Einstein

A GREAT MYSTERY LIES HIDDEN HIGH ON A PERMA-nently snow-covered mountaintop in eastern Turkey. This mystery has influenced all the civilizations of the world and is reflected in their literature throughout the ages. This mystery has perplexed and challenged explorers for nearly 5,000 years.

A man-made artifact, the object of this mystery has attracted the attention of the CIA and the Russian KGB. Both Russian and U.S. spy satellites as well as reconnaissance planes from these countries and NATO allies have secretly photographed this strange object protruding from the snow-capped summit. The photographs remain "top secret" and are stored in underground military vaults in the United States and hidden in the KGB chambers of the Kremlin.

TREASURE OF AGHRI DAGH

For centuries hundreds have traveled to Aghri Dagh
—in Turkish, *Ağri Daği,* "the Mountain of Pain"—
hoping to get even a glimpse of this legendary treasure. Many explorers have not survived the arduous
climb up into steep, unstable slopes covered with
volcanic rock, ice, glaciers, and deep, snow-covered
crevasses. On this mountain, violent storms with
high winds can develop, quickly dropping temperatures to more than 50 degrees below zero. The
hazards to climbers from avalanches, thieves, wild
animals, poisonous snakes, and even modern-day
terrorists have taken the lives of many adventurers.

The very few who have been fortunate enough to
avoid injury or death and have come back with eyewitness accounts of this ancient artifact—even with
photographs to back up their stories—have met with
calamities. All the privately held photographs of this
mysterious object have disappeared. In one case, the
owner was murdered for his pictures. Many of the
other eyewitness photographers have long since
died, taking to the grave the whereabouts of their
pictures documenting this ancient mystery.

What is this mysterious artifact explorers risk
their lives trying to find? Why is it so important for
the superpowers to keep the photographs locked in
top-secret military vaults? Why do Washington and
Moscow refuse to declassify these pictures? The only
specific historical document that can be used to
identify this object is the Holy Bible. In the Book of
Genesis, the Bible records the landing of a large,
wooden boat "on the mountains of Ararat." Could it

really be the biblical ark of Noah that rests on Mount Ararat? Maybe it's some other large boat or even an ancient building. And if it's not Noah's ark, how did this other artifact get buried in the ice and snow at such a high elevation? What ancient people would have put it there, and why?

A FARFETCHED IDEA

The very idea of Noah's ark on Mount Ararat does seem farfetched. Just as Pompeii was buried and thought to be only a legend for 1,500 years, and the Great Sphinx of Giza was hidden in sand with its existence questioned for 2,000 years, the mysterious Noah's ark hidden for nearly 5,000 years may still be waiting to be discovered. Critics, however, scoff at the biblical account as mere legend.

The ancient city of Troy was also considered to be a legend until Heinrich Schliemann, who dreamed of finding it from the time he was a boy, hired diggers and found this notable city in Turkey. Maybe once again Turkey is about to reveal to the world the greatest archaeological find of this millennium. Mount Ararat could indeed be the resting place of the ark of Noah that the Bible claims saved mankind and the animal species from the devastating global flood described in Genesis.

Still, this is one mystery in which answering questions only raises more. If it's Noah's ark, why all the secrecy by our government? Does disclosing the photographs of this wooden boat endanger U.S. national security? What scientific evidence substantiates the incredible claims that Noah's ark not only exists but has been found on a mountaintop? How could a wooden ship possibly survive to the present day when many ancient cities made of stone have already crumbled into rubble?

Consider this even more provocative question: How could Noah—a citizen of an ancient civilization —build a giant vessel sturdy enough to survive a cataclysmic worldwide flood? Where did he get his engineering plans and tools to build the ark? And where is the evidence that the flood described in Genesis even occurred?

WHAT SOLVING THE MYSTERY COULD MEAN

Even if we can answer scientifically all the questions that surround this mysterious and controversial biblical account, does finding Noah's ark have any real relevance in our world today?

"For many of us today, religious beliefs seem old-fashioned, unscientific, and not particularly relevant in people's lives," says Dr. Tim LaHaye, author of more than thirty bestselling Christian books and Washington, D.C., radio commentator on the syndicated radio program, *Capitol Report.* "If the ark of Noah can be discovered, it will mean that the Bible cannot be written off as just a collection of legends, but must be considered more as fact.

"The discovery of the ark will make us reexamine what religious teachings of all faiths have to say about very important issues such as death, immortality, and how we live our daily lives," explains Dr. LaHaye.

Another perspective on the significance of finding Noah's ark comes from Jack Donohue, who has been a U.S. presidential advisor and consultant to heads of state around the world. "The three major religions in the world, Judaism, Christianity, and Islam, all have in their sacred writings the story of Noah's ark. Suppose we can prove the ark exists. Suppose we can prove that the Genesis account is not a fairy-tale. These groups have been tearing each other apart in the Middle East for centuries. Just think what a unifying force the ark could be for the Jews, Moslems, and Christians—for all the peoples of the world!"

As the late editor of *National Geographic* said several years ago regarding Noah's ark: "It will be the greatest archaeological find in human history and the greatest event since the resurrection of Christ. It will alter all the currents of scientific thought."

BEGINNING YOUR JOURNEY

Join us now for a thought-provoking journey as we turn back the hands of time and look at the world through the eyes of Noah—as we scientifically examine the entire Noah's ark and Flood accounts recorded in the Bible.

Modern technology and experts in virtually every scientific field have been utilized to objectively and thoroughly scrutinize all of the available evidence regarding this biblical ship. Reports of those who claim to have been inside of this mysterious vessel have been carefully examined, and satellite photos obtained from foreign governments have been analyzed in an effort to verify the accounts. Wood brought back from the ship by eyewitnesses has been scientifically tested and dated.

Absolutely nothing in our investigation of the mystery of Noah's ark has been intentionally eliminated or overlooked. This book is not a religious quest to prove the Bible, but rather a scientific and archaeological search to discover, identify, and report the truth.

The evidence alone will challenge your understanding of our past and stimulate your thinking about our future as we journey along the path to the incredible discovery of Noah's ark.

Our journey begins with a highly probable event one day long, long ago . . .

2

PREPARING FOR DOOMSDAY

It is a blessed thing that in every age
someone has had the individuality enough
and the courage enough to stand by his own
convictions.

Robert G. Ingersoll (1833–1899)

SALTY BEADS OF SWEAT BURNED AS THEY FELL INTO
Noah's eyes. He stopped hammering the heavy
plank above his head and wearily wiped the perspiration away with his dusty forearm. Stepping back on
the platform, he surveyed the noisy activity around
him—pounding hammers, the cracking of huge
beams, men cursing and shouting commands.

Almost twenty men were working on the third
level of the ark—and he could have used fifty more.
It had been a long, difficult job to build this enormous craft; a task filled with delays, injuries, and
unforeseen dangers.

Noah cupped his mouth with his callused hands.
"Stop working!" he yelled. "Let's rest for a while
and get a cool drink. Go tell the others." Noah
waited patiently as his message was called down to

those working at the other end of the massive structure—nearly 450 feet away.

The sounds of hammering and sawing quickly died down and Noah took a deep breath. The rich, warm air was filled with the smells of freshly hewn wood and boiling sap resins. Lost in his thoughts, Noah sat on a stack of planks and drew a long drink of water from his goatskin bag before splashing a little on his face.

His rough, sweat-drenched tunic clung to his body, and he seemed to ache all over. But nagging worries irritated him more than sore muscles. Finding and keeping good workers was a constant and growing problem. He also had difficulty keeping the materials and completed work safe from thieves and vandals. Noah and his sons took turns guarding the construction site at night, but even that wasn't always enough.

Silently, he cried out to God in sheer frustration. He wondered how and when they would ever be able to finish this monumental project. Nothing seemed to go smoothly anymore, and no one seemed to care that the end was so very, very near.

"Something troubling you, Father?" Japheth, the "fair one" jumped down on the platform from the scaffolding above. The youngest of Noah's sons, he was slender but strong, with a smile just like his mother's. He drank from Noah's goatskin bag.

"Oh, I am just thinking about the work that still needs to be done and the number of men we'll need when it's time to load the provisions. The grain . . ." Noah paused and dropped his head, sighing deeply.

"We finished fifteen cubits of wood this morning and if we have enough men tomorrow, we can probably make fifteen more," Japheth said encouragingly. "The ark will be finished soon. You should be happy, not sad. So what's troubling you?"

Noah gave Japheth a doleful glance. "It's nothing, son. You and your brothers have done a good job and the work will be over soon. I just . . ."

"You're really thinking about the workmen who will die if they still refuse to believe, aren't you, Father?" Japheth sat quietly beside Noah. "You've done your best to warn them; each man must decide for himself." Noah looked up and smiled at the son too young to be so wise. Japheth gave his father a reassuring pat on the shoulder before scrambling back up the scaffolding again.

Noah was a man of extraordinary courage and faith who found favor in the eyes of God. He lived with his wife, Naamah, and their children in the lush, green valley of Mesopotamia surrounded by gently rolling hills. The land was beautiful, but the people were violent and cruel.

UNIMAGINABLE WICKEDNESS

In the Bible, Genesis, chapter six, tells us:

> The Lord saw how great man's wickedness on the earth had become, and that every inclination of the thoughts of his heart was only evil all the time. The Lord was grieved that he had made man on the earth, and his heart was filled with pain. So the Lord said, "I will wipe

mankind, whom I have created, from the face of the earth—men and animals . . ."

Genesis 6:5–7, NIV[1]

So God said to Noah, "I am going to put an end to all people, for the earth is filled with violence because of them. I am surely going to destroy both them and the earth. . . .

I am going to bring floodwaters on the earth to destroy all life under the heavens, every creature that has the breath of life in it. Everything on earth will perish."

Genesis 6:13, 17

Although the people of Noah's day were intelligent and advanced in their achievements, they sought pleasure through unimaginable wickedness. They flaunted their evil in blatant sexual abuse. They sacrificed their children to pagan gods. They practiced violence and lawlessness as a way of life. Finally, their evil became intolerable to God.

"Whatever other sins that ancient man was guilty of . . . the biblical record, anthropological findings, and archaeological evidence indicate ancient civilizations were violent and in continuous conflict," according to Dr. Clyde McCone, professor emeritus of anthropology at California State University in Long Beach, California.

"Apart from the Bible, we find independent accounts telling us much the same story about the conditions in civilization at the time," says Father Michael Hanifin, an Old Testament Bible educator and parish priest in southern California. "Both ancient Greek and Hebrew writings indicate that there was a great deal of corruption and brutality among the populace. There were many murders—human life was cheap indeed."

The world had become such an evil place that it had even lured away some members of Noah's own family—a fact that was a constant source of pain in his heart. Only his wife, Naamah, and their three sons, Shem, Ham, and Japheth, believed God and his instructions to Noah—and even they had moments of doubt.

His sons loyally worked on the ark in spite of the mocking, brutal people who took great delight in harassing them. The ark was a burning reminder of Noah's preaching of repentance, and it seemed to make the people angrier all the time. Although it was a dangerous time to go against the crowd, the young men and their wives believed the warnings of God's coming judgment and chose to trust Noah. His fate would be theirs, too.

Out of the corner of his eye, Noah noticed a loud group of extremely tall men talking to some of his workers and offering them wine. They were the Nephilim. Giants, these men were enormous, cunning, and evil. Their presence meant trouble. Noah scanned the platforms and dirt below for his oldest son, but the brawny Shem was nowhere in sight.

"Hey, old man," one of the giants yelled, scooping up a rock from the dark soil and hurling it in Noah's direction. "We'll turn this into a nice big brothel when you finally finish it. There'll be plenty of room for everyone—even animals!" The men howled with laughter as they passed around a jug of wine.

Some of the workers resting in the shade laughed,

too, and quietly started egging the Nephilim on, hoping for a fight that would delay their return to work.

Noah faced the giants squarely, his voice firm and bold. "You will soon face God's judgment if you . . ." But they drowned out his words with swearing, crude gestures, and laughter as they turned to walk away, beckoning the workers to follow.

"Judgment from God? What god? And rain?" they sneered. "Who's ever heard of water falling from the sky? You're crazy, you old fool, and one of these days . . ."

"Back to work men—now!" Noah shouted as he quickly descended the ladders. "There will be no pay if you do not work a full day."

On the ground, the Nephilim looked even more imposing than from above. Noah was dwarfed by the fierce-looking men with the bronzed, muscular bodies. As he marched closer to them he was almost overwhelmed with the stench from their wine and filthy clothes. Their piercing eyes were filled with a wild hatred. Noah suppressed the uncomfortable fear welling up inside and spoke in forceful tones.

"If you want to go with these men, then go, but if you are here to work, then get back to work now! I will only pay if you work a full day."

"Don't listen to him; come and have some fun," one of the drunken Nephilim demanded. Then he stepped forward and pointed at Noah. "And as for you, old man, you haven't seen the last of us."

With a silent prayer and steely determination, Noah stood his ground and repeated his command.

His second son ran up and stood by his side. Together they stared silently at the giants and their crew, wondering what would happen next. . . .

SUPERMEN

Who were the Nephilim? We know very little about them apart from what is recorded in the Bible. Genesis 6:4 tells us:

> The Nephilim were on the earth in those days—and also afterward—when the sons of God went to the daughters of men and had children by them. They were the heroes of old, men of renown.

"The Nephilim were the unnatural offspring of man and fallen angels," says Bible commentator Chuck Missler, author of twenty books, including *The Flood of Noah*, *The Rise of Babylon*, and *The Persian Gulf Crisis*. "This unnatural intervention in the lives of mankind was the reason for the Flood, and Noah's uncontaminated genealogy was a factor in him being selected to survive it."

The theory that the Nephilim were the offspring of demonic beings and humans is still controversial. Some scholars maintain that the term only refers to the line of Cain, the wicked son of Adam and Eve, intermarrying with righteous descendants who followed God. Many believe the Nephilim were giants, as the King James version of the Bible translates. Whether giants or normal-sized human beings, they had become very evil and violent. The results of their immoral carnage are well documented by ancient historians.

THE WORLD OF NOAH

The world Noah and his family lived in was quite different than you might imagine. Instead of being primitive, the ancient civilizations destroyed by the Flood were highly advanced in many fields, including astronomy, metallurgy, agriculture, weaponry, mathematics, and architecture. Their remarkable intelligence, abilities, and accomplishments have intrigued scientists for centuries.

But when did Noah live? What do we know about the pre-Flood world? How do we know that ancient men even had the tools and technology necessary to build a great ship like the ark?

Chronology is the science dealing with the division of time, enabling us to arrange events in order of their occurrence, or to assign correct dates to ancient events—such as when Noah lived! We can use one or more of four different types of chronology to determine this answer: astronomical, geological, archaeological, and political-historical.

"We can accurately calculate when Noah lived," says Gene Faulstich, founder of the Chronology History Research Institute in Ruthven, Iowa, "using astronomical data and historical data from the Bible and other ancient manuscripts. The ancients kept very accurate and detailed records of their observations of the sun, moon, and sky.

"Astronomy is an exact science, and by examining the astronomical information recorded by these ancient astronomers, it's possible for us to determine on our calendar when these events actually took place. In other words, based on Noah's records found in the Genesis account, and astronomical computer analysis, we have determined that he began building the ark in 2465 B.C., with the first rains falling in 2345 B.C.," explains Faulstich.

ANCIENT MAN'S ACHIEVEMENTS

Let's look at some of the archaeological evidence of ancient man's abilities and achievements to get a better idea of the world in which Noah lived before the Flood and immediately thereafter. According to Roger Oakland, a respected author-lecturer and science educator, "If we look at the evidence left to us by ancient civilizations, we find that the further back we go, the more amazing are the accomplishments.

"The ancient Minoans on the island of Crete were highly advanced. Some of the reconstruction of their temples that were destroyed catastrophically reveals that they had tremendous abilities, architectural skills, and artistic design in their buildings. They used inlaid stone, natural ventilation and air-conditioning.

"We can look at ancient Egyptian artifacts such as daggers—some of which are electroplated. Electroplated artifacts have been found literally around the ancient world.

"The ancients were also able to make batteries and generate electricity. The ancient Mayans were able to calculate the solar year to be 365.2420 days—accurate within 2/10,000th of a day.

"Even more amazing is the recent discovery of a Chinese woman buried over 2,100 years ago. Today, her body is still so perfectly preserved that X-ray technicians were able to determine the contents of her last meal. Her body was buried at the base of a mound and when it was excavated, they found a very complex system of coffins. Within the sarcophagus, they found many interesting things—a compact containing rouge, lipstick, powder, brush, silk gloves, and a silk scarf. They also found lacquerware and musical instruments—exactly what the Bible claims the people of the past were able to do!"

Other ancient achievements are just as amazing and leave researchers with numerous difficult questions. For instance, the largest stone in the Third Pyramid in Egypt weighs more than 319 tons and was cut with a precision that rivals what modern man can cut using lasers and computers today. Many of the stones in this pyramid and in ancient temples around the world fit together so perfectly that you can't even slip a piece of paper between them— astounding architectural achievements by ancient man.

In England, researchers have found that the stones composing the strange ruins of Stonehenge weigh fifty tons each and apparently had to be moved uphill at least a hundred miles to their present location. Scientists still can't be certain what Stonehenge was used for, but popular theories include one or more of the following: an enormous lunar calendar, a pagan temple, a navigation school, an eclipse predictor. A worship site is the most likely explanation, as pagan worshippers still periodically assemble there for rituals.

How could ancient people construct temples and pyramids so mathematically and astronomically precise? Such incredible feats can be compared with the information we are only able to obtain today through the latest satellites and computers. Were these people really that advanced?

"We tend to think of ancient man as being very uncivilized," says Dr. Donald Chittick, holder of several patents in alternate fuels, and a retired professor of earth science and chemistry, who has lectured around the world. "However, archaeological evidence shows us that the contemporaries of Noah had a very high level of scientific activity. For example, researchers have found ancient electric batteries in the Middle East. They used copper and iron instead of carbon and zinc like we do, but the batteries definitely worked and were used to electroplate daggers and other objects with gold."

Besides electroplating applications, it's believed these "Baghdad" batteries, found in 1936 in an archaeological site near Baghdad, Iraq, were used to illuminate underground crypts and tombs. Both Babylonian and Egyptian high priests, and perhaps even common folks, may have been adept at producing electrical energy.

The world's first known working seismometer—a device that registers earthquakes—was built in A.D. 132. More than 2,000 years ago a Chinese astronomer noted the moons of Jupiter—long before Galileo "discovered" them. The first model airplane, found in 1898 in a Middle East archaeological dig and now on display in the Cairo Museum with a replica shown at the Smithsonian Aviation Museum, shows ancients understood flight. This 2,200-year-old model airplane has wings that angle slightly downward at the ends—the exact same improved wing design first used in modern times on the supersonic Concorde!

"Archaeologists have also found an analog computer on a sunken ship in the Aegean Sea," notes Dr. Chittick. "It was used to make maps that were generally more accurate than the ones we could make before the advent of satellites. In fact, until very recently, we believed that their maps were in error because they showed two bodies of land representing Antarctica. Now we've found that their maps were accurate and ours were in error.

"In California," Dr. Chittick says, "a geode was found with an ancient version of a spark plug inside. . . . Now, these artifacts are not unique. There is ample evidence to show that there were very advanced civilizations spanning the globe. Then they were inexplicably wiped out—presumably by the Flood."

TUBAL-CAIN FORGED METALS

The Bible gives us another clue to the abilities of the people in Noah's day. According to the Book of Genesis, Tubal-Cain "forged all kinds of tools out of bronze and iron." The Bereshith Rabba Jewish tradition tells us that Naamah, the sister of Tubal-Cain, was Noah's wife. If that is true, then it would be logical to assume that Noah had access to metal tools to aid him in the construction of the Ark. Artifacts found in that region of the Middle East confirm that the people of Noah's day not only had metal tools but also metal household objects and metal pagan idols, some with elaborate decorations.

"There was an exciting discovery in 1934 of a wood-handled metal hammer encased in sedimentary deposited limestone (Ordovician stone)," says Carl Baugh, a Texas paleoanthropology educator and museum curator. "The metal was analyzed and found to contain 96.6 percent iron, 0.74 percent sulfur and 2.6 percent chlorine. In order to compound chlorine with metallic iron it requires a process perfected only within the last ten years. Therefore, it had to be natural circumstances under which this ancient hammer was forged because of the elemental constituency requiring complete elimination of ultraviolet radiation. This artifact confirms that ancient man had extensive knowledge of metallurgy and used metal tools before the Flood."

According to Roger Oakland, ancient belt buckles have been found in China that were made from an alloy of 5 percent manganese, 10 percent copper, and 85 percent aluminum. Scientists are amazed that ancient man knew how to extract aluminum from bauxite ore because it involves using temperatures in excess of 1,000 degrees plus electrolysis!

Also in China, archaeologists have found swords dating back more than 2,200 years that were made of thirteen different metals alloyed together. In the Mount Ararat region alone, Russian scientists have found 500 ancient furnaces presumably used for smelting bronze. The ability of ancient man to mine and use a number of different metals has been proven by artifacts found around the world.

It seems obvious, then, that the tools and technology necessary to construct an enormous ship were available to Noah. But what do we know about the ark itself? Let us again turn back the hands of time and view the ark under construction.

BUILT TO LAST

"Now compress the pieces of wood together with these rocks," Shem instructed the workman struggling under the weight of a stack of unfinished beams and planks. "Once the gopherwood is cured, it will be as strong as your ax."

The man muttered something under his breath as he stacked the planks.

Using a coarse brush, Shem spread some of the boiling sap resins on a huge strip of wood and then added another layer. The air was filled with the fragrance of freshly hewn wood and the sticky resins boiling over a fire nearby. Several men were using the same procedure on another stack of planks not far away—layering strips of wood with sap resins, then using large stones to compress the boards as they dried.

All around them were thick planks drying in the sun and stacks of hardened wood ready to be used on the ark. Workmen were swarming over the massive three-story ship now nearing completion. The man by Shem broke off a toothpick-size sliver from a plank and put it between his teeth as he stretched his arms in the bright noonday sun. "Why not just use whole beams of wood to build this crazy ship?" he asked, helping Shem lift the heavy planks up to the workbench. "Why go through all of this extra work?"

"Because, my friend, once these strips are coated with that boiling sap, they'll be so strong nothing can break them. This great ark will last forever."

"It may last forever," the man laughed, "but it's never going to see any water this far inland. ... ."

The historical account in Genesis 6:14–16 outlines God's instructions for building the ark:

> So make yourself an ark of cypress wood; make rooms in it and coat it with pitch inside and out. This is how you are to build it: The ark is to be 450 feet long, 75 feet wide and 45 feet high. Make a roof for it and finish the ark to within 18 inches of the top. Put a door in the side of the ark and make lower, middle and upper decks.

What is "cypress wood," or "gopherwood," as it is called in some translations? The answer is still being debated, but for many years scientists believed that the gopherwood referred to in the Bible was either white oak, cypress, cedar, or larch. All of these species are strong and durable. They were used by various ancient civilizations for shipbuilding and could be found growing in the rich, pre-Flood area of the Middle East.

"GOPHERWOOD" WAS LAMINATION PROCESS

Dr. Don Shockey, a cultural anthropologist and founder of the Foundation for International Biblical Exploration and Research, has recently discovered a

startling new explanation for the term "gopherwood."

The ancient term for "gopherwood" in Hebrew was not
the name of a particular species of wood but rather the
term for a unique lamination process using resins made
from sap. It's ingenious. I met a man raised in
Jerusalem and he told me that in the past, they would
cut the bark of a certain tree and collect the sap. Then,
if you put this protective sap on two pieces of wood,
clamped them together and left them overnight, by the
next day, you could not break the splice. The wood on
either side would break first.

He said that they don't use this system any more
because it discolors the wood. After he told me that, a
light went off in my head. We obviously don't have a
"ply" tree, yet we have plywood. The idea of
"gopherwood" being a process rather than a species
makes perfect sense to me. From an engineering point
of view, a laminated beam made from several different
types of wood glued together, cured and hardened,
would be structurally superior, in terms of tension and
resiliency, than just a single block of wood.

We've found that this process is currently being used
in Canada to commercially produce a laminated wood
product. In this process, they take small strips of wood
with resin hydrocarbons, heat and pressurize it and then
cure it with microwaves. Once it's cured, the wood
becomes harder than steel. We know that in England
and in Russia, they have been using this process to
make weapons of war—including gun barrels—and there
are indications that our own Stealth bomber has some
of this in it because it's vegetable material and can't be
detected like metal.

It is absolutely amazing, and there are endless uses
for it. Insects won't bother it, and this process makes the
wood water-resistant, fire-resistant—practically

indestructible. I am convinced that Noah had this
technology and used it building the ark.

It is interesting to note that several of the eyewitnesses who have reported seeing the ark on Mount
Ararat specifically mentioned that the mighty beams
they saw looked as if they were made of laminated
wood. A piece of wood brought back from Mount
Ararat by a twentieth-century ark expeditioner, and
believed to be from the ark, generated this unusual
note from a carbon-14 lab:

> The dark bituminous-like coating turned out not to be
> just surface coating but distributed throughout the
> wood. This was very surprising as we have only
> encountered this before in dealing with pressure-
> penetrated woods. Still further of a mystery is how this
> material [bituminous coating] could be impregnated so
> deeply within the wood fibers without the use of
> present-day technology.

Noah was also instructed to cover the ark with
"pitch" inside and out. Webster's dictionary defines
"pitch" as a thick, dark, sticky substance derived
from either the sap of a conifer or made from the
distillation of coal tar, asphalt, or petroleum. Pitch, a
bituminous substance, is found in oil-bearing regions
like the Middle East, and during Roman times, it
could even be found floating in great lumps on the
Dead Sea. It was usually mixed with straw or reeds
to fill cracks in the hull of a ship to make it water-
proof. However, it was generally used only to coat
and seal the exterior of a ship.

Why would God tell Noah to coat the ark inside

and out—especially if gopherwood was actually the name for laminated beams glued together and covered with resins? Wouldn't that be overkill? Or is it possible that God wanted the ark to be waterproofed and completely sealed inside and out to ensure that it would survive all of the natural elements—to the present day?

THE SIZE OF NOAH'S ARK

God told Noah to build the ark and make it 300 by 50 by 30 cubits. In ancient times, the cubit was defined as the distance between an average man's elbow and fingertips, ranging anywhere from 17 inches to 24 inches in length. Using 18 inches as the cubit measurement most frequently cited by the ancient Hebrews, this would make the ark 450 feet long, 75 feet wide, and 45 feet high. An enormous craft by any definition.

Presumably constructed out of laminated wood, stained dark with resins, and covered with a shellac-like pitch, the ark would have resembled a dark brown, rectangular barge or a shoe box. Not pretty, but very functional. Once again, that's essentially the same description as that given by many of the eyewitnesses, including those who have never read or heard the biblical account.

Let's use some comparisons to visualize the size of the completed ark. Experts tell us that the ark was the length of one and one-half football fields, or approximately the size of a four-story apartment building a block long.

"Noah's ark is one-half the size of the great ocean

liner, the *Queen Mary*," says George Williamson, an avid ark researcher and hobbyist from the Chicago area. "The roof of the ark could have easily held twenty volleyball/basketball courts and the interior of the ark contained 1.5 million cubic feet—enough room for 170 railroad boxcars!"

Imagine! It would have taken 280,000 cubic feet of timber—between 9,000 and 13,000 planks—to construct the ship, which has been estimated at a little more than 4,100 tons deadweight.[2]

With ocean water figured at 35 cubic feet per ton, the ark, completely empty, would float with its bottom about 4.3 feet below water. Loading the ark to where it would sink to a depth of 15 feet would require 10,000 tons of cargo, and to 20 feet, 15,000 tons. Assuming the weight of the animals as 100 tons, and allowing each animal twenty times its own weight in food plus twenty times its weight in water for a year, the cargo would weigh about 4,000 tons. We don't know, of course, how many tons of animals were aboard, but these calculations are within reason and extremely conservative. It is calculated that the fully loaded ark probably weighed about 24,300 tons.

The ark was undoubtedly a great ship, very different from the Sunday school drawings and cartoons so many people are familiar with. A massive vessel, it was built to withstand the violent forces of the greatest catastrophe the earth has experienced to date.

WINDOWS IN THE ARK

"The design is absolutely ingenious," claims Dr. El-fred Lee, an internationally acclaimed archaeological illustrator and college professor. He has worked with several of the ark eyewitnesses to re-create what they've seen on Mount Ararat. "The only window on the ark was about eighteen inches high and spanned the center of the ship for 450 feet. There was a small overhang that covered this window to keep the rain out. It would have appeared kind of like a catwalk down the center of the rooftop. This unique design provided light and ventilation to all three levels and, because of its position, probably kept out the water from even the most violent waves. It was a simple, yet marvelous design."

Shipbuilders have discovered that the ark's length to breadth equals a ratio of six to one, meaning it would be a slow-moving vessel. In 1604, Pieter Jansen, a Dutch merchant, commissioned a shipyard to build a scale model of the ark according to the measurements given in the Book of Genesis. This craft proved to be not only more seaworthy than contemporary vessels, but its gross tonnage was one third larger than ships built to more modern designs.[3]

Rev. Eddie Atkinson, a pastor and model ark builder who has studied the design of the ark for many years, explains,

> The ark was exactly six times longer than it was wide, and it set the standard for all other oceangoing vessels. Had the ark been square, for instance, it would have just spun around in circles. The dimensions of the ark

made it so stable in rough seas that the same length-to-width ratio is still being used by modern shipbuilders today. In fact, during World War II, the USS *Oregon* and the USS *New Mexico* were built specifically on this model, using the same length-to-width ratio as the ark.

It wasn't until 1884 that a ship larger than the ark was built and that was the passenger ship *Eturia,* built by the Cunard line. Also, the *Guinness Book of World Records* claims that the ark was the longest wooden ship ever built.

ARK WAS EXCEPTIONALLY STABLE

Marine engineering experts agree that with its low center of gravity, the ark was exceptionally stable and could have remained seaworthy indefinitely—even through the most violent waves and storms.

"In terms of the hydrodynamic forces," says Dr. Henry Morris, professor emeritus of hydraulics engineering, "this ark would have been very stable. In fact, the balance between the buoyant force, the gravitational force, and the wave force would be such that the ark would right itself if it were tilted anywhere from zero to 90 degrees. It would be practically impossible to capsize."

We wanted to test the various stability theories put forth by Dr. Morris. So we had a model ark built to the same proportions as the biblical ark. We had our tests conducted in San Diego, California, by an internationally known hydraulics laboratory that asked us not to disclose its name. The following interview was conducted with the hydraulics lab project director after the testing:

Q. *How high a wave could the ark have survived?*
A. The tests showed that the ark could survive waves higher than you would ever encounter in the ocean.
Q. *What is the maximum height of a wave the ark could have survived based on your test results?*
A. More than a 200-foot wave without capsizing. But there are no waves that large in the ocean.
Q. *What about tidal waves—would they ever be high enough to capsize the ark?*
A. A peaked up tidal wave could maybe reach 100 feet or more, but this would happen only close to shore in shallow water, not in the ocean.
Q. *Then because of the ark's unique design ratio, it could have survived any type of wave produced by the ocean?*
A. If it were hit broadside by a gigantic wave, it's conceivable that it could have been capsized. However, the surprising thing revealed by the tests was that the ark naturally propelled its bow into the waves. It's a remarkably stable vessel.[4]

Like the giant ships of today, the ark's low center of gravity gave it remarkable stability. The deeper it sank in the water because of its heavy cargo, the more stable it became. The results of these tests proved conclusively that the ark was not only seaworthy and remarkably stable, but that it had a natural tendency to propel its bow into the waves—making it almost impossible to capsize.

ARK INSPIRED LATER SHIPBUILDERS

The ark was a masterpiece of engineering that has inspired shipbuilders and mariners throughout history. Our investigation of other aspects of this mysterious vessel will continue in later chapters, but let's examine what we know to be true about the ark so far.

We know that Noah had access to the metal tools and technology necessary to build this great ship and that it was begun in 2465 B.C. The ark was constructed with a variety of indigenous woods laminated together with resins, then coated inside and out with pitch. It had three levels, with a window down the length of the roof, and it didn't have sails or a rudder.

This incredible design, as given to Noah by God, kept a very precious cargo—the only remnants of selected human and animal life on earth—safe and dry for a year while floating on the dark, cold turbulent seas that covered the entire planet.

"We'll go with them to have some fun," one of the builders of the ark scoffed with wine dripping from his chin, "but we'll be back after we've used up our money. And when this ship is finished, we'll put it to good use—long after you're gone."

Five of the workers left with the Nephilim, and Noah turned back toward the ark without a word.

"Father, aren't you going to try to stop them?" Ham demanded angrily. "We need their help."

"No, son, it would be useless. Besides, what good will they be to us full of wine? We can finish with the men we have left. Come now, the time is short and we have much to do to get ready. . . ."

Notes

[1] All scripture quotations, unless otherwise indicated, are taken from the Holy Bible, New International Version®. NIV® Copyright© 1973,

1978, 1984 by International Bible Society. Used by permission of Zondervan Publishing House. All rights reserved.

[2]Frederick A. Filby, *The Flood Reconsidered* (Grand Rapids: Zondervan Corporation, 1971), p. 88.

[3]Ibid., p. 100.

[4]David W. Balsiger and Charles E. Sellier, *In Search of Noah's Ark* (Los Angeles: Sun Classic Books, 1976), pp. 117–118.

3

CREATURES ON THE ARK

By perseverance the snail reached the ark.
Charles Haddon Spurgeon (1834–1892)

HEAVY CRATES, BAGS OF GRAIN, AND ENORMOUS water jugs were stacked all over the compacted dirt near the massive wooden loading ramp of the ark. The air was heavy and still cool in the early morning light.

Japheth yawned and stretched his back and was bending down to pick up another crate when he spotted them.

"Father, look!"

"It's unbelievable!"

"Shem, Naamah, everyone come quickly!" Noah cried out. "Hurry, we must help them."

"Quick. Open the cages," Naamah called to her daughters-in-law. "Put the birds inside. Gently . . ."

From every direction—walking, crawling, or drifting down from the sky—animals and birds of every kind were making their way to the ark. All were moving quickly as if they were being driven by an unseen force.

Noah and his family had been loading provisions on the ark when Japheth first spotted the deer tentatively coming close to the ramp—the only door to the ark.

"Look, they're coming to us on their own! They're walking into their cages. It's amazing!"

"Here, drop some grain and see if they'll follow you inside."

"Look, Father, they want to come inside," Japheth laughed. One deer was eating grain out of his hand and the other was nuzzling his leg as he backed up the ramp. "All right, all right, come with me. . . ."

"Look at all the birds. Here. Scatter grains near the cages. See if they'll go inside."

"They trust us."

"I can't believe it. They want to come inside!"

"It's wonderful. . . ."

"This is just as the Lord said it would be," Noah laughed. Suddenly his voice turned somber. "We need to get them all safely into their stalls and cages because the time is short." He surveyed the darkening sky. "Very short. The animals can sense it."

In chapters six and seven, the writer of Genesis records this spectacular event. God told Noah:

"I am going to bring floodwaters on the earth to destroy all life under the heavens, every creature that has the breath of life in it. Everything on earth will perish. But I will establish my covenant with you, and you will enter the ark—you and your sons and your wife and your sons' wives with you. You are to bring into the ark two of all living creatures, male and female, to keep them alive with you. Two of every kind of bird, of every kind of animal and of every kind of creature that moves along the ground will come to you to be kept alive. You are to take every kind of food that is to be eaten and store it away as food for you and for them."

Noah did everything just as God commanded him.

The Lord then said to Noah, "Take with you seven of every kind of clean animal, a male and its mate, and two of every kind of unclean animal, a male and its mate, and also seven of every kind of bird, male and female, to keep their various kinds alive throughout the earth. Seven days from now I will send rain on the earth for forty days and forty nights. . . ."

On that very day Noah and his sons, Shem, Ham and Japheth, together with his wife and the wives of his three sons, entered the ark. They had with them every wild animal according to its kind, all livestock according to their kinds, every creature that moves along the ground according to its kind and every bird according to its kind, everything with wings. Pairs of all creatures that have the breath of life in them came to Noah and entered the ark. The animals going in were male and female of every living thing, as God had commanded Noah. Then the Lord shut him in.

Genesis 6:17–22; 7:1–4, 13–16

Probably nothing in the biblical account of Noah's ark and the Flood creates more controversy than the animals themselves. Critics pose a number of tough questions that need scientific answers: How did Noah capture the animals? How many different kinds of animals were aboard? How could eight people care for the animals? With the help of scientists and Bible scholars, these questions can possibly be answered.

HOW NOAH CAPTURED THE ANIMALS

First, how could Noah possibly gather or "trap" representatives of every kind of animal on earth?

Dr. Arthur J. Jones, a scientist at Bournville College in Birmingham, England, who has done years of research on the questions raised by the Genesis account of Noah's ark, has carefully studied the original Hebrew terminology in his search for answers. Writing an article in the *Ararat Report,* the world's only regularly published newsletter on Noah's ark research activities, Dr. Jones says,

> The Lord commanded Noah to "cause [the animals] to come into the Ark" [Genesis 6:19] and to "take to you [into the Ark—Genesis 7:1] all the behemah and birds [Genesis 7:2–3]." He was told that they would come to him for this purpose.[1]

The Bible says in several other places that the animals came to Noah. There wasn't any need to trap them. "Genesis 6:20 says 'pairs of all shall come unto you.' Genesis 7:9 says 'two by two they came unto Noah.' Genesis 7:15 says 'they came unto Noah unto the ark two by two.' Genesis 7:16 says 'the coming ones came male and female of all flesh.' "[2]

But why would the animals go to the ark on their own? It doesn't seem to make sense; we do not see wild animals walking up to people in today's world.

"Animals are directed by instinct to respond naturally to numerous stimuli," says Dr. Ken Cumming, Harvard-trained professor of biology at the San Diego–based Institute for Creation Research. "Scientifically, we've learned that animal response to potential disaster seems linked to magnetic field fluctuations in the brain—and it's also connected to how they respond to polarized light.

"You can actually see many animals react to imminent danger right before natural disasters such as hurricanes or earthquakes and before magnetic disturbances such as thunderstorms.

"The earth-shattering tectonic events that released the waters from under the surface of the earth," says Dr. Cumming, "would have affected the earth's magnetic fields and could have produced the stimuli that warned the animals of pending danger. Their natural instinct to seek safety and shelter may well have been what drew them to the ark."

Interestingly, even today predators and prey will run together or stay in close proximity for long periods without incident while fleeing forest fires and other natural disasters.[3]

Also, we know from the fossil record that the climate of the pre-Flood earth was very different from that of the post-Flood earth—something we'll discuss in a later chapter. Tropical plants have been found frozen in Arctic regions, and fossil evidence has shown that desert regions were once covered with lush vegetation. If the entire pre-Flood earth had a similar temperate climate, it's possible that representative animals of all kinds on the earth at that time could have been found in the general area where Noah built the ark. They wouldn't have had far to travel after they sensed the coming disaster.

HOW MANY ANIMALS
CAME ABOARD?

Another frequently asked question involves the number of animals on the ark. According to taxonomists, there are more than 1,072,000 known species of animals in the world today.

Dr. Richard N. Vineyard, a biology professor in Utah and a critic of the biblical account of Noah, says, "The question I would ask is quite simple: How could two of every living animal be brought aboard any vessel? The sheer numbers and weight would overwhelm a fleet of arks. I don't believe we can take the story of the ark literally."

But Dr. John Whitcomb, a retired professor of Old Testament Studies at Grace Theological Seminary who co-authored the book *The Genesis Flood,* explains this.

It doesn't say in the biblical account that "two of every single animal on earth was taken aboard the Ark." There were certain animals that didn't have to go on board, such as fish, water snakes, whales, insects, and other marine life that could survive in the water.

Also, it says that only two or seven of each "kind" were taken. The extra animals taken aboard the ark fell into the clean-animal categories and were to be used for sacrifices to God following the Flood. Some may have also been used for food and clothing in the post-Flood world.

"Each family of creatures on the earth today has a single pair of ancestors," says Dr. Kenneth Ebel, professor of biology at Christ College in Irvine, California. "Even though there are over 300 varieties of dogs in the world today due to selective breeding . . . they all have a single common ancestor. Considering the number of kinds of animals required to be put aboard the ark, there would have been ample room to load the ancestors of all the species we know today."

Well, just how many common-ancestor kinds went aboard the ark? According to Dr. Whitcomb, "We can deduce that only the following numbers of animal groups would have possibly been on the ark—3,700 known kinds of mammals; 8,600 kinds of birds; 6,300 kinds of reptiles; and 2,500 kinds of amphibians."

This would leave hundreds of thousands of different kinds of fish, tunicates (marine chordates like sea squirts), echinoderms (marine creatures like starfishes and sea urchins), mollusks (mussels, clams, oysters), coelenterates (corals, sea anemones, jellyfish), sponges and protozoans (microscopic single-cell creatures) to survive in the water.

In addition, aquatic mammals (whales, seals, porpoises), certain amphibians, a large number of the arthropods (lobsters, shrimps, crabs, water fleas, barnacles), as well as many species of worms and some insects could have survived outside the ark.

"According to my calculations," says Dr. Whitcomb, "there could have been as few as 2,400 animals on the ark or up to as many as 50,000 animals on the ark. While that seems like a huge discrepancy, it can be explained by the different estimates and definitions of the kinds of animals on the earth before the Flood.

"These 'kinds' never evolved or merged into each other by crossing over the divinely established lines of demarcation, but they have been diversified into so many varieties and sub-varieties (like the races and families of humanity) that even the greatest taxonomists have been staggered at the task of enumerating and classifying them.[4]

"Noah did not have a hopelessly impossible task," concludes Dr. Whitcomb. "The biblical record is totally credible." Dr. Ebel agrees, saying there would have been ample "room left over for Noah's family and supplies."

Genesis classifies some animals as "clean" and some as "unclean."

> Pairs of clean and unclean animals, of birds and of all creatures that move along the ground, male and female, came to Noah and entered the ark, as God had commanded Noah.
>
> Genesis 6:8–9

What do "clean" and "unclean" mean? Clean animals are generally described as non-flesh-eating, chewing a cud, and having a divided hoof. Many nonpredatory birds are considered clean, while camels (which chew the cud but do not have a divided hoof) and pigs (which have a divided hoof but do not chew the cud) are considered unclean.

Unclean animals are ones that do not have a divided hoof or chew the cud, and eat flesh.

It is difficult to determine exactly which animals in the "clean" and "unclean" categories were on the ark, but after studying numerous other biblical references, Dr. Jones came up with the following list of "clean" animals: deer, giraffes, pronghorns, cattle, antelopes, sheep and goats, pigeons, dodos, sand grouse, megapodes, curassows, grouse, pheasants, guinea fowl, turkeys, sparrows, finches, ducks, geese, and swans.

The "unclean" animals would include predatory and scavenging land birds, most water birds, bats, small rodents, lizards, and predatory mammals.

God's first instruction to Noah was that he bring the animals into the ark in pairs. Later, Noah was told the number of pairs. There would be one pair—male and female—of the unclean animals, but seven pairs of the clean animals—male and female—or fourteen animals in each clean group.

Bible students disagree on this point. Some contend there were only seven of each clean group, or three pairs plus one which Noah would sacrifice after the Flood.[5]

Dr. Jones, however, argues the seven-pair theory:

Four times (Genesis 6:19–20; 7:2–3, 8–9, 15) the account emphasizes that all the animals were taken into the ark in pairs. The account also makes it clear that the purpose was propagation: "to keep seed alive upon the face of all the earth" (Genesis 7:3).

The reasons for taking seven times more clean animals than unclean seems straightforward: first, clean animals were required for sacrifice; second, they would be required to provide clothing and food (Genesis 9:3) after the Flood (the environment being radically changed); third, as these were becoming vulnerable prey animals they required a head start for survival (Genesis 7:3).[6]

Assuming the average size of all the animals on the ark was about that of a sheep (since there are very few large animals, and even those could have been represented by young of their kind), how many animals would the ark hold?

Railroad stock cars carry approximately 120 sheep per deck which would be 240 sheep per standard, two-decked stock car. Since the ark had the volumetric capacity to carry approximately 100,000 animals the size of sheep, there was obviously more than enough room.[7]

It has been estimated that only 36 percent of the ark would have been filled with animals. However, since the ark was designed for long-term living rather than short-term transport, extra room would have been needed. Some of this space would have been taken up by the subdividing created for stalls, cages, and ramps and by all of the food required for man and animals for one full year. There also had to be enough internal free space for ventilation and water storage, and plenty of room for waste disposal, which most experts believe filled the bottom deck.

How could eight people possibly care for that many animals? Wouldn't it have been impossible? Let's imagine what it was like for Noah and his family after all the animals were on board.

HOW NOAH CARED FOR
THE ANIMALS

"Father, all of the animals are locked in their cages," Shem said, chewing on a piece of straw.

"Yes, we checked on all of them," Ham interjected wearily as he slumped down on a pile of rugs stacked against the dark brown wall.

"All of them?" Noah asked, surprised.

"Yes, all of them." Japheth nodded with his arm wrapped around his new bride. He squeezed her gently and she giggled.

"Good. Now we must divide up the responsibilities."

Noah looked around the large room at his tired family. This room on the first floor of the ark would be their communal kitchen and main living area for more than a year, so they had worked together to make it as comfortable as possible. It had a large, low table surrounded by cushions and blankets. Covered storage boxes that could be used for sitting or sleeping lined the walls.

Sunlight streamed through their only window, which ran the length of the ship high above them. They had oil lamps to use when it became dark, but for now, the sun cast streaks of light across the dark wood of their living area.

This was the first time they had stopped moving and come together since the door of the ark had been sealed shut. Looking at his beloved family, Noah felt a tightening in his throat as his eyes filled with tears.

"First, we must thank the Lord for bringing us

safely . . ." Noah paused, listening to the muffled voices of people laughing and yelling outside.

"Hey, Noah, what are you doing in there? We don't see any water yet. . . ."

"Yea, what are you doing in there? Trying to make water yourself?"

"You'll have to come out and face us sometime. . . ."

Noah shook his head and spoke softly to his family, his voice cracking. "They will not be laughing soon." Clasping his rough, callused hands together, he bowed his head and led his family in a prayer.

The voices outside caused Noah pain—but not because the people were mocking him. Even though the end was just a few days away, the people still did not believe; there would be no other chance to escape the coming judgment. The door was sealed.

"Oh, my loved ones," Noah said, turning to look at each of them before glancing sadly toward the voices outside, "this has been a difficult journey already—just building the ark and getting the animals safely inside. It's . . . it's impossible to imagine what it will be like when the waters come and all life outside . . ."

"We'll take care of preparing the food," Naamah interrupted, nodding her head toward her daughters-in-law. "And we will help to feed the birds and the other small animals on this level, dear." She looked down at her lap and smoothed out the folds in her skirt, unable to look at her husband's distraught face any longer.

"Yes," Japheth's beautiful young wife encouraged, "and we'll help with the larger animals too. It'll all work out."

"Good. Thank you. Your youth will serve you well." Noah smiled faintly. "This voyage to our new life will not be easy, but God will be with us and see us safely through this terrible time. . . . It is good to know that the Lord is merciful to those who seek his mercy." Noah bent down and kissed Naamah on the top of her head, then straightened up and smiled.

"Now, with all of the larger animals on the second level . . ."

"Father, I'll take the cats," Ham offered.

"I'll be happy to feed the elephants and the other large animals in the middle cages," Shem chimed in.

"I don't mind taking care of the livestock, Father," Japheth pronounced.

"Good. Thank you, my sons. Well, then . . . Let's rest for a short time. The judgment of the Lord on the earth will begin soon. . . ."

Skeptics discard the possibility that eight people could have fed the thousands of animals on board the ark. To support their argument, some have pointed out that during a twelve-hour day, each member of Noah's family would have had to feed one animal every three minutes.

Scientists tell us, however, that the living conditions on the ark, including the falling temperature, the reduced light, the restriction of movement, and the rocking of the ship would have caused most of the animals to go into a state of inactivity—like cows locked in their barn stalls during Midwestern winters. Motion and semidarkness are both known to have a calming effect on animals. These circumstances would have also caused most of the animals to eat less and sleep more than normal, and many animals would have gone into some form of hibernation.

Hibernation is only a small part of a wide spectrum of animal behavior. In the tropics, for example, many small animals go to sleep to avoid the peak of the dry season, a phenomenon called *aestivation,* which is very similar to hibernation. Even an occasional short period of unfavorable conditions is slept through by many animals. As for larger animals, such as bears, they will remain in a semidormant state in their dens for months at a time during the winter.

"Practically all reptiles and amphibians have the capacity of hibernation," says Dr. Henry Morris, coauthor of *The Genesis Flood.* "Mammals, being warm-blooded, do not have as great a need for it, and so at present, relatively few practice it. Nevertheless, it is probable that the latent ability to do so is present in practically all mammals."[8]

When animals are hibernating, they do not remain in that condition indefinitely, but arouse periodically in a rhythmic manner every few days or weeks. As soon as conditions on the ark improved, the animals probably awoke and ate. The ability to enter a prolonged sleeping period, however, is a fairly common property among animals.

"In the ark, we would expect that there would be a lot of darkness, mainly due to the storm above," says Dr. Cumming. "Under these quieting conditions, with lack of food and sleep in semidarkness— all of this added together would make the family of Noah more than adequate to care for the animals for even up to a year."

So the experts tell us that it would not have been difficult for eight people to look after their animal cargo. "The ratio of human caretakers to animals on the ark is similar to that in many modern zoos around the world," according to Dr. Whitcomb.

From what we are told through the Genesis account, it appears, then, that Noah would not have had an impossible task collecting or caring for the animals put into his care on the ark.

Rev. Eddie Atkinson, an ark-model builder and pastor in Dallas, Texas, has studied the account of Noah's ark in the Bible as well as numerous other ancient flood traditions. He has built several scale models of the ark. The most elaborate one contains more than 1,100 hand-carved animals and includes minute detail of what the ark's interior was like fully loaded with animals and supplies. Based upon his research, he believes that animals were placed only on the top two levels of the ark.

The top floor held all of the birds from one end to the center of the Ark. Then, there was probably a catwalk over the cages of the elephants and giraffes on the second floor. The other half of the top floor held the rodent cages, storage, the kitchen and living quarters for the eight members of Noah's family.

Then, on the second floor, there would be all the different kinds of cats including lions and tigers in cages at one end, then the cages for hippos and rhinos, with the cages for the elephants and giraffes in the middle, open from above. Next would come the horses, zebras, sheep and livestock and storage areas of food for the animals on the second level. The bottom level was undoubtedly used for garbage and waste.

Animal care involved more than feeding, of course. Stalls and cages would have had to be cleaned daily—at least when the animals were not hibernating. Manure would most likely have been stored on the lower deck. Computations by some San Diego zoologists indicate that up to 800 tons of manure accumulated in the lower deck during the year aboard the ark.[9]

HOW NOAH AND FAMILY LIVED IN THE ARK

How Noah and his family lived in the ark is also intriguing. Room would have been ample for food, water, and sanitation storage, and for exercising of the animals, with sufficient internal free space to prevent unbearable fouling or heating of the air. So the ark was built to maintain the best possible conditions for life.

With such provision for the animals, it is logical to assume the eight persons aboard also were comfortable. We must not ignore, either, the woman's touch to the living quarters. We can surmise Noah's wife and daughters-in-law made their cabins as pleasant as possible under the circumstances.

What kind of beds did they sleep in?

A bed in Bible days was simply a mat or blanket that could be carried in the hands. The poor often had no bed, except their outer garment. We can hardly consider Noah poor; he would have had to have wealth to hire work crews for the ark. Wealthy people had quilts or mattresses filled with cotton, which they spread on the floor or on a divan.

Divans were platforms about three to four feet wide. Sometimes they extended across one end of the room or around three sides and were elevated from six inches to a foot above the floor. By day they were used as a sofa; by night for sleeping.[10] It is possible that there were built-in divans in the family's living quarters.

Noah's family probably had other furniture, maybe even crude wooden tables for eating. Modern Arabs usually have nothing but a piece of skin or leather, a mat, or a linen cloth spread upon the ground for a table. Ancient Hebrews are supposed to have used a similar "table."

We don't know, of course, what the living customs were during pre-Flood times, but can assume that furnishings after the Flood evolved from the craftsmanship, designs, and traditions of Flood survivors.

What did the people on the ark eat?

Noah was commanded to bring food aboard the Ark for both the animals and his family.

Genesis 9:2–3 implies that before the Flood, people were vegetarians. After the Flood, God put the fear of man in the animal kingdom and told Noah, "Every moving thing that liveth shall be meat for you; even as the green herb have I given you all things." Meat became part of the post-Flood diet. The phrase, "even as the green herb," strengthens the evidence that Noah and his family were vegetarians before and during the Flood.

We can assume their diet included milk, eggs, bread, nuts, fig cakes, raisins, cheese, grains, grapes, herbs, olives, wheat, and other similar foods, since all these existed in ancient biblical times.

To make bread, Noah's family would have needed some means for baking. One type of oven still used in the Middle East is a great stone pitcher. A fire is made in the bottom among small flints and the dough is soon baked. Sometimes the dough is rolled out very thin and stuck on the outside surface of the heated pitcher. When it's baked, it falls off. Perhaps such an oven existed in Noah's day.

Frying pans existed in Old Testament times (Leviticus 7:9). There were deep vessels of iron used for boiling meat or baking bread. Also in existence were thin, flat iron plates on which bread could be quickly baked as on the griddles we have today. Conceivably, such baked foods were part of Noah's diet.[11]

Other cooking and eating utensils could have included earthenware pots and bottles, and skins. These were common in Bible days. We also know from the Bible that pre-Flood craftsmen were skilled in metalworks. It is conceivable that some of Noah's utensils were made of copper, gold, or silver. They could have been quite fancy.

Noah and his cargo were aboard the ark for about one year and ten days. They undoubtedly had their hands full feeding and caring for the animals and looking after their own needs, but it's obvious that their task was not impossible. Their ingeniously designed craft was well suited for the needs of both people and animals on a long voyage into a new world.

The account of Noah's ark raises other questions that critics are quick to point out in discrediting the story. If a flood was going to destroy the earth, where would all the water come from? And where would it all go afterwards? Even the people of Noah's day scoffed at the sight of the enormous barge resting on a dry plain near Shuruppak in Mesopotamia—now modern Iraq.

Notes

[1] Bill Crouse, *Ararat Report* 19 (Nov–Dec 1988), pp. 1–5. Published by Christian Information Ministries International, Richardson, TX.

[2] Ibid., pp. 1–5.

[3] Tim LaHaye and John Morris, *The Ark on Ararat* (Nashville: Thomas Nelson, Inc., 1976), p. 251.

[4] John C. Whitcomb and Henry M. Morris, *The Genesis Flood* (Phillipsburg, NJ: Presbyterian and Reformed Publishing, 1961), p. 66.

[5] Dave Balsiger and Charles E. Sellier, *In Search of Noah's Ark* (Los Angeles: Sun Classic Books, 1976), pp. 129–130.

[6] Ibid., p. 130.

[7] Whitcomb, *The Genesis Flood,* p. 69.

[8] Ibid., p. 71.

[9] Balsiger, *In Search of Noah's Ark,* p. 134.

[10] Ibid., p. 135.

[11] Ibid., p. 136

4

A WATERY GRAVE

Fear God, and give him glory . . . Worship
him who made heavens, the earth, the sea,
and the springs of water.

Revelation 14:7

SEVEN DAYS HAD PASSED SINCE THE DARK, MONO-
lithic ark had been sealed shut. On the first day,
many of Noah's neighbors had come to jeer and
watch the last of the provisions and animals being
taken aboard. But the number of people had dwin-
dled as the days went by and nothing happened.

It was a hilarious sight to the people, and travelers
went out of their way to see the huge ark. Strangers
couldn't believe the gossip that there were actually
thousands of animals inside, so big discussions
would ensue with the local experts. Men would
stroke their beards and sometimes share a jug of
wine as they pontificated on why a wealthy man
would lose his mind and build a great ship so far
inland—and then fill it with animals!

Everyone wanted to know what was going on in
there, and many hurled more than just insults at the
ark.

"Noah, when's your water falling from the sky?"

"Hey, did your gods forget?"

"Maybe you just heard them wrong . . ."

"You'll have to come out and face us sometime . . ."

But mocking and laughing at Noah's folly could only consume so much of one's time. Only a passionate few spent their days and nights outside of the ark —mostly watching to make sure that Noah and his family didn't try to sneak out and slip away unnoticed.

"Noah, we're still waiting."

"Hey," a man yelled, laughing, between bites of fruit, "it doesn't look like your boat has gone very far yet."

Preaching judgment to the people and calling for their repentance over the years, Noah had made many bitter enemies—enemies who wanted to humiliate him and settle the score.

"He's not going to tell us how to live our lives," a large woman with only a few teeth was telling a stranger. "We made sure of that. And when he comes out, I want to be here. Some of the men have plans for that Noah."

"Yes, that will be a celebration day," a young Nephilim sneered. "They have to come out eventually, and we'll be ready for them when they do."

The soft magenta sky was unusually dark this seventh morning, but no one was alarmed at first. Even when the first drops of rain fell, everyone had an explanation for them—birds, most likely.

But the sky, brewing ominously, grew very dark. Even the "ark-watchers" dismissed the idea that

Noah was right until the sky became like a dam bursting in the heavens.

Great sheets of rain pelted the earth and quickly turned the dust into puddles of mud.

The earth groaned like a woman about to give birth, and people became terrified as wrenching earthquakes below and thunderous explosions above signaled the violent pangs of judgment.

The shrill whistling sound of objects falling through the sky was carried in every direction by the wind. In a panic, the people who had been laughing and cursing Noah for years raced to the ark, covering their ears, screaming.

"The sky is falling!"

"Help us! The sky is falling!"

"Get out of my way," a man yelled, viciously knocking an old woman out of his way.

"We're going to die. . . ."

They pounded on the solid, high walls and clawed at the only entrance, begging Noah to open the ramp. In desperation, people climbed on top of others in an effort to reach the roof of the ark.

"Please, Noah. Save our children. . . ."

"Open the door—now!"

"Let us in there you. . . ."

Their unanswered pleas quickly turned into vile cursing as they kept pounding on the walls and screaming in vain. The wind lashed the rain like a whip, stinging their unprotected faces.

More and more people came running to the ark, shrieking at Noah and his family to let them in as the muddy fields turned into deepening lakes and the rumbling in the earth turned into a roar.

Their muffled pleas could be heard by everyone inside, who stood in stunned silence, eyes wide with horror. There was nothing they could do. The door had been sealed shut. No one could come in.

Noah shook his head sadly and gazed at Naamah. "It's started. The judgment has begun."

Genesis, chapter seven, gives us only a brief account of this event:

Noah was six hundred years old when the floodwaters came on the earth. And Noah and his sons and his wife and his sons' wives entered the ark to escape the waters of the flood. . . . And after seven days the floodwaters came on the earth.

The animals going in were male and female of every living thing, as God had commanded Noah. Then the Lord shut him in.

For forty days the flood kept coming on the earth, and as the waters increased they lifted the ark high above the earth. The waters rose and increased greatly on the earth, and the ark floated on the surface of the water. They rose greatly on the earth, and all the high mountains under the entire heavens were covered.

The waters rose and covered the mountains to a depth of more than twenty feet. Every living thing that moved on the earth perished—birds, livestock, wild animals, all the creatures that swarm over the earth, and all mankind. Everything on dry land that had the breath of life in its nostrils died. . . . Only Noah was left and those with him in the ark.

The waters flooded the earth for a hundred and fifty days.

Genesis 7:6–7, 10, 16, 17–23

FLOOD STORY RAISES QUESTIONS

This passage leaves us, once again, with many questions. Where did all of the water come from, and where did it all go after the Flood? Forty days and nights of rain alone couldn't provide enough water for a worldwide flood, could it? How could floodwaters possibly cover all the highest mountains? And what would have sparked such a massive deluge?

Critics quick to discount the Flood story because of these questions include a California field geologist, Tom Hill, who says, "There have been many devastating floods throughout man's recorded history. However, scientists and geologists have found no evidence of a single massive flood covering the entire earth in water for one hundred and fifty days."

Modern-day meteorologists tell us that even if all of the water in our atmosphere were to precipitate at the same time, it wouldn't produce more than two inches of water—hardly enough to float the ark, much less destroy all life on earth. We're talking about a global flood—not a big regional catastrophe like the 1931 Yellow River flood in China that covered an area the size of New Jersey and killed one million people.

We asked a number of scientists as well as Bible scholars to help us answer these difficult questions and explain some of the prevalent theories regarding our ancient earth.

WHERE DID THE WATER
COME FROM?

"The Bible says that water both from above and below flooded the earth," says California Bible educator and parish priest Father Michael Hanifin. "Rain from the heavens fell and the oceans flowed up over the land. There are different theories to explain where the water came from and why, but the Bible is clear, this Flood covered the entire earth."

"Most people don't realize how much water is on the earth," says Dr. Walter Brown, the former chief of science and technology at the Air War College and a retired professor of the U.S. Air Force Academy. "There's actually ten times more water in our oceans than land above sea level. In fact, if we could flatten out our earth and make it as smooth as a billiard ball, the water would cover the earth to a depth of nearly 9,000 feet. The earth could actually be called the water planet."

To put it another way, approximately 70 percent of the earth's surface today is covered by water. Only a little more than one quarter of the entire globe is not covered with water, and not even all of that is available for use by man. Large areas, including deserts, mountain ranges, and both polar regions, are closed to human habitation because of climate or other environmental limitations. That leaves only about one half of the land suitable for habitation by man.

We also know that while there is a great deal of water on and in our planet, very little moisture exists in the atmosphere above. What was the pre-Flood atmosphere like? Was it significantly different from ours today?

The fossil record and other evidences show that the earth and its atmosphere experienced a radical change during the Noachian Flood. The Chronology History Research Institute has analyzed the Flood astronomically and concluded that it began on Sunday, May 14, 2345 B.C.—but more about this in a later chapter.

The climate of the pre-Flood earth was moderate around the globe. Many scientists attribute this to a so-called "greenhouse effect" on ancient earth. This enormous global canopy of water existed as vapor, or in a frozen, crystallized form at the upper levels of our atmosphere.

"The first chapter of Genesis describes a firmament or atmosphere above the earth," says Dr. David Clark, a professor of New Testament Studies and chairman of the Division of Religion at Southern California College. "God created this to separate the waters above the firmament from the waters below the firmament. In describing the waters above the earth, the Bible suggests that in the time before the Flood, there was a water vapor or canopy surrounding the earth. This rich, dense cloud cover protected the earth, moderated the climate, and provided dew instead of rain prior to the Flood, as we see from Genesis 2:5–6."

"The idea of a water vapor or canopy surrounding the earth sounds somewhat bizarre," says Dr. Larry Vardiman, a professor of atmospheric science who has spent fifteen years researching the concept that a water-vapor canopy surrounded the earth in pre-

Flood days. "But actually, canopies are quite common among the planets of our solar system. Venus, Jupiter, and Saturn all have cloud canopies and thick gaseous envelopes surrounding them. Unlike the clouds and water-vapor canopy on earth, however, these clouds and gases are made up of carbon dioxide, sulfur dioxide, hydrogen, helium and ammonia."

Dr. Vardiman further explains,

> Under a water-vapor canopy, earth would have had a relatively warm, uniform temperature, high humidity, and increased atmospheric pressure. The climate may have been tropical from pole to pole and may have contributed to giantism in plants and animals and much longer life spans.
>
> The vapor canopy would have precipitated at most 40 feet of water directly. In addition, water released by volcanic eruptions during the flood would have kept heavy rain falling for forty days and nights becoming lighter as our present-day weather regime came into existence. Soon after the Flood, precipitation would have turned to snow on high mountains and in the polar regions causing the "ice age."

According to Donald W. Patten, a Seattle, Washington, based geographer and planetary catastrophist, the earth's pre-Flood atmosphere was comprised of approximately three to five times as much water vapor as is in today's atmosphere. And, like today, this water vapor was concentrated in the lower troposphere.

Dr. Patten, author of *The Flood of Noah,* has conducted extensive research on the evidence for a pre-Flood canopy. He also believes the sea-level surface temperature under this canopy was between 60 degrees and 70 degrees Fahrenheit and that the canopy was 3,000 to 5,000 feet thick and ranged between 5,000 and 10,000 feet above sea level. However, other scientists believe that the surface temperature of the earth under the canopy was closer to 90 degrees Fahrenheit.

While the canopy theory is somewhat controversial and still being studied, a great deal of growing scientific evidence supports it. However, the majority of water involved in the Flood did not come from the canopy, but from water already on or under the surface of the earth. Before examining where the waters "of the great deep" came from and what caused their sudden violent flooding of the earth, let's examine some more evidence for a pre-Flood canopy.

Imagine a world of huge dinosaurs, gigantic flying birds, and enormous plants and you probably have a good picture of what the earth was like in Noah's time. But with their relatively small lung capacity, how did these creatures get enough oxygen to stay alive? And why did plants grow so much larger before the Flood than they do today?

Explains Dr. Carl Baugh, a Texas museum curator and paleoanthropology educator,

> We've been doing extensive research into the context that produced the enormous sizes of plants and animals that can be found in the fossil record, and this equates with a pre-Flood model mandating that there had to be a pre-Flood canopy of some sort compressing the atmosphere.
>
> We know that the great dinosaurs such as Tyrannosaurus Rex had a relatively small lung capacity,

and yet tests indicate paleontologically, from the fossil record that is, that some of the dinosaurs reached tremendous heights. Seismosaurus, for example, could raise his head almost 70 feet in the air. Now something has to explain this anomaly compared to today's atmosphere. How could the largest dinosaurs oxygenate their deep cell tissues with such a small lung capacity?

At sea level today we have 14.7 pounds per square inch of atmospheric pressure. The largest dinosaurs needed more atmospheric pressure than that to oxygenate their deep cell tissues. Tests have determined that at two atmospheres of pressure, the entire blood plasma becomes saturated with oxygen. Therefore, a canopy, a firmament above the earth, compressing the atmosphere, would explain how the dinosaurs were able to survive and why plants were able to grow so much larger than they are today.

Also, from analyzing air bubbles trapped in fossilized tree resin, we have found that the pre-Flood atmosphere contained 30 percent oxygen as compared to our 21 percent oxygen today. With the ancient canopy over the earth creating approximately 27 pounds per square inch of atmospheric pressure and the air containing 30 percent oxygen as compared to our present 14.7 pounds per square inch of atmospheric pressure and 21 percent oxygen today, tests have determined that a man would have been able to run approximately 200 miles without getting winded.

We know that this canopy surrounding the entire earth performed several different functions. Water by its very nature filters out the ultraviolet rays that are harmful to man. In addition, the charged hydrogen in this water vapor or canopy of crystalline content would glow a magenta—that we would call pink. This perfect wavelength would have created a gentle pink glow in the sky.

Researchers have found that this is the exact wavelength that encourages the large growth and reproductive cells of plants. That means that this canopy would have increased the life span of man and the longevity of all biota.

In the mid-1980s, Dr. Kei Mori, professor of science and technology at Keio University in Tokyo, Japan, while testing light energy transmission systems for future consumer applications, unknowingly applied some pre-Flood atmospheric conditions to a tomato-plant test. To a cherry tomato plant he added increased atmospheric pressure around the stalk and filtered out the ultraviolet radiation. After two years his cherry tomato plant had not only thrived, but was a tree—sixteen feet tall—and had produced 903 tomatoes. Eight years later his plant was thirty feet tall and had produced more than 8,000 tomatoes. His test was an excellent scientific verification that the pre-Flood context would produce very large sizes such as we find in the fossil record.

A canopy, then, would also help to explain why tropical plants and fossils of tropical plants have been found frozen under Arctic and Antarctic ice.

James L. Hall, associate professor of biology at Liberty University and curator of the Museum of Earth and Life History in Lynchburg, Virginia, sums it up:

> Evolution is based on the principle of uniformitarianism, which says that the present processes were in operation in the past. But since animals were huge in the past, physical processes were much different.
>
>   The increased oxygen, two atmospheres of pressure produced by the canopy filtering out shortwave radiation, would have contributed to long life spans and hugeness in the fossil record.

The canopy would have moderated the temperature on the earth by filtering and diffusing the sunlight during the day and keeping the warm air from dissipating at night. Humidity, then, would rise to a saturation or near saturation level. As dewpoint was reached, a thick layer of nocturnal dew would have formed. Evaporation during the day would have been slow because there probably was no wind. Therefore, the earth would have been sufficiently and continuously watered by abundant condensation and slow evaporation.

In conjunction with the collapse of the canopy surrounding the earth's atmosphere, many scientists believe that water from subterranean sources also helped to cause torrential rains for forty days and nights.

What do we know about the floodwaters that came according to the biblical account? Genesis 7:11–12 says,

In the six hundredth year of Noah's life, on the seventeenth day of the second month—on that day all the springs of the great deep burst forth, and the floodgates of the heavens were opened. And rain fell on the earth forty days and forty nights.

From this account we can surmise that there were three sources that produced enough water for a global flood: the water-vapor canopy, subterranean pressurized reservoirs, and the sinking of land-masses or the rising of the ancient ocean seabeds.

Is there any significance in the fact that Genesis

7:11 says the subterranean waters "burst forth" before the "floodgates of heaven were opened?"

On the pre-Flood earth, a secondary source of water existed in vast subterranean heated and pressurized reservoirs either in the primeval crust or in the earth's mantle. Such a situation still exists today, although in lesser quantity.

A number of things could have triggered the eruption of the underground waters and caused the cataclysm. Dr. Henry Morris suggests a simple explanation: "The pressurized waters below the crust suddenly erupted at a point of weakness. Collapse at one point would cause a chain reaction leading to similar eruptions at many other points around the world."[1]

The resulting atmospheric turbulence, combined with immense amounts of dust blown skyward from erupting volcanoes, would begin condensation and precipitation of the canopy, he says. The process would be similar to modern-day cloud seeding to cause rain.[2]

Thus we see the possible significance of the order of destruction mentioned in Genesis 7:11. Subterranean upheavals within the oceans, volcanic eruptions and earthquakes, and the gushing forth of those waters triggered the opening of the windows of heaven, and the canopy waters poured upon the earth as torrential rains for forty days and forty nights before slacking off to light rain for the next 110 days.[3]

Dr. Frederick A. Filby, in his book *The Flood Reconsidered,* says,

Using the metaphors of ancient languages, the Bible records that the *windows* of heaven were opened and the *fountains* of the Great Deep (Abyss) were broken up. In other words, Noah was conscious of torrential rain and the oncoming of a huge tide, not from swollen rivers, but from the Great Deep, the ocean.

That the latter (ocean and subterranean water) was much greater than the former is clearly shown by the fact that the ark (both in the biblical and the Babylonian accounts) was carried northwards towards Armenia, whereas a river flood resulting from rain and geyser-type eruptions would have carried it out to the Persian Gulf.

Dr. Filby contends that many of the great earth movements happened during recent periods and are no doubt directly related to the biblical Flood catastrophe. "In fact, they increased to a tremendous crescendo."[4]

Picking up on Dr. Filby's contention that great earth movements occurred during the year-long Flood, we again turn to Dr. Brown. This former professor of mathematics at Massachusetts Institute of Technology (MIT) has advanced the scientific hydroplate theory to explain the geological and other events that took place during the Flood.

We can see on our planet seventeen very strange features that can now be systematically explained as a result of a cataclysmic, global flood—whose waters erupted from subterranean chambers with an energy release exceeding the explosion of thirteen billion hydrogen bombs.

This hydroplate explanation solves the origin of the Mid-Oceanic Ridge, salt domes, metamorphic rock, volcanoes, and magnetic patterns on the ocean floor and shows us just how rapidly our major mountain ranges formed. It explains coal and oil deposits, rapid continental drift, shelves and slopes, and why on the ocean floor there are huge trenches and hundreds of canyons and volcanoes. It accounts for the many things we see in our layered strata, including many fossil graveyards, the frozen mammoths, the so-called ice ages, and major land canyons—especially the Grand Canyon.

According to Dr. Brown, the pre-Flood earth probably had only one very large supercontinent, covered with lush vegetation. There were seas and major rivers. The mountains were smaller than today's—perhaps 9,000 feet high.

According to the hydroplate theory, the pre-Flood earth had a lot of subterranean water—about half of what is now in our oceans. This water was contained in interconnected chambers forming a thin, spherical shell, about half a mile thick, perhaps ten miles below the earth's surface.

If so, what would cause these chambers to erupt and flood the world? Dr. Brown explains,

> Increasing pressure in the subterranean water stretched the overlying crust layer, just as a balloon stretches when the pressure inside increases. Failure in the crust began with a microscopic crack which grew in both directions at about three miles per second. The crack, following the path of least resistance, circled the globe in about two hours.
>
> As the crack raced around the earth, the overlying rock crust opened up like a rip in a tightly stretched cloth. The subterranean water was under extreme

pressure because of the weight of the ten miles of rock pressing down on it. So the water exploded violently out of the rupture. All along this globe-encircling rupture, fountains of water jetted supersonically almost twenty miles into the atmosphere. The spray from this enormous fountain produced torrential rains such as the earth has never experienced—before or after.

The Bible states that "all the fountains of the great deep burst open" on one day, and it describes these events, about 5,000 years ago, which we can now tie together scientifically.

The high-pressure fountains eroded the rock on both sides of the crack, producing huge volumes of sediments that settled out of this muddy water all over the earth. These sediments trapped and buried plants and animals, forming the fossil record. The flooding uprooted vegetation, moving it to regions where it accumulated and quickly became coal and oil by processes we can duplicate in the laboratory today.

The "fountains of the Great Deep" and the expanding steam produced violent winds. Some of the water, jetting high above the cold stratosphere, froze into supercooled ice crystals and produced some massive ice dumps—burying, suffocating, and instantly freezing many animals—including the frozen mammoths of Siberia and Alaska.

This erosion widened the rupture, according to Dr. Brown. Eventually the width was so great that the compressed rock beneath the subterranean water chamber sprung upward—giving birth to the Mid-Oceanic Ridge that wraps around the earth like the seam of a baseball. The continental plates (the hydroplates), still with lubricating water beneath them, slid downhill away from the rising Mid-Atlantic Ridge.

"After the massive, slowly accelerating continental plates reached speeds of about 45 miles per hour, they ran into resistances, compressed and buckled," says Dr. Brown. "The portions of the hydroplate that buckled downward, formed ocean trenches. Those that buckled upward formed our mountain ranges. This is why the major mountain chains are parallel to the oceanic ridges from which they slid."

According to Dr. Brown, the hydroplates, in sliding away from the oceanic ridges, opened up very deep ocean basins into which the floodwaters retreated. On the continents, each basin (or bowl-shaped depression) was naturally left brimful of water—producing many post-Flood lakes. He describes it this way:

> Each lake that gained additional water from rainfall or drainage, spilled over its rim at the lowest point on the rim. That eroded a little notch in the rim, which allowed even more water to flow through the notch faster, eroding it even deeper. This process accelerated until the entire contents of many post-Flood lakes dumped through very deep slits forming canyons. The largest of these was the Grand Canyon. Just north and east of the Grand Canyon was a huge post-Flood lake that I have identified and named Grand Lake. It held more water than five of our Great Lakes combined. Grand Lake spilled over and eroded its dam just south of Page, Arizona, forming the Grand Canyon.

Wait just a minute. What a compelling theory of what happened during the Flood! But could the Grand Canyon really have been formed during or shortly after Noah's flood within a few days? Most scientific theories advocate that it formed over millions of years. Is there any hard evidence that canyons can form rapidly, as Dr. Brown contends?

Dr. Steven A. Austin, professor of geology at the ICR Graduate School in San Diego, California, has been studying the Mount St. Helens eruption and comparing what is observable there to the possible formation of the Grand Canyon. He claims this eruption is the most significant geological event of the twentieth century because it tells us much about strata, coal, and canyon formations.

The eruption of Mount St. Helens in Washington State on May 18, 1980, was initiated by an earthquake and rock slide. Pressure was released inside the volcano where superhot water turned to steam. The northward-directed steam explosion released energy equivalent to twenty million tons of TNT, which toppled 150 square miles of forest in six minutes. An enormous waterwave in Spirit Lake, north of the volcano, stripped trees from slopes as high as 850 feet above the lake. The total energy output, on May 18, was equivalent to 400 million tons of TNT—20,000 Hiroshima-size atomic bombs.

"Deposits of strata up to 600 feet in thickness have formed at Mount St. Helens since 1980," says Dr. Austin. "What is unique is that this strata accumulated in short periods of time—in some cases in less than a day. In the past, it was thought that these strata layers were formed slowly over hundreds or thousands of years.

"Rapid erosion occurred during the volcanic eruptions of Mount St. Helens. Mudflows were responsible for the most significant erosion. A mudflow on March 19, 1982, eroded a canyon system in the headwaters of the North Fork of the Toutle River Valley. This canyon, known as the 'Grand Canyon of the Toutle River,' is a one-fortieth scale model of the real Grand Canyon—and, it was formed in less than a week," explains Dr. Austin.

So eyewitness scientific evidence does exist confirming that not only can layered strata be laid down rapidly, but hills and gullies resembling badlands topography—or even the Grand Canyon—could have formed in very short periods of time instead of during the course of thousands or millions of years.

THE CATACLYSMIC TRIGGER

Getting back to the global Flood, we must ask the question, what was the trigger that set the events of the Flood in motion?

Some scientists theorize that the gravitational pull from a close planetary flyby caused the waters to "burst from the deep," and they cite numerous evidences to support this theory. A "domino effect" may have actually combined the cataclysmic results of a close planetary flyby with the hydroplate action, or the tearing apart of the earth's surface, releasing the subterranean waters to flood the earth.

"We have records from ancient civilizations around the world," claims Donald Patten, a geographer and planetary catastrophist, "that say the Flood was caused by a close planetary flyby and the ancient astronomers all state in their accounts that it was caused by Mars. In the Sumerian account it was Mars, in the Assyrian account it was Mars, and in the Chaldean account it was Mars. In India it was Mars and in the Egyptian Book of the Dead it was Mars. Almost all of the ancient civilizations left records of catastrophic flybys attributed to Mars.

"The Flood then," Patten continues, "was caused by the gravitational conflict created when Mars flew perilously close to the earth. The tides arose in the Indian Ocean to 5,000 or 6,000 feet high because the gravitational pull on the water was such that which way was up and which way was down became totally confused."

In his book *Worlds in Collision,* Immanuel Velikovsky also examines the records of ancient civilizations and concludes that they were almost universally afraid of Mars and/or Venus and worshipped them or tried to appease them—sometimes with human sacrifices. In addition to the civilizations cited by Mr. Patten, Dr. Velikovsky also lists the Romans, Greeks, Aztecs and Voltecs, Mayans, Chinese, Indo-Iranians, Pawnee Indians, and Israelites as recording catastrophic events on earth caused by close flybys of either Venus or Mars.

Still, many scientists are not convinced that a close planetary flyby caused the worldwide Noachian Flood, because only legends and traditions exist supporting that idea. Some scientists offer other, more plausible theories for the spark that set off the Flood.

California astronomer David F. Coppedge says, for example, "It's clear from observation of the moons and planets of the solar system that many of them have undergone periods of heavy meteorite bombardment. Even on the earth, with its higher erosion rates, over a hundred such ancient impact sites have been discovered. It is certainly plausible that one of these triggered several cataclysmic events that resulted in the Great Deluge."

According to Jeremy Auldaney, a science researcher and meteoricist,

> The most likely cause of the Flood was the close approach of an astronomical meteoroid or the impact of one or more asteroids. An asteroid is actually a very large meteorite or group of meteorites which contain iron, carbonaceous chondrites or other elements. It's very common for small meteorites to hit the earth. An iron meteorite, for example, is very rare in space, but very common on the earth.
>
> We have found elements of carbonaceous chondrites meteorites in the iridium layer found in the last strata left by the Flood, leading us to believe that a carbonaceous chondrite meteorite exploded coming through the upper atmosphere, destroying the canopy, and that an iron meteorite possibly penetrated the earth, releasing the water inside.

While doing research for a previous book, *In Search of Noah's Ark,* the authors of the present text found sufficient evidence to suggest that it's plausible that a gigantic meteorite colliding with Earth could have jarred the Earth's crust so tremendously that it set off the universal cataclysmic conditions necessary to have caused the rising of sea-beds, earthquakes, volcanoes, and the collapse of the water canopy.[5]

The *Encyclopedia Britannica* states that the number of meteorites falling in the centuries before Christ was higher than today. Indeed, in early times, men regarded iron as the metal that fell from the sky.[6]

The meteorite that fell in prehistoric times near Winslow, Arizona, made a hole 4,500 feet across and 600 feet deep. It flung out masses of rock weighing up to 7,000 tons and is estimated to have hurled out altogether 400 million tons of rock. The pressure of the impact exceeded 1,000,000 pounds per square inch, turning silica into new forms known as cocsite and stishovite.

How big would a meteorite have had to be to cause the Flood? And how would it have sparked the Flood?

For answers, let's look at information gathered by satellite photos of Mercury and our moon.

When a huge meteorite, say up to 500 miles in diameter, hits a planet, fast-moving compressive waves move through the globe, followed by slower surface waves. They converge at a point opposite the meteorite impact, shattering land forms and leaving the area in a shambles.[7]

Scientists are quite sure this happened when a huge meteorite collided with Mercury and created the 800-mile wide Caloris basin. The fast-moving compressive waves followed by surface waves moved through the planet, shattering the land forms opposite Caloris and creating what scientists call the "weird terrain." Similar shattered land forms exist on the Moon opposite great crater basins.[8]

There is little need to speculate on what such an impact would do to the earth in ancient biblical times when atmosphere, continents, and oceans existed. It would start an indescribable series of events that could easily have sparked the Flood.[9]

OFF ITS AXIS

The earth's axis was also changed dramatically during the Flood. This change gives us some fascinating clues as to what took place during that horrific time of multiple cataclysmic events. While researchers can't say definitively what caused the earth's axis to change, the data show conclusively that it was changed around the time of the Flood.

"The tilt of the earth's axis today," says Dr. Bill Overn, visiting professor of physics at Concordia College and an aerospace computer engineer, "is about 23½ degrees. In the past, it was changed quite radically, and we know this from reliable ancient records as well other data."

According to Dr. Overn, there is a grave misconception among many scientists today that the ancients did not know the earth was round. The Babylonians and Assyrians measured the tilt of the earth's axis, and in 250 B.C. the Greeks measured the circumference of the earth to within less than 25 miles of its present value. Dr. Overn asserts:

Using ancient records and artifacts along with other data, we can see there has been a change in the earth's axis and we know that that change occurred during the Flood. Right after the Flood, the tilt of the earth's axis was about 27 degrees and it has since changed to its present 23½ degrees.

It is normally accepted that the less the tilt of the earth, the less severe the winters are. Under the old, higher tilt caused somehow during the Flood, the earth would have experienced an ice age for 300 to 400 years, becoming less severe as the value or degree of the tilt decreased.

And if the earth's axis tilted at the time of the Flood, bringing on the Ice Age and other events relating to our weather regime, is there any scientific evidence that might document the exact date of this shift?

Scientists writing in the May 15, 1970, edition of *Science* magazine were able to determine that the axis shifted by studying data on the position of the sun and the solstices (positions of the sun creating the longest and shortest days of the year). The date they said this shift occurred—2345 B.C.—is the same that, according to its astronomical analysis, the Chronology History Research Institute says Noah's Flood started.

VIEWING THE EVIDENCE

In summary, we know there is sufficient evidence to suggest that a canopy of water vapor or ice covered the planet before the Flood. This canopy compressed the earth's atmosphere and helped to moderate the temperature and climate. In addition to the atmosphere, the earth's axis and geology were also vastly different than they are today.

In or around 2345 B.C., we know the earth's surface was drastically affected and a Flood that covered the entire earth for a year was created by water from underground reservoirs combined with surface water and the water from a collapsing canopy. This

Flood could have been caused by any number or combination of widely divergent factors, but the fact remains that solid evidence supports its occurrence and that the Flood changed our planet forever.

As we shall see in a later chapter, this Flood is the only event in human history that can be found in some oral or written form in practically every culture and civilization subsequent to Noah's. No other single event in human history carries this distinction. Now let's return to our passengers aboard the ark to see how they're weathering the Flood.

WEATHERING THE STORM

The violent waves rocked the great ship and the darkness made the wind cold. The animals settled down and made little noise. Most huddled together for protection from the rocking and the unknown sounds carried by the wind.

Noah's family eventually got their "sea legs," too, and were able to walk down the hallways to check on the cages without falling over.

Naamah took an oil lamp and followed her worried daughter-in-law down a dark hallway to the room she shared with Japheth. He had been very sick and looked pale by the light of the lamp. Naamah gently brushed his hair off his forehead, and he opened his eyes halfway.

"How are you feeling, son?" Naamah asked Japheth as she felt his forehead and cheeks.

"Oh, better. I just need to . . ."

"It's okay. You rest for now. Your father and brothers have all of the animals under control, so you just lie here until you feel better." Naamah adjusted the wet cloth on his forehead and smiled at Japheth's young wife.

"He'll be fine. It's just the rocking of the waves that has made him sick."

Naamah walked unsteadily back down the hall to the small private room she shared with Noah. She lay down on the blankets next to him in the semi-darkness and stared up at the ceiling, unable to go back to sleep. Even though she trusted God, she couldn't help wondering how they would all survive this terrible ordeal.

Notes

[1] Henry M. Morris, *Scientific Creationism* (San Diego: Creation-Life Publishers, 1974), pp. 124–125.

[2] Dave Balsiger and Charles E. Sellier, *In Search of Noah's Ark*, (Los Angeles: Sun Classic Books, 1984), p. 58.

[3] Ibid., p. 59.

[4] Frederick A. Filby, *The Flood Reconsidered* (Grand Rapids: Zondervan Publishing Corp., 1970), pp. 7–8.

[5] Balsiger and Sellier, *In Search of Noah's Ark*, p. 62.

[6] *Encyclopedia Britannica*, Vol. 15, pp. 275–276 (1966).

[7] Balsiger and Sellier, *In Search of Noah's Ark*, p. 62.

[8] Kenneth F. Weaver, "Mariner Unveils Venus and Mercury," *National Geographic*, June 1975, p. 861.

[9] Balsiger and Sellier, *In Search of Noah's Ark*, p. 63.

5

EVIDENCE FOR A
WORLDWIDE FLOOD

Facts do not cease to exist because they are
ignored.

Aldous Huxley

NOAH REACHED INTO A CAGE AND GENTLY GRABBED
one of the gray doves with one hand while stroking
its head tenderly with the other. Birds of all types
and colors in the other cages were making a variety
of sounds—cooing, clucking, chirping, and squawk-
ing at him in the semidarkness. Noah spoke to them
softly, reassuringly, with a chuckle as he latched the
cage and then, holding the dove, walked back down
the dark hallway to the main living area.

Noah took the dove and climbed up a ladder to
the window he had made and set it free.

"Go, little dove, and find us dry land."

It spread its wings and was lifted high by the gentle breeze. He watched it soaring in the pale blue sky
until it flew out of view. The breeze was still such a
new sensation, he stuck his hand out of the window
to feel it on his skin.

"Father, how soon can we leave the ark?" asked Shem.

"Soon, my son. Very soon."

"What will it be like, Father?"

Noah turned away from the window and looked at his son.

"I don't know. We'll just have to wait and see. If this dove doesn't return, it'll be a sign that enough dry land is above water for the dove to live outside the ark."

Noah and his family had already been in the ark several months. Tired of being locked up in it, they all wanted to look at the sky and walk on dry land again. They had many questions on their minds, and the waiting for the waters to subside was getting frustrating for everyone.

"We're running out of food for ourselves and the animals," Ham reminded Noah.

"We'll be starting over with nothing. We need to start building right away. . . ." Shem implored.

"God will let us know when it is safe to leave the ark," Noah reassured them. "He will tell us through the birds when it's safe to leave. Until then we must wait."

"Well, I'm sick of waiting," Ham huffed. Kicking a wooden crate, he stormed out of the room. "I'm sick of all of this, and I'm sick of all of you!"

Noah shook his head sadly, but made no attempt to stop him.

"Let him cool off," Shem suggested. "He'll be okay."

Waiting had been the hardest part all along. They had huddled in fear during the rumbling explosions that started the Flood and thankfully waited as the storms slowly subsided and the mighty ark drifted endlessly day after day after day. Finally, seven months after the Flood began, the ark came to rest on the mountains of Ararat.

During the many long months, they had finally grown used to the gentle rocking of the boat, the sound of the water lapping against the hull and the creaking of the great timbers inside. They had settled into the routine of caring for the animals and now had plenty of time on their hands to think. Too much time.

They couldn't see anything outside—which added to their frustration. The warm sunlight came in from above, but there was nothing they could see in any direction except water and the pale blue sky. Even though the ark had already run aground on Mount Ararat, other mountain peaks were not yet visible. It was difficult and frustrating not being able to see other land and never really knowing what would happen next. Every day required blind faith and trust in God. Everything about their lives had been changed forever, and it scared them.

Their goal for so long had been to build the ark and to survive the destruction all around them. Now all they could do was care for the animals and wait. Caring for the animals kept them occupied, but they couldn't help wondering what would be out there— what would be left of the world they had been wrenched from so violently so long ago. Or how long they would have to wait to find out what had happened.

The water all around them carried an eerie silence and they believed that no one outside their immediate family had survived. No one. They were all alone in the world; the thought was frightening.

"Come and help me get some fresh feed for the livestock, and we can talk," Noah said to Shem. "Maybe we can find your brothers and talk to them, too. The wait will be over soon, you'll see. . . ."

VIEWING THE BIBLICAL RECORD

As we leave our passengers aboard the ark, let's briefly examine the biblical account to determine if we can get a more accurate picture of what was taking place during this period of time. According to Genesis, chapters seven and eight,

> Every living thing on the face of the earth was wiped out; men and animals and the creatures that move along the ground and the birds of the air were wiped from the earth. Only Noah was left, and those with him in the ark.
>
> The waters flooded the earth for a hundred and fifty days.
>
> But God remembered Noah and all the wild animals and the livestock that were with him in the ark, and he sent a wind over the earth and the waters receded. Now the springs of the deep and the floodgates of the heavens had been closed, and the rain had stopped falling from the sky. The water receded steadily from the earth. At the end of the hundred and fifty days, the water had gone down, and on the seventeenth day of the seventh month the ark came to rest on the mountains of Ararat. The waters continued to recede until the tenth month, and on the first day of the tenth month the tops of the mountains became visible.
>
> After forty days Noah opened the window he had

made in the ark and sent out a raven, and it kept flying back and forth until the water had dried up from the earth. Then he sent out a dove to see if the water had receded from the surface of the ground. But the dove could find no place to set its feet because there was water over all the surface of the earth; so it returned to Noah in the ark. He reached out his hand and took the dove and brought it back to himself in the ark. He waited seven more days and again sent out the dove from the ark. When the dove returned to him in the evening, there in its beak was a freshly plucked olive leaf! Then Noah knew that the water had receded from the earth. He waited seven more days and sent the dove out again, but this time it did not return to him.

Genesis 7:23–24; 8:1–12

Although this part of the story raises many key questions, it also tells us much about the developing post-Flood era and how things were done in Noah's world. The account indicates that a new weather regime had started with the blowing of wind. It reveals how ancients kept their calendar, where the ark landed, and how the post-Flood culture used birds for gathering important information.

Still the perplexing questions remain—are there any nonbiblical cultural records of a global Flood? What geological proof exists that such an event actually happened? If man lived before the Flood, wouldn't it be logical to assume that artifacts of this pre-Flood civilization were encased in sedimentary deposits?

"I would say that proving a single, worldwide deluge would be necessary to prove the story of Noah. If a single worldwide flood cannot be conclusively proven, then neither can the Genesis story of the ark," claims California field geologist Tom Hill.

Hill raises a valid point. But before addressing it, let's reexamine cultural or historical evidence for a Flood.

A UNIVERSAL STORY

The Noachian Flood is the only event that appears in the oral history or written records of almost every society on earth. It was the last event shared by all of mankind. Critics who claim that this is a result of teaching by Christian missionaries can't explain why no other event or story in the Bible is so universally known.

If Flood traditions around the world stemmed from missionaries teaching Bible stories, then one could conceivably find widespread variations of the story of Jonah and the whale, Sodom and Gomorrah, the feeding of the 5,000 by Jesus, or many of the other miracles found in the Old and New Testaments. Noah's Flood stands alone because the eight members of Noah's family were the only human survivors of this unique worldwide catastrophe, and this is their personal story.

These eight survivors passed the story on to their descendants, and it has continued to be passed on—although being altered somewhat—by succeeding generations to the farthest reaches of this planet.

According to historians and cultural anthropologists, stories of the Flood can be found in more than 217 different cultures around the world. In the Middle Eastern and African cultures, for example, there are 17 Flood traditions; in the Pacific Islands, 38; in the Far East, 21; in Europe and Asia, 34; and, among North American Indians, 58 Flood accounts. Additional accounts exist in Central and South America.

Three different ancient Babylonian Flood stories remain on cuneiform tablets—all are intimately related to the biblical Flood story. Some of these tablets were found in the ancient library of King Ashurbanipal in Ninevah.

George Faber, in his book *Origin of Pagan Idolatry,* published in London in 1816, says, "A very large part of heathen mythology originates from the history of the deluge, and many of the more ancient nations have preserved almost literal accounts of an universal deluge, which corresponds in a very wonderful manner with the history of it as detailed by Moses."[1]

"I have researched the story of the great Flood in languages and cultures throughout the world," says Dr. Charles Berlitz, author of more than 200 books and one of the fifteen most eminent linguists in the world, who speaks twenty-five different languages. "Not only does it appear in the Christian Bible, but also in the *Koran,* the bible of Islam. There it tells the story of Noah—'Nuh' in Arabic—who escapes the Flood and survives with his family.

"In all the stories of the Flood I've studied, the stories are practically identical in all different sorts of languages whether Persian, Babylonian, Assyrian, Egyptian, Chinese or Sanskrit. The only thing that changes is the name of Noah but the story is essentially the same. This is a worldwide phenomenon."

In his book *The Lost Ship of Noah,* Dr. Berlitz

says, "There are over 600 variations of this legend among the ancient nations and tribes, and the story has been told through the millennia in all quarters of the globe. The variations in accounts of the catastrophe, as could be expected, occur principally in regional modifications of the same story, such as the description of the ark, the reasons for heavenly displeasure, the way chosen individuals were saved, and even the possibility of the doom happening again.[2]

Dr. Steve Deckard, a professor of science education at a California graduate school, gives us an interesting comparison of the Flood legends from around the world. "Similar Flood legend accounts in various cultures imply a common source for the cultures or a common event, or both."

According to Dr. Deckard, "The eleventh tablet of one of the Babylonian Flood stories known as the *Gilgamesh Epic* is considered to be a remarkable confirmation of the Genesis account. This cuneiform fragment was found near the Israelite city of Megiddo. The date of this cuneiform account is unknown but it most likely dates back to the time of Moses—about 1400 B.C. Comparison of the Genesis Flood account with the *Gilgamesh Epic* and more than 200 other Flood legends show a remarkable similarity in a number of respects." Dr. Deckard's similarities include:

95% talk about a global Flood.
95% state the catastrophe was a Flood alone.
88% report there was a favored family.
73% say animals played a part.
70% claim the people survived due to a boat.

67% say the animals were saved.

66% say man's wickedness was the Flood's cause.

57% report survivors ended up on a mountain.

35% claim birds were sent out.

13% state survivors performed a sacrifice afterward.

However, critics of the Noah account point out that Flood traditions name more than fifty different mountains as the landing site of the boat. What sets apart the biblical Flood story from all the others?

"This is one area where the Hebrew account in the Bible is unique from the other Flood accounts," says cuneiform expert, Dr. Arthur Custance, a fellow of the Canadian Royal Anthropological Institute. He has authored fifty-two treatises relating to ancient history, anthropology, archaeology, biblical history, and philosophy. Dr. Custance explains,

> In extra-biblical accounts, the survivors always land on a local mountain. In the Hebrew account, the ark lands far from Palestine in a distant country "on the mountains of Ararat"—a place of which most Hebrew people had no firsthand knowledge.
>
> This circumstance surely suggests that here in the Bible we have the genuine account. And it also underscores the great respect that the Hebrew people had for the Word of God and the requirement that they never tamper with it. It would surely, otherwise, have been most natural for them to land the ark on their most famous mountain, Mount Zion.[3]

Dr. Ethel Nelson, a Chinese pictograph linguist who has authored two books on ancient Chinese pictography, has made some startling discoveries about some of the oldest Chinese pictograph characters found written on the inside of Chinese bronzeware and on ancient oracle bone.

"The Flood record," says Dr. Nelson, "has been found on such artifacts as the Akkadian, Sumerian, and Babylonian cuneiform tablets now on display at the British Museum. These tablets date back to about 700 B.C. But there is a more ancient pictograph record found in ancient Chinese bronzeware and oracle bone pictograph writing. This pictograph writing dates back to about 1700 B.C.—within 600 years after the Flood!"

Dr. Nelson, writing in her book, *The Discovery of Genesis,* with coauthor C. H. Kang, states that by dissecting ancient Chinese characters, they found that many of the characters ideographically explain the story of Noah and the Flood, and other parts of the book of Genesis.

In addition to ancient Flood traditions providing evidence for Noah's Flood, a large bronze coin struck 1,700 years ago at Apameia Kibotos in Asia Minor (modern Turkey), near the mountains of Ararat, depicts the story of Noah's ark. The coin, now on display at the Israel Museum, is believed to be the only coin type known to bear a biblical scene. Containing Greek inscriptions, the coin pictures three portions of the Flood story on one side. Noah and his wife protrude from the ark, the dove with an olive branch rests on the ark's roof, and then Noah and his wife are shown standing to the right of the ark with arms upraised in prayer. The side of the ark is inscribed with the Greek letters for *Noah.*

In addition to numerous cultural and linguistic records of Noah's Flood, does substantial geological evidence exist to support this worldwide catastrophe? Roger Oakland, science author and former biology professor at a Canadian college, says,

> There's an extensive amount of evidence for a global Flood. And I see most of that evidence in the fossil record. Worldwide fossils of animals and fish have been found buried in swimming positions, suddenly and catastrophically preserved in a moment in time.
>
> One of the most fascinating fossil finds which show animals in swimming positions including rhinos, hippos, and zebras is found in Nebraska. Hundreds of dinosaurs in Alberta, Canada, drowned in flood-deposited volcanic ash. In Scotland, tons of fish have been found in positions of terror, fins extended and eyes bulging. Another fossil graveyard in Geiseltal, Germany, shows a mixture of plants and insects from all climatic zones.
>
> When these kinds of fossils are found together at such a great distance from their apparent place of origin, this is usually indicative of widespread global flooding and rapid burial. The only conclusion anyone can make is that it was caused by a flood of a universal nature.

Harry S. Ladd of the United States Geological Survey tells of a petrified "fish bed" in Santa Barbara, California, where "more than a billion fish, averaging 6 to 8 inches in length, died on four square miles of bay bottom."[4] The question is, how did they get trapped there, if not by a flood?

Another graveyard believed to be related to flood action is found near Diamondville, Wyoming. This deposit, now a tourist attraction, is furnishing some of the most perfect specimens of fossil fish and plants in the world. Fish from 6 to 8 feet in length and palm leaves from 3 to 4 feet wide have been uncovered.

This confirms the geological theory that the climate was tropical, unlike the blizzard-ridden, rugged terrain of Wyoming today. The deposit contained an assortment of other odd remains—alligators, garpike, deep-sea bass, sunfish, chubs, herring, pickerel, crustaceans, birds, turtles, mollusca, mammals, and varieties of insects.[5]

Such a mixture of organisms from different habitats and climatic regions of the world is characteristic of the most important fossil deposits. Many scientists believe this happened by the *allochthonous process* in which materials are rapidly transported to their final locality and deposited under flood conditions.[6]

This is illustrated by the famous Baltic amber deposits in Eastern Europe, extensively investigated by Dr. N. Heribert-Nilsson, late director of the Swedish Botanical Institute. He says, "The insects discovered there are of fairly modern types (not prehistoric) and their geographical distribution can be ascertained. It is then quite astounding to find that they belong to all regions of the Earth."[7]

"The Morrison Formation," says Dr. Ariel Roth, the director of the Geoscience Research Institute at Loma Linda University in California, "is spread over 400,000 square miles in the western United States. It runs from Texas to Canada and is well-known because it contains lots of dinosaur fossils. This formation is indicative of what you'd expect to be laid down during a global flood because of its uniformity in strata layers and its widespread coverage. This is what you would expect from a worldwide catastrophe such as described in the Bible."

"My view," says Dr. M. E. Clark, a professor of hydraulics as well as theoretical and applied mechanics at the University of Illinois, "is that the whole geologic column is composed of conformal layers laid one on top of the other with usually a fine line of demarcation between them. This necessitates a very rapid deposition of these individual layers.

"The most compelling evidence, however, is that of polystrate fossils—a fossil tree or animal that is evidenced in the rock layers of having been covered up by ten or 20 layers," says Dr. Clark, who has studied flood sedimentation deposits worldwide. "The tree could not have stood for thousands of years while that many layers were being laid down gradually. This is very compelling evidence for very rapid deposition of the sedimentary layers that we see throughout the geologic column."

According to Mace Baker, a paleontological researcher and author,

The dinosaur fossils point to a worldwide Flood. Dinosaurs are often found in mass burials with up to 100 dinosaurs in one location such as the ones that have been found in New Mexico and Germany. These mass burials are encased in enormous quantities of rapidly formed sedimentary rock layers which are deposited by water. These mass quantities of dinosaur fossils indicate that they were buried catastrophically and very rapidly.

Ordinarily, when animals die their flesh is soon consumed by scavengers and their bones are left to decay and return to the soil. During the time in which the bones are decaying they most generally may be found in one of two positions: (1) they may be found on their side with their legs outstretched, or (2) the bones are sometimes found in a disarticulated condition. The latter condition is due to the work of scavengers.

In the case of armored dinosaurs, we find that a large number of them have been overturned and then fossilized in an upside-down position. To find one dinosaur fossil in this position would not be significant. To find so many in the upside-down position, however, speaks very clearly of a great catastrophe involving the force of raging waters.

Another example of rapid burial is a fossil of a *Compsognathus,* a small bipedal dinosaur, that was found in Germany with the fossil remains of a lizard in its stomach, and a *Pterosaur,* a type of flying reptile, [that] was found with food in its stomach and in its beak. So these, among many other evidences, clearly indicate that the dinosaurs did not perish over a long period of time as most scientists believe, but were wiped out and covered very rapidly by a catastrophic flood.[8]

Seashells and fossils of fish and marine mammals have been found on the highest mountain ranges on earth—further evidence of a universal deluge. Skeletons of whales have been found in the Himalayas, the world's highest mountain range. The bones of crocodiles have been found in the Swiss Alps.[9] Fossils of fish, sea snails, and clams have been found atop Mount Everest.

Geologists who have climbed Mount Ararat—the landing site of Noah's ark—have discovered a variety of seashells and other evidence that this mountain was once underwater.

"I've noticed two things in particular on Mount

Ararat from a geological point of view that indicates this 17,000-foot volcanic mountain was once underwater," says Grant Richards, a geologist-geophysicist and field associate with the San Bernardino County Museum in California. "First is the occurrence high on Mount Ararat of what is called pillowlava. This alone indicates that the mountain was at one time underwater. Secondly, we have found salt crystals on Mount Ararat which could only have been formed under water."

Dr. Clifford Burdick, a geologist commissioned by the Turkish government many years ago to study Mount Ararat, discovered more impressive evidence of a flood. He found cube-shaped salt clusters as large as grapefruit near the 7,000-foot elevation of Mount Ararat.[10]

Pillow lava has been found as high as the 14,000-foot level of Ararat, implying that lava issued from inside the earth while Ararat was underwater. The water rapidly chilled the lava, creating circular formations resembling pillows. This would support Genesis 7:20, which says the flood covered the highest mountains to a depth of 22½ feet.

Dr. Burdick says most of Ararat was formed by volcanic action, and if the glacial ice cap on Ararat did not exist, one would probably find pillow lava all the way to the summit.[11]

Could this pillow lava have been formed during the time of the Flood or because of it?

"Presumably so," Dr. Burdick says. "We don't know of any other time that a mountain that high—17,000 feet—would have been underwater. You just have to connect the two. There's no other historical or geological record of the ocean being that high except at that time."[12]

Conglomerate cones found on Ararat, Dr. Burdick says, are further evidence of a universal flood. The conglomerates are various sizes of rocks fused together. They are a mixture of rounded stones, solidified by a cementing medium like calcium carbonate. Lava flow and violent water action are needed to produce them. Finding a conglomerate cone at the 12,000- or 13,000-foot level of Ararat indicates that at one time the area was underwater.[13]

Exciting evidence of a global flood can also be found in the study of coal deposits. Coal is formed by compacted, decayed vegetation, and scientists estimate that it takes anywhere from 5 to 10 feet of compacted plant material to form 1 foot of coal. At a ratio of seven to one, then, a 10-foot seam of coal represents 70 feet of compacted plant material.

When we realize that coal seams can be up to 400 feet thick, we begin to understand how much more vegetation flourished in the pre-Flood world than exists on earth today.

Dr. Harold Coffin of the Geoscience Research Institute has done extensive research into the formation of coal beds and has concluded that a 400-foot seam of coal would represent a fantastic 4,000 feet of peat at an average of 10 feet of peat or vegetable matter for 1 foot of coal. Few peat bogs, marshes, or swamps anywhere in the world today reach even 100 feet, and most are less than 50 feet. The only logical conclusion to explain the creation of a 400-foot seam of coal, then, is a tremendous force collecting and compressing all of this vegetable matter.[14]

"The concept of a global deluge," Dr. Coffin says, "that eroded out the forests and plant cover of the pre-Flood world, collected it in great mats of drifting debris, and eventually dropped it on the emerging land or on the sea bottom is the most reasonable answer to this problem of the great extent and uniform thickness of coal beds."[15]

The fossil record, then, clearly indicates that the fish and animals found perfectly preserved in sedimentary layers worldwide were not a result of these animals dying naturally and then being slowly covered with sedimentary layers over a long period of time. They had to have been caught suddenly in a tremendous deluge that compressed them quickly between various sedimentary layers before they could decompose. There is absolutely no other logical explanation for the fossils and enormous coal deposits other than a worldwide Flood.

It's pretty much of a settled issue that the Flood can be proven by cultural traditions and by a variety of fossil and geological evidence. Traditional scientific thought, however, rejects the idea that the major coal layers of the world were deposited during Noah's Flood.

"The age of the coal layers in the earth's crust varies from more than 300 million years for anthracite coal to a few million years for low-grade coal such as lignite," claims field geologist Tom Hill of Irvine, California.

But in any global flood that destroyed all mankind, you would expect to find some artifacts from Noah's pre-Flood civilization. If there are human artifacts found among the fossils in the flood sedimentary layers or even in coal deposits, then academically, one would have to conclude that the entire Noah's Flood account is factual.

"I would seriously doubt and question that any so-called man-made objects would be found in ancient coal beds," says geologist Hill.

Critics want to know, what does the evidence say? If human artifacts can be found in either sedimentary rock layers or in coal deposits, only two conclusions can be made—either man was on the earth millions and millions of years ago, or the widely accepted "geologic column" taught in schools is in error.

Bible scholars estimate that the pre-Flood population numbered in the millions. They could not have disappeared without a trace—and they didn't!

Many such human artifacts have been found encased in either coal or sedimentary rock layers. Examples of such finds include an eight-carat gold chain, a clay figurine, a spoon, a thimble, an iron pot, nails, and other items.

An engraved metal bowl, for example, was found in conglomerate rock near Dorchester, Massachusetts, in 1851. An article in *Scientific American* indicates that a powerful blast made in rock near Dorchester threw out an immense mass. Some of the pieces weighed several tons. The blast scattered small fragments in all directions. Among the fragments was a bell-shaped metal pot, $4\frac{1}{2}$ inches high, $6\frac{1}{2}$ inches at the base, $2\frac{1}{2}$ inches at the top, and about $\frac{1}{8}$-inch thick. It had a zinc color.

On the sides were engraved bouquets of flowers

beautifully inlaid with silver. The carving and inlaying were done exquisitely by a cunning workman.[16]

Still another mystery is the discovery in England of a gold thread embedded in stone quarried from a depth of 8 feet. No one knows how long this remnant of a former age had been embedded.

The late M. A. Kurtz, of Nampa, Idaho, in 1889 discovered a clay female doll at a depth of about 300 feet in a layer of coarse sand as he was boring for an artesian well.

His discovery, called the "Nampa Image," gained the attention of the scientific world.[17] The 1 1/2-inch doll figurine was found after Kurtz had drilled through about 15 feet of lava rock, 100 feet of quicksand, then 6 inches of clay, 40 more feet of quicksand, more clay, more quicksand, more clay, then clay balls mixed with sand, then coarse sand.

It has since been called one of the most curious archaeological discoveries of the nineteenth century and is currently on display at the Idaho Historical Society Museum in Boise.[18]

The significance of the image is this: It is a man-made object discovered at a depth of about 300 feet, meaning that whoever shaped it lived on that land 300 feet below the present surface, or it was washed there by the Flood. In either case, it was buried by flood action, based on what scientists know of the way sedimentary deposits are laid down.

In 1822 British surgeon Gideon Mantell chronicled that in 1791 M. Leisky of Hamburg, Germany, discovered an "ancient iron pin" in a piece of fractured flint.

The *London Times,* in 1851, reported that a miner

returning from the California goldfields found an iron nail embedded near the center of a gold-bearing quartz rock.

The *Zanesville Courier,* in 1853, reported the Cusick's Mill quarry near Zanesville, Ohio, yielded the bones of a woman completely entombed in sandstone that also retained the full impression of her once fleshly form.

J. Q. Adams, writing in an 1883 issue of *American Antiquarian,* reported the discovery of a thimble trapped in a lump of lignite coal mined from the Marshall Coal Bed in Colorado.

In June 1891 Mrs. S. W. Culp of Morrisonville, Illinois, found a 10-inch gold chain embedded in a lump of coal she was breaking apart for her stove.

More recent finds include a small iron pot found in 1912 encased in a block of coal at the Municipal Electric Plant in Thomas, Oklahoma. The coal was traced to the Wilburton Oklahoma Mines. The pot, with an affidavit from the pot finder, is now on display at the Miles Municipal Museum in Eureka Springs, Arkansas.

Newton Anderson, a chemist and retired science educator living in Florida, recently told how he found a bell in coal while living in West Virginia.

I found the bell in a lump of coal when I was ten years old. I was asked to fire the furnace. I got a large lump of coal, and when I got it to the furnace I dropped it. The coal broke and the top of the bell—the stem—was sticking out of the coal. Later, I carefully rendered the coal from the bell base.

The bell has an unusual pagan god on top of the stem with both arms and wings raised upward. The god is in a kneeling position and the rest of the top is an ornate stem. This brass bell has an iron clapper inside.

For a long time we've tried to learn about the bell. Historically, this pagan ceremonial bell is described very well by an account in Genesis 4:22 that says Tubal-Cain was an artificer of brass and iron. This quite likely is a pre-Flood civilization object, and it could have been carried over by Noah's Flood into the coal.

Interestingly, Anderson had a special scanning electron elemental analysis test performed on the bell and determined the elemental composition of the bell couldn't be reproduced by today's metallurgy technology. Was the pre-Flood civilization more advanced in metallurgy, or did the pre-Flood atmosphere somehow impact the elemental composition?

Another equally interesting find of a human artifact occurred in 1934 when Emma Hahn of London, Texas, discovered a rock with a fragment of wood protruding from its surface. After breaking open the rock, she was surprised to find that the wood was in fact the splintered handle of a hammer—whose iron head remained intact.

Rock formations where the hammer was found have been reliably dated to the Ordovician geological period nearly a half-billion years ago. The rock encasing the hammer has similar characteristics. Either the evolutionary geological dating column is wrong, or an intelligent ancient man lived a half-billion years ago—499 million years earlier than scientists say man lived on earth!

Critics of these conclusions regarding the hammer say that the artifact is a result of a natural process of accretion. This occurs when mineral-rich water evaporates, leaving behind deposits that build up until an object becomes completely encased.

For this book, we decided to examine the still rock-encased hammer and learn what scientific tests reveal about it. We contacted Carl Baugh, museum curator in Glen Rose, Texas, who keeps the hammer in a local bank vault.

"The wood in the interior of the handle is partially turned to coal," Baugh says. "The structure of the hammer has been compared to known historical hand tools recorded in the United States, and no historical equivalent could be found after an exhaustive search. Furthermore, the hammer does not rust, with scratch marks from 1934 remaining shiny bright to this day."

Baugh then took the hammer to Batelle Laboratories—the labs that analyzed the Moon stones—to determine the composition of the hammer head through a scanning electron elemental analysis. The analysis by weight shows that the hammer head is made of 96.6 percent iron, 2.6 percent chlorine and 0.74 percent sulphur, with no silicon or nickel—a highly unusual combination. The absence of silicon and the high amount of chlorine would indicate, according to Baugh, that the hammer was not formed by any known modern means.

"It's our belief that the hammer has been formed by a totally unknown manufacturing process and that it had been formed a long time before modern manufacturing processes were developed," Baugh says. "The strength of the hammer appears to come from the strange concentration of chlorine in the iron. If the chlorine is throughout the hammer, it would account for the fact that the hammer head does not appear to corrode very easily."

Next Baugh had a tomography analysis done on the hammer at the largest tomography lab in the world, located in Texas. Tomography is a technique using X rays for examining the internal structure of solid objects.

> The tests revealed it was the most homogenous implement ever seen by the lab technicians. Nothing in modern technology or in ancient metallurgy can compare to the uniformity of the hammer's interior. It's impossible to produce this hammer today.
>
> Physicists say the only way this hammer could be produced would be under a different type of atmospheric pressure. The only historical record of atmospheric conditions being different was in the biblical days of Tubal-Cain and Noah. The biblical account also states Tubal-Cain was a maker of metal tools—meaning this hammer is probably a pre-Flood civilization tool deposited sedimentarily in the worldwide flood of Noah's day.

Was this hammer and the other artifacts found in coal and sedimentary rock layers pre-Flood tools deposited by the the Flood? This may never be conclusively proven, but evidence certainly supports the biblical account and seriously calls into question the evolutionary geological dating column.

ON THE WINGS OF A DOVE

As we rejoin our passengers aboard the ark, it has seemed a long time since Noah released the dove to search for dry land. Having finished their chores for the day, the family sits quietly eating meager portions of their evening meal. Suddenly, Noah spots the dove outside of the window. Excited, he goes to the window and reaches out his hand. The dove alights on it. Under the watchful eyes of his family, he carefully draws the little bird back inside the ark and gently strokes its head.

"Well, family, it looks as if we will still be on the ark for a while. This little dove wasn't able to find dry land or else she wouldn't have come back to us."

"How long do you think we'll have to stay on the ark?" Shem asks.

"I don't know. We'll send her back out in a few days and see what happens then. I know waiting is difficult," Noah says, looking around sympathetically at his loved ones. "We have no other choice than to trust God. He knows how we are getting low on food and water. He will make a way for us."

"You hope . . ." Ham says disparagingly.

"No, my son, I know," Noah reassures him as he takes the dove back to its cage.

It was natural for Noah to send out a raven and a dove to determine if the flood waters had subsided. In ancient times, animals often were used for communication and navigational purposes. Doves or pigeons, with their powerful homing instincts, have always been famous for their ability to undertake long, swift flights. To assume that Noah knew this is more than reasonable.[19]

Pigeons were used as messengers in the days of Solomon.[20] The Romans used them during battles, and the Greeks used them to carry the results of the Olympic games. Many amazing flights were made by these birds in World Wars I and II. Through mist and storm and shrapnel, literally hundreds of pigeons carried their messages that saved the lives of thousands of wrecked airmen and troops cut off by enemy forces.[21]

Noah waited a week and again took the little dove to the window and released her into the strong wind that was blowing outside the ark. He watched her for as long as he could, then turned away from the window and silently prayed.

Noah and his family had been on the ark for almost a year now, and their food and water supplies were dangerously low.

"If it doesn't rain again soon," Naamah worried, "we're going to run out of water." She spoke softly so her daughters-in-law talking and sewing in the corner couldn't hear.

"Yes, I know." Noah nodded. "We'll have to cut down our usage even more."

"What's left to cut? We're already using it only for drinking."

Noah sat down at the table and put his weary head in his hands. He didn't have any answers for his worried wife other than to trust God to supply all of their needs. Summoning all his courage, he lifted his head and spoke reassuring words to Naamah.

"God kept us safe during the destruction of the earth. He chose to warn us and save us and the animals through this ark. We have no reason to believe He won't continue to keep us safe and provide for all of our needs. God keeps his promises."

"I don't know, Noah." Naamah stood and began pacing the floor. "I'm getting worried," she scowled, biting her lower lip. "I just don't know . . ."

"Father, come quick!" Japheth was out of breath as he ran into the room. "The dove has returned with a freshly plucked olive leaf."

"Are you sure?" Noah felt a rush of excitement. "An olive leaf?"

"Land . . . things growing again . . . can it really be true?" Naamah clutched her hands to her chest and danced around. Her daughters-in-law joined in exhilaration. "Oh, Noah, our trial is over! We can finally leave the ark! Praise be to God!"

"Just a minute, my love," Noah said gently, walking quickly toward the door. "Let me go up to the roof and look around."

"But, Noah, the olive branch. Surely . . ."

"We can't leave the ark until God tells us that it's time," Noah cried out to his family as he headed up the stairs to the roof. "But maybe, just maybe, the dove brings us news that that day may be soon . . . very, very soon!"

WHAT THE OLIVE LEAF PROVED

According to Greek tradition, the first olive branch to reach Greece was brought by a dove from Phoenicia. Olive groves are favorite places for doves to build their nests. No wonder Noah's dove returned to the ark with "a freshly plucked olive leaf."[22]

Noah apparently knew the habits of animals, and

he knew that the raven—a scavenger bird—would not return to the ark if the water had subsided enough for it to perch on some slimy surface or carcass. And this is exactly what happened.

The dove is a clean bird; it would not perch on such a surface. Noah sent it out three times. The second time, the dove returned with an olive leaf in its mouth. This told Noah that the earth was returning to its fruitfulness.

While an olive tree may grow in water, it doesn't thrive at mountaintop heights and as a rule prefers slopes below 3,000 feet. Thus, Noah knew that the lower elevations were beginning to produce vegetation.[23]

In their book *The Genesis Flood,* John Whitcomb and Henry Morris say that before it was discovered by the dove, the olive leaf would have had as much as four months' exposure to sunshine in order to sprout from an asexually propagated olive branch buried near the surface of the soil.[24]

And the olive, one of the hardiest of all plants, would be one of the first to sprout after the Flood. Full-grown olive trees can survive extremely harsh treatment. Only a few months are needed from the time of implantation of olive cuttings until the leaves sprout. Branches of olive trees apparently were buried near enough to the surface of the soil to sprout shoots, thus producing a new generation of trees from asexually propagated plants, says Dr. Walter Lammerts, a California horticulturist.[25]

About a month later, Noah removed part of the ark's roof (Genesis 8:13), and saw the ground was dry. Noah waited another fifty-six days before disembarking into a world that was as different as night and day from what he knew before the Flood.

Notes

[1] Violet Cummings, *Noah's Ark: Fact or Fable?* (San Diego: Creation-Science Research Center, 1972), p. 132.

[2] Charles Berlitz, *The Lost Ship of Noah* (New York: G. P. Putnam's Sons, 1987), p. 110.

[3] Donald W. Patten, *A Symposium on Creation* (Grand Rapids: Baker Book House, 1972), pp. 9–10, 17.

[4] Harry S. Ladd, "Ecology, Paleontology and Stratigraphy," *Science* 129 (January 9, 1959), p. 72.

[5] "Fishing for Fossils," *Compressed Air Magazine* 63 (March 1958), p. 24.

[6] John C. Whitcomb and Henry M. Morris, *The Genesis Flood* (Phillipsburg, NJ: Presbyterian and Reformed Publishing Co., 1961), pp. 158–159.

[7] N. Heribert-Nilsson, *Synthetische Artbildung* (Stockholm, Sweden), pp. 1195–1196.

[8] Mace Baker, *Evidences of a World-Wide Flood from a Study of the Dinosaurs* (Roseville, MN: Twin-Cities Creation Conference, 1992), p. 147.

[9] Berlitz, *The Lost Ship of Noah,* pp. 141–142.

[10] Dave Balsiger and Charles E. Sellier, *In Search of Noah's Ark* (Los Angeles: Sun Classic Books, 1976), p. 48.

[11] Ibid.

[12] Ibid.

[13] Ibid., pp. 48–49.

[14] Rene Noorbergen, *The Ark File* (Mountain View, CA: Pacific Press Publishing Association, 1974), p. 64.

[15] Ibid., pp. 64–65.

[16] *Scientific American* 7 (June 5, 1952), p. 298.

[17] Balsiger and Sellier, *In Search of Noah's Ark,* p. 44.

[18] Ibid., p. 45.

[19] Ibid., p. 138.

[20] *Chambers Encyclopedia,* Article "Dove."

[21] Balsiger and Sellier, *In Search of Noah's Ark,* p. 139.

[22] Ibid.

[23] Ibid.

[24] Whitcomb and Morris, *The Genesis Flood,* p. 8.

[25] Balsiger and Sellier, *In Search of Noah's Ark,* pp. 139–140.

6

REPLENISHING THE EARTH

Society is always taken by surprise at any
new example of common sense.

Ralph Waldo Emerson (1803–1882)

IN THE TENTH MONTH OF THEIR JOURNEY ABOARD
the ark, Noah climbed up a ladder to the roof and
made a hole large enough to crawl through. He then
climbed out onto the roof of the massive wooden
barge to look around. The ship was perched on the
upper slope of a mountain that one day would be
known as Mount Ararat, among the mountains of
Ararat in eastern Turkey. Noah found it difficult to
keep his balance in the brisk wind, but the view was
spectacular.

Scattered huge clouds billowed into the pale blue
sky, and the bright sunlight made him squint at first.
He could see in every direction—valleys, hills, and
mountain lakes brimming with water. Land! Just
seeing the hills springing forth with new plant life
filled him with tremendous comfort and joy.

"Oh, God, thank You for preserving us and bringing us safely through the rebirth of Your earth," he

cried with outstretched arms. "How magnificent are Your works. . . ."

Noah laughed and spun around, giddy with sheer exuberance over finally being out of the confines of the ark. Pacing from side to side and from one end of the roof to the other, he relished the nearly forgotten feelings of freedom and openness. His senses were bombarded with the fresh smell of the seawater, the sight of new colors everywhere, and the breathtaking view in every direction. This was his first, unobstructed glimpse of the landscape around him, and he felt mesmerized. Out of a tragic death was emerging glorious new life, and he knew that at that moment, he alone was privileged to witness it.

The harsh, blowing wind was cold, however; and even though he kept moving, he was shivering. Regretfully, he crawled back down into the warmth, the earthy smells, and the semidark confines of the ark.

"What is it like outside, Father?"

"Yes, is the water all gone?"

"Can we leave now?"

"What did you see?"

"Whoa," Noah said, laughing. "One at a time. We're high up on a mountain slope and the view is unbelievable . . . very different. There's still a lot of water on the land below, so we will probably need to wait at least until the next new moon to leave the ark—maybe longer. In the meantime, we'll need to make warmer clothing. The land that I can see has changed much since we came on board, and the weather is different."

"Can we go up and have a look?" Shem asked eagerly.

"Yes." Noah nodded. "But be careful. The wind is blowing very strong and it is not warm up there."

Without another word, Shem, Ham, and Japheth crawled up through the hole in the roof and strode around, stunned and awed by the changes they could see in every direction.

"Shem, please be careful," his wife called up through the hole. But her voice was lost in the howling wind. A few minutes later, the young men reluctantly went back inside to escape the cold.

The family chatted excitedly for hours about the new world awaiting them and even forgot about their boredom.

Noah and Naamah lay down that night with hearts full of joy, thanksgiving, and praise. Their trust in God's promises had been rewarded in the most remarkable ways, and they knew that in spite of the hardships, the best was yet to come.

"Naamah, I want to plant a vineyard when we leave the ark. I want to plant grapes and many grains and . . ."

"We will have much work to do," Naamah said with a yawn, "but can we talk about it more in the morning? You can't plant anything while we're still on the ark, my love. Good night."

"You're right," Noah chuckled. "I'm just so excited about the possibilities . . ."

As the days passed, everyone except Naamah went on the roof daily to view the landscape as it grew more lush and green. Finally, some 375 days after they boarded the ark, Noah announced that God had told him it was time to break open the seals on the ramp and lower it.

As the first one down the ramp, Noah stepped onto the dry earth and dropped to his knees. His family joined him on the rocky soil, and they offered a prayer of thanksgiving to God. Then they hugged and danced around in joy—not minding the cold wind that blew in the crisp, early morning air.

They were finally on land again. They had survived and they were finally free. . . .

SEARCHING FOR CREDIBLE ANSWERS

The biblical account picks up the story of Noah disembarking from the ark:

> By the first day of the first month of Noah's six hundred and first year, the water had dried up from the earth. Noah then removed the covering from the ark and saw that the surface of the ground was dry. By the twenty-seventh day of the second month the earth was completely dry.
>
> Then God said to Noah, "Come out of the ark, you and your wife and your sons and their wives. Bring out every kind of living creature that is with you—the birds, the animals, and all the creatures that move along the ground—so they can multiply on the earth and be fruitful and increase in number upon it."
>
> So Noah came out, together with his sons and his wife and his sons' wives. All the animals and all the creatures that move along the ground and all the birds —everything that moves on the earth—came out of the ark, one kind after another.
>
> Then Noah built an altar to the Lord and, taking some of all the clean animals and clean birds, he sacrificed burnt offerings on it. The Lord smelled the pleasing aroma and said in his heart: "Never again will I

curse the ground because of man, even though every inclination of his heart is evil from childhood. And never again will I destroy all living creatures, as I have done.

"As long as the earth endures, seedtime and harvest, cold and heat, summer and winter, day and night will never cease."

Then God blessed Noah and his sons, saying to them, "Be fruitful and increase in number and fill the earth. The fear and dread of you will fall upon all the beasts of the earth and all of the birds of the air, upon every creature that moves along the ground, and upon all the fish of the sea; they are given into your hands. Everything that lives and moves will be food for you. Just as I gave you the green plants, I now give you everything.

And God said, "This is the sign of the covenant I am making between me and you and every living creature with you, a covenant for all generations to come: I have set my rainbow in the clouds, and it will be the sign of the covenant between me and the earth. Whenever I bring clouds over the earth and the rainbow appears in the clouds, I will remember my covenant between me and you and all living creatures of every kind. Never again will the waters become a flood to destroy all life. Whenever the rainbow appears in the clouds, I will see it and remember the everlasting covenant between God and all living creatures of every kind on the earth."

The sons of Noah who came out of the ark were Shem, Ham and Japheth. (Ham was the father of Canaan.) These were the three sons of Noah, and from them came the people who were scattered over the earth.

Noah, a man of the soil, proceeded to plant a vineyard. . . .

After the Flood, Noah lived 350 years. Altogether, Noah lived 950 years and then he died.

Genesis 8:13; 9:3, 12–16, 18–20, 28–29

If you thought some of the other parts of the Noah account were unbelievable before we explained them scientifically, you will not be surprised that this part of the story raises additional questions that challenge various fields of science for credible answers.

Critics are quick to call this part of the Noah account unbelievable: Noah was 601 years old when the ark came to rest on Ararat, and he died at 950 years of age. And how could he have lived so long? How could all the races have come from Noah and his family? Furthermore, how could all the languages of the world result from a family that spoke only one? How did the animals and birds spread all over the world? Critics also dispute the belief that the Ice Age and today's weather regime came into existence as a result of the year-long Flood. Good questions from the critics—and they all need good answers from the scientific community.

THE DAY OF DELUGE

Before we deal with these difficult questions, let's set the stage by clarifying some items regarding the Flood. First, when did the Flood occur?

Dr. Gerald E. Aardsma, a nuclear physicist from Canada, believes the Flood may have occurred as far back as 12,000 B.C. However, most biblical scholars and chronologies suggest the Flood occurred about 5,000 years ago—somewhere between 2390 B.C. and 2103 B.C. Rabbi Jose, writing in A.D. 150, set the Flood in the year 2103 B.C., while chronologist Philip Mauro placed the date at 2390 B.C. Chronologist

Gene Faulstich, founder of the Chronology History Research Institute in Iowa, uses astronomical dating to confirm biblical events. He says,

> Ancient people did not have clocks and calendars as we do today. They dated events from the position of the sun and moon. For example, the rains began, according to Noah in the second month, on the seventeenth day. We understand that to be one lunar month after the first day of spring—two days after the full moon.
>
> Astronomical dating is an exact science in which we can, with the aid of computers, examine biblical events in light of astronomical occurrences. We can take the chronology data given by Noah in Genesis during the Flood and with computers, convert this data into a meaningful calendar. We also note that Noah was on the ark for one solar year of 365 days, observed the Sabbath day, and even more important, the Noah Flood events synchronize perfectly with the solstices and equinoxes, as well as with the days of the week.
>
> In 1650, Irish chronologist James Ussher, without the aid of computers, placed the Flood in 2348 B.C. However, with today's astronomical computer technology, we're able to accurately determine that the Flood occurred in 2345 B.C., and that the first Flood rains started to fall on May 14, 2345 B.C. We're able to confirm all the events surrounding the Flood due to a solar eclipse which occurred at sunrise on May 16, 2344 B.C.—when he observed a bow in the sky after they left the ark three days earlier.

Once Noah's Flood chronology data is matched with astronomical-dating information on computer, Faulstich says the following scenario emerges (assume Noah is speaking):

We had the ark loaded on May 12, 2345 B.C., and we rested on Saturday, May 13th. The rain broke loose on May 14th, and the rains continued until the first day of summer. I could not see any land for six months, but on the first day of winter, I saw a mountain peak. The water continued to subside, and on the first day of spring, I looked out to see dry land. This was also New Year's Day in 2344 B.C. After sending birds away from the ship, I decided to leave the ark on the anniversary of my entrance into the ark.

On Sunday, May 13th, I left the ark. I built an altar for God, and on the morning of May 16th, I made the first offerings. As the sun rose, the moon came up below it and eclipsed it. This caused an awesome sight in the eastern sky, but an equally beautiful rainbow in the western sky.

Some scholars believe the Flood began and ended in our present-day month of November. Many cultures around the world recognize a "Day of the Dead" that apparently was originally a commemoration of the destruction of all life on earth due to the Flood. The November celebration date may have been connected with the Christianizing of the event, as Christmas, December 25th, is the celebration of Jesus' birth although He was not born on Christmas but rather in the spring.

Dr. Filby, in his book *The Flood Reconsidered,* explains,

November 2nd is All Souls' Day—the Day of the Dead. In France it is *Le Jour des Morts*—Christianized now for centuries but still at heart the old Day of the Dead when flowers are taken to the tombs. From South America to Northern Europe, from Mexico to Polynesia, gifts and flowers are placed on tombs on this anniversary of the Day of the Dead.

The Persians commenced their New Year in November in a month which was named Mordad—meaning month of the angel of death. In Peru the New Year commenced in November. Mexicans, too, kept the Day of the Dead at the same time of the year.

Natives in parts of Australia at this time of the year paint white stripes on their legs and arms and ribs to resemble skeletons. Our Anglo-Saxon ancestors called November Blood-month! The Celtic inhabitants of England—whose traditions incidentally are among the most ancient in the world—kept their New Year in November.

The ritual has in some cases been absorbed into, or modified by, later religions but the recollection of that Day of Judgment and Death has never ceased.[1]

HOW FAR DID THE ARK FLOAT?

Another unanswered question is—if Noah's Ark landed on Mount Ararat, where was it built, and how far did it float?

According to Donald W. Patten, a geographer and author of *The Flood of Noah,* "The ark was built near a pre-Flood city named Shuruppak—it is so identified in the *Gilgamesh Epic,* which is a cuneiform story of the Flood found in Assyria. Shuruppak also became a post-Flood city and is located in southern Iraq.

"We know where the ark landed. It was in eastern Turkey. We know it moved 520 miles or more. It was swept north by slightly northwest high into the mountain basin of eastern Turkey."

THE POST-FLOOD EARTH

In addition to all of the other changes in the post-Flood earth, it is apparent from the Bible text that Noah and his family entered the ark as vegetarians but were allowed to eat meat when they disembarked.

They may not have had any choice but to eat meat when they left the ark. The new earth probably would not have produced any fruits, grains or vegetables by the time Noah's family disembarked, and they may have prudently chosen to save or ration what food they had left—especially in light of the fact that they may have been entering an "ice age" or "winter season" where nothing could grow. They may also have needed to use the skins and fur of some animals for protective clothing, leading them naturally to make use of the meat. Certainly, meat was available, as Noah was instructed to take seven pairs of clean animals aboard the ark. They obviously had a purpose beyond reproduction of the species, and sacrificial offering didn't require that many extra animals.

Regardless of the reasons, Noah and his family faced a traumatic adjustment to a world that must have been as shocking to them as it would be for us to land on the moon.

The world following the Flood was not as stable as the pre-Flood earth. For at least 700 years, volcanic eruptions and earthquakes were common, and weather patterns were severe and erratic. This worldwide instability resulted in the Ice Age.

Three conditions resulting from Noah's Flood

would have caused the snow and ice of the Ice Age to accumulate: extensive evaporation from oceans, extensive snowfall, and reduced snowmelt.

The glacial sheets did not cover Bible lands, but they no doubt affected its climate, producing more rain, snow, and ice than occurs there today.

The patriarch Job lived in Arabia during this time. There are more references to cold, snow, ice, and frost in his book than in any other book of the Bible. For example:

- "Thawing ice and swollen with melting snow" (Job 6:16).
- "If I washed myself with snow" (Job 9:30).
- "They have nothing to cover themselves in the cold" (Job 24:7).
- "Heat and drought snatch away the melted snow" (Job 24:19).
- "He says to the snow, 'Fall on the earth' " (Job 37:6).
- "The tempest comes out from its chamber, the cold from the driving winds. The breath of God produces ice, and the broad waters become frozen" (Job 37:9–10).
- "Have you entered the storehouses of the snow, or seen the treasures of the hail, which I reserve for times of trouble, for days of war and battle?" (Job 38:22–23).
- "From whose womb comes the ice? Who gives birth to the frost from the heavens? When the waters become hard as stone, when the surface of the deep is frozen?" (Job 38:29–30).

During the Ice Age, so much water was frozen that the sea level was lowered several hundred feet. Ice shelves covered parts of the oceans. This made all the continents accessible, thus allowing migration to occur. Furthermore, no competition for the uninhabited land was necessary, and since food was scarce, migration was encouraged.

Volcanic eruptions, glaciation, an unpredictable environment, a varying food supply, and intermittent warmth from the sun would present unique challenges to the animal population.

Animals inhabiting areas affected by these conditions tended to exhibit longer hair, more massive bones, and heavier teeth. Typical Ice Age mammals included the giant ground sloth, giant beaver, mammoth, saber-toothed tiger, and giant kangaroo. Most of these mammals have smaller, modern-day counterparts.

Episodes of melting snow, catastrophically ruptured glacial lakes, and sudden storms produced many fossils of land animals. Many animal types became extinct at this time. The vast numbers of mammoth fossils in Alaska and Siberia are preserved in frozen soil, not in the rocks. Only a few specimens, usually incomplete, retain frozen flesh.

LONG LIVE MAN

One of the truly monumental questions of this biblical account is how Noah could have lived for almost a thousand years? Impossible, say the critics. You might be surprised to find out just how reasonable the explanation really is.

"A lot of people question the Bible," says Dr. Jonathon Henry, chairman of the Department of Natural Sciences at Tennessee Temple University, "when they read of pre-Flood life spans that averaged 872 years as compared to 72 years today. There are, however, other, nonbiblical documents such as cuneiform tablets with the Sumerian King's List and the Akkadian King's List telling of kings who lived similarly long life spans.

"The famous Sumerian King's List (circa 2,000 B.C.), which makes a passing reference to the Flood, lists eight kings, each of whom is said to have ruled for an average of 30,000 years before the Flood. '[Then] the Flood swept over [the earth].' After the Flood, the reigns of kings are listed as being much lower."[2]

The idea that Noah lived 950 years is incredible enough, but for kings to live 30,000 years is totally unbelievable! But there is an explanation. "According to the ancient Sumerian King's List, preserved on the Weld-Blundell prism, eight pre-Flood rulers reigned over the lower Mesopotamian cities of Eridu, Badtibira, Larak, Sippar, and Shuruppak for phenomenally long time periods. The shortest reign is 18,600 years and the longest is 43,200 years," writes Merrill F. Unger in his famous book, *Archaeology and the Old Testament.*

The *Pictorial Biblical Encyclopedia,* written by Israeli author Gaalyahu Cornfeld, points out how the duration of these reigns are incorrectly stated because the numbering system used by the Sumerians is misinterpreted. For instance, Cornfeld points out that "King Ziusudra reigned 36,000 years" is "equivalent to 600 'ner' in the Mesopotamian numerical pattern." Therefore, the age ranges are similar to the biblical pre-Flood ages of the ten patriarchs from Adam to Noah.

Why did the people in the pre-Flood world live so much longer than we do today? In our research, we discovered a number of intriguing known and implied factors.

It was a different world after the Flood.

As we have shown, the earth before the Flood was encircled by a water-vapor canopy that created a greenhouse effect on the planet. Temperatures were tropical and mild from pole to pole, preventing air-mass circulations and resultant rainfall. The canopy also filtered out harmful radiation from space, reducing the rate of somatic mutations in living cells, which drastically decreased the rate of aging and death.[3]

The Flood, which marks the great division between the original and present worlds, altered the structure of the earth's atmosphere, hydrosphere, lithosphere, and biosphere by a cataclysmic change in the external behavior of the processes of nature.[4]

With earth's protective canopy gone, destructive forces were loosed. For the first time, man, animals, and plant life felt the sting of cold, the ravages of winds and storms, and the blistering temperatures of desert and tropical heat. The ravaging Flood and resultant climatic changes left Planet Earth virtually ruined, its vast, once fertile land areas submerged in great oceans or under barren sands driven by hot winds.[5]

Before the Flood, man lived more than 900 years.

Adam, for example, lived for 930 years (Genesis 5:5); Enos lived to be 905, Cain lived to be 910; Jared, the father of Enoch, died at age 962. Methuselah lived the longest of all—969 years. Noah's father, Lamech, died at age 777 (Genesis 5:31). Noah lived to be 950 years, 350 of which were after the Flood (Genesis 9:28–29).[6]

After the Flood, man's life span eventually decreased to only "threescore and ten" (on the average). Shem, Noah's first son, lived to be 600. He was about 97 when the Flood began. Shem's son, Arphaxad, lived only 438 years. By the first generation after the Flood, the life span had decreased nearly 500 years.[7]

By Abraham's time, life was considerably shorter. Abraham is described as an "old man, full of years" who died "in a good old age" at 175 years (Genesis 25:8). His wife, Sarah, was 127 years old when she died. Isaac lived 180 years, Jacob 147, and Joseph 110. A few hundred years later, King David lived to be only 70, which is the present average life span promised by God ("threescore and ten," or occasionally "fourscore"—Psalm 90:10). Even with modern science's war against major diseases and with far better nutrition, we haven't been able to advance the average life span much beyond God's 70- to 80-year average.[8]

The declining life span seems to be linked to the dissipation of the earth's vapor canopy, say Whitcomb and Morris.[9] The most important effect of the canopy was its shielding action against the intense solar radiation bombarding the earth from space.

The canopy protected life against lethal longwave radiation. Today, ozone is concentrated in the ionosphere and fluxes down because of the global wind systems. Ozone is a highly toxic gas that reacts with the hemoglobin and lipids to create a domino chain reaction among the molecules in the human system. We breathe in ozone in two or three parts per 100 million.

Experiments have shown that not only do white blood cells rush to the lungs when ozone enters the system of an organism, but all the vital processes react. And one of the effects of ozone poisoning is aging. Ozone did not filter down before the Flood. Today it does, and is a major cause of aging.[10]

On the other hand, we can be thankful for this ozone layer in the upper atmosphere of the earth, according to the *Encyclopedia of Atmospheric Sciences* (p. 720). This very thin, protective layer—now a major concern of scientists who believe the use of fluorocarbons in aerosol sprays is destroying it— does stop a tremendous amount of lethal solar radiation from reaching the earth's surface.[11]

Scientists have definitely discovered that overdoses in radiation can contribute to premature aging. According to Dr. Jacob D. Liedmann, a neurosurgeon living in Israel, the human body is capable of living about 1,000 years if certain glands were to continue functioning. He agrees that increased radiation does play a role in shorter life spans, but believes God discontinued the functions of some human glands after the Flood.[12]

He explains that the pineal gland, located close to

the third ventricle of the brain, just below the corpus callosum, has never functioned in modern man. The thymus gland, located in the breastbone area, stops functioning at puberty. A third group of glands, known as the parathyroids, located between the thyroid and thymus glands, undergoes functioning adjustments in puberty that can directly relate to the proper or improper action of other organs.

Dr. Liedmann says the function of the pineal gland is unknown, but is believed to have been connected with the renewal of cell structures. "Even though it doesn't appear to have any function today, its removal or the severing of connective tissue will result in death," Dr. Liedmann says.

Most medical specialists agree that the thymus is a remnant of an organ functional in our ancestors. Dr. Liedmann believes that when it did function, the thymus contributed to man's life span.

"The functioning changes in these three glands are most likely the major reason for our life span's reduction to about 70 years," he says. "The key to life spans like those mentioned in the Bible is within these glands. People who believe victories over disease and better nutrition will result in considerably longer life spans can only hope to add a few years to man's longevity. The expansion of our longevity is controlled by these glands."

According to Dr. David A. Kaufmann, a professor of human anatomy and physical education at the University of Florida,

A commonly accepted but erroneous view is that man's life span is lengthening because of improvements in evolutionary development of human tissues helped along with so-called advances of evolutionary medicine and technology. The world human life expectancy, once one has survived infancy, has not improved since the "threescore and ten years" of King David as prophesied in Psalm 90:10.

The Bible actually states in Genesis 6:3 that our life span potential in the post-Flood world is 120 years. Human-aging research with mice in the early 1990s has clearly demonstrated that 120-year life spans are very achievable.

"There are three main factors that affect one's total health and longevity. First, the inherited, programmed aging process in one's cells. Secondly, one's total living environment at work, play, and at home, and thirdly, one's lifestyle. We have little control over the genetically controlled aging process, limited control over our living environment and much control over our lifestyle.[13]

Dr. Kaufmann also says that increasing pollution shortens life spans. Dr. Ethel Nelson, a pathologist and medical missionary from Tennessee, adds,

We note in the Bible that the Lord permitted the eating of flesh foods immediately after the Flood, and now we also know that eating large amounts of protein will shorten the life span considerably.

One of the most ancient civilizations was that of Egypt. Paleopathologist Dr. Marc Armand Ruffer and his associates, who have done over 36,000 autopsies on Egyptian mummies, concur . . . that the arteries of the well-fed royal bodies reveal cholesterol deposits with narrowing of the artery lumens. Here is evidence that arterial disease (atherosclerosis) was shortening the life spans of humans enjoying flesh foods only ten to fifteen generations after the Flood.[14]

Dr. Kaufmann believes that modern man could maximize his own life span to potentially 120 years by adopting certain regimens.

He suggests following the seven known traits of centenarians: enjoyment of work, strong will to live, quiet independent lifestyles with contentment, eating a variety of natural foods, being devoted to family and faith, keeping mentally and physically active, and having no high ambitions, regrets, self-pity, or combativeness.[15]

Men had large families in pre-Flood days and there is evidence of this practice after the Flood. The age of fathers at the birth of each of the *named* sons ranged from about 30 years in the case of some of Shem's descendants to 500 years in Noah's. Longevity declined after the Flood, but for centuries after the Flood, men still lived and procreated for hundreds of years at a time. Due to the combined effect of long lives and large families, mankind rapidly filled the earth (Genesis 1:28, 6:1, 11) before and after the Flood. The table of nations in Genesis, chapter ten, and the account of dispersion in chapter eleven also indicate large early post-Flood population explosions.[16]

Whitcomb and Morris estimate that the earth's population was as high as 1 billion at the time of the Flood. Others have estimated it at only a few million.[17]

ORIGIN OF RACES

A question often heard from skeptics of the Noah's ark account is, how could all of the races and languages on earth today have possibly come from one family? We asked Dr. Richard Bliss, author of twenty-five professional scientific articles and books and the chairman of the Science Education Department at a California graduate school, if he could shed some light on racial and ethnic characteristics. His answer:

> When it comes to the development of ethnic characteristics, the human genes allow for variations based upon natural selection, cultural preferences and isolated population groups. A geneticist named Punnett developed a mathematical or statistical formula called the Punnett Square which shows how, from brown-skinned males and females, you can easily and quickly get every racial color in the world.
>
> Theoretically, all of the genetic changes that can be formulated for sexually reproducing species in the Punnett Square could happen in as little as one generation, as documented by the case of a family in Australia. This family, with one Nigerian black parent and one English white parent, produced twin boys who have completely different ethnic characteristics—one white son and one black son!

"Technically, the term 'race' should never have been applied to humans, since there is only one race —the human race," says Dr. Walter Brown, author and former director of a U.S. Defense Department laboratory. "One should realize that the word 'race,' referring to physical characteristics, hardly ever occurs in the Bible. Instead, the word 'nation' is used over 200 times. Common usage of the word 'race' today refers to groups of people with distinguishing physical characteristics such as skin color, physical structure, shape of eyes and other facial features, and type of hair."

According to Dr. Brown, to really appreciate how minor these variations are in humans, consider the large variations in the canine family. Most varieties of domestic dogs were produced in the past 300 years. The sizes, colors, fur (or hairlessness), bone structure, abilities, and temperaments of dogs can vary tremendously. For example, look at the differences between a Great Dane or a Chihuahua or a St. Bernard. Since dogs can also interbreed with the wolf, coyote, and the jackal, all are part of the dog "kind."

"By comparison, human variations are relatively few and minor," Dr. Brown says. "We must remember that in every kind of life, there are vast numbers of genes that permit these variations, allowing successive generations to adapt to environmental changes. Without this design feature, extinctions would be much more common."

THE TOWER OF CONFUSION

After Noah and his family left the ark and established homes near the mountains of Ararat, their descendants populated the "land of Shinar," or the Mesopotamian region that has been called "the cradle of civilization." They continued to procreate, and their descendants are named in Genesis, chapter eleven, as building a great city with a tower "that reaches the heavens." According to the Bible, this displeased God, and he confused their languages so they couldn't understand one another. Then he dispersed them from the Tower of Babel in every direction throughout the world.

But the critics disagree. "Fundamentalist Christians have tried to teach that the confusion of the languages came as a result of the building of the Tower of Babel," claims J. David Davis, a U.S. representative of the Temple Institute in Jerusalem and leader of the B'nai Noah Community in Tennessee. "This cannot be proven from either historical data or archaeological evidence. The word Babel has its origin in a Semitic word, which is actually two words, 'ba' and 'bel,' meaning 'the gate to God.'"

The critics also disagree with the fundamental viewpoint on the purpose of the Tower. "Just exactly what the tower was for," says William Curtis, a former college professor and now the director of the Institute for Scientific and Biblical Research, "is open to much interpretation. The tower may have been an astronomical observatory or its purpose may have been as a central rallying point.[18]

"Whatever the tower's purpose was, it is clear from both secular and biblical history that such a tower existed. Ancient historians Herodotus and Eusebius wrote that the remains of such a tower existed in Babylon in their day, and many archaeologists today confirm that the tower ruins they have found in Babylon are that of the time era circa 2200 B.C."[19]

Since linguistics is the study of languages and language origins, let's consider the position taken by Dr. John Oller, professor of linguistics and educational foundations at the University of New Mexico and author of *Language and Experience* and nine other books in the field of linguistics.

Dr. Oller says, "Actually, as remarkable as it may seem, the biblical story of the Tower of Babel is completely consistent with all of the evidence. Anyone who denies this fact is simply engaging in fantasy or speculation.

"There are roughly 5,000 languages in the world today and 50 to 60 stocks. We can trace the best-known of those languages, the Indo-European system, back to about 3,000 B.C., roughly the time of Babel. There is simply no evidence that existing stock can be traced back further."

Dr. Steven Collins, a researcher in Europe and the Near East and professor of biblical studies for Trinity Theological Seminary, offers further evidence for the credibility of the biblical story of Babel and the confusion of languages.

"It is common knowledge in anthropology that the growth of world populations began in the Near East, primarily between the Black Sea and the Caspian Sea. But it all started in the Middle East. The interesting thing about this is that we have a document in the Book of Genesis that describes this ancient process as having begun in and around the Tower of Babel. And, of course, this is exactly what modern anthropology knows by way of the evidence."

Dr. Jonathon Henry, professor of mathematics and science at Tennessee Temple University, explains,

Genesis, chapter ten, lists seventy ethnic groups which dispersed from the Tower of Babel and from which the earth's human population is descended. The fate of these groups is traceable from biblical statements and secular sources. These are said to be the progenitors of all the nations on earth after the Flood, and accordingly, Genesis, chapter ten, is often called the "Table of Nations."[20]

Noah had three sons—Shem, Ham, and Japheth. The descendants of Japheth experienced remarkable prosperity and dispersion, and their names make it clear that they inhabited vast portions of the earth, migrating westward to the Aegean, northward into Europe, and eastward into the Asian subcontinent. Japheth's descendants, then, are the Indo-Europeans. They are identified as the Gentiles in Genesis 10:5, and about 65 percent of Japhethite lines retain their identity today.[21]

The name of Japheth himself is found in ancient literature as Iapetos, the legendary father of the Greeks, and Iyapeti, the reputed ancestor of the Aryans in India. In Australian aboriginal legend, he was Yaperi.[22]

The descendants of Ham migrated mainly into Africa. However, it is incorrect simply to identify Hamites with Africans. Some Hamites eventually migrated to what are now the Oriental countries—China, Japan, and Korea. Still other of Ham's descendants ultimately crossed the Bering Strait which was then a land bridge into North and South America and became the native American peoples. In more recent millennia, other non-Hamitic peoples—the Muslims, a Semitic people—have conquered and settled huge portions of Africa. Of the thirty Hamite lines, only about 20 percent retain their identity today.[23]

Shem's descendants are the Semites, of which the

Jews and Arabs are the only major Semite lines surviving today. They settled mainly in the Bible lands. None of the Semite family lines seems to have left any lasting mark on history except the descendants of Eber, ancestor of Abraham. Most lines seem to be extinct today. Approximately 5 percent of Semite lines can be traced in history.[24]

"In general," Dr. Henry says, "the fate of the families in Genesis, chapter ten, has included the following outcomes—retention of lineage or identity for some peoples such as the Jews, Greeks, and Armenians; apparent extinction with no mention later in the Bible or in history; and loss of identity now, but a re-emergence in later times as indicated by biblical prophecies."[25]

Let's return to Noah's ark, where all this began, and see how the unloading process is moving along.

HOW THE ANIMALS MIGRATED

The animals were led from the ark in such a way as to give the "prey" plenty of time to disperse before the "predators" were released.

"Look!" Japheth's wife exclaimed, opening the smaller cages outside of the ark. "Some of the birds seem confused. Shoo, go on now, that's right, you're free!"

"After the birds are all out, let's release the rodents," Naamah suggested. "Then we'll ask the men to release the reptiles, okay?"

Her daughters-in-law laughed. Naamah couldn't bring herself to even go near the snakes in the ark for more than a year and she certainly wasn't going to start now.

"Isn't this fresh air wonderful!" Shem's wife took a deep breath and stretched. "I can't believe we're finally free."

"Our child," said Ham's very pregnant wife, patting her stomach, "will be born into a new world. There is so much to be done, though, before the baby comes . . ."

Naamah hugged her. "Don't worry, we'll all help you."

"Yes, we'll all help each other and this will be a wonderful new start for all of us," Japheth's wife laughed.

"Come with me." Naamah smiled. "I want to show the three of you something that may just surprise you. . . ."

Just how did all the animals, reptiles, birds, and insects repopulate the new world?

Although billions of insects and fish perished during the Flood, many species survived. Fish that did not get trapped in the sedimentary deposits laid down by receding floodwaters were able to weather the Flood. Most insects reproduce by eggs and therefore many were easily capable of surviving the Flood. Furthermore, the strong evidence suggests that many insects rode out the deluge aboard floating debris atop the floodwaters. Finally, it would not be difficult to believe that some varieties of insects made it aboard the ark as stowaways or as planned passengers even though Noah was not required to include them on his embarkation list. Thus, the repopulation of insects and fish throughout the world was no doubt easily accomplished.[26]

Present-day animal distributions can be explained on the basis of waves of migrations from the mountains of Ararat after the Flood.[27]

Dr. Frank Lewis Marsh in his book *Evolution, Creation and Science,* makes these helpful suggestions as to how the migrations went:

> The journeys from the mountains of Ararat to their present habitats were made in an intermittent fashion, each generation sending representatives a little farther from the original home. The presence of tapirs today only in South America and the Malayan Islands, opposite sides of the Earth, is indicative of the fact that animals migrated in more than one direction. . . .
> There is no reason for believing that this distribution of animals was accomplished by any other processes than those employed in distribution today. . . . Increase in number of individuals of any one kind causes a necessity for spreading outward toward the horizon in search of food and homes. . . .[28]

It is quite unnecessary to assume that hundreds or even thousands of years were required for animals to attain their present geographical distribution. There is some evidence that animals could have reached their present habitats with amazing speed, crossing continents and even large stretches of open sea on their way.[29]

In 1883 the island of Krakatoa was left destroyed by a volcanic eruption. For nearly twenty-five years, practically nothing lived on the remnant of that volcanic island.

"But then the colonists began to arrive—a few

mammals in 1908; a number of birds, lizards, and snakes; various mollusks, insects, and earthworms," says Rachel L. Carson, in her famous book, *The Sea Around Us.* "Ninety percent of Krakatoa's new inhabitants, Dutch scientists found, were forms that could have arrived by air."[30]

Professor Paul A. Moody of the University of Vermont explains how large land animals have been able to cross oceans on natural "floating islands":

> In times of flood, large masses of earth and entwining vegetation, including trees, may be torn loose from the banks of rivers and swept out to sea. Sometimes such masses are encountered floating in the ocean out of sight of land, still lush and green, with palms twenty to thirty feet tall. It is entirely probable that land animals may be transported long distances in this manner.[31]

We know little of the migrations of animals in the past. But what we do know shows clearly the possibility of rapid colonization of distant areas, even though oceans had to be crossed in the process.

"It would not have required many centuries to migrate from Asia to South America over the Bering land bridge," Whitcomb and Morris say. "Population pressures, search for new homes, and especially the impelling force of God's command to the animal kingdom (Genesis 8:17) soon filled every part of the habitable Earth with birds, beasts, and creeping things."[32]

THE SEARCH IS ON

Today the search is on for Noah's ancient ark that preserved mankind and the animals. Some artifacts of this historic event have already been found. In 1943 "Believe It or Not" columnist Robert Ripley discovered enormously huge anchors in Kairouan, Tunisia. Ripley says the anchors were used for tying Noah's ark to Mount Ararat. So far, no one has been able to refute Ripley's report or offer an alternative explanation for the anchors.

Also, Ripley reported in 1941 that he found the tomb of Noah in the Lebanon Mountains of Syria. The tomb is 120 feet long and frequently has clothing—shawls and turbans—draped on it. The sick who often come to sleep by the tomb relate stories of miraculous healings as a result of their visits.

But let's not settle for anchors from the ark, or a tomb visited by sick pilgrims. Rather, let's journey to Mount Ararat where the ark is buried under ice and snow—where on rare occasions it is revealed to a few fortunate climbers.

Notes

[1] Frederick A. Filby, *The Flood Reconsidered* (Grand Rapids: Zondervan Corp., 1971), pp. 107–108.

[2] John C. Whitcomb, *Chart of the Period from the Creation to Abraham* (Hagerstown, MD: Whitcomb Ministries, n.d.).

[3] Dave Balsiger and Charles E. Sellier, *In Search of Noah's Ark* (Los Angeles: Sun Classic Books, 1976), p. 140.

[4] Henry M. Morris, *Scientific Creationism* (San Diego: Creation-Life Publishers, 1974), p. 213.

[5] Balsiger and Sellier, *In Search of Noah's Ark,* p. 140.

[6] Ibid., p. 141.

[7] Ibid.

[8] Ibid.

[9] John C. Whitcomb, Jr., and Henry M. Morris, *The Genesis Flood* (Phillipsburg, NJ: Presbyterian and Reformed Publishing Co., 1961), p. 399.

[10] Donald Patten, "Cataclysm From Space" filmstrip (American Media, 1971).

[11] Balsiger and Sellier, *In Search of Noah's Ark,* p. 142.

[12] Dr. Jacob D. Liedmann, statements made during a March 1976 interview.

[13] David Kaufmann, "Creation Medicine and the Aging Process," Twin Cities Creation Conference, Northwestern College, Roseville, MN, 1992, p. 36.

[14] Ethel R. Nelson, "The Eden Diet and Modern Nutritional Research," Twin Cities Creation Conference, Northwestern College, Roseville, MN, 1992, p. 58.

[15] Kaufmann, "Creation Medicine," p. 36.

[16] Balsiger and Sellier, *In Search of Noah's Ark,* pp. 145–146.

[17] Whitcomb and Morris, *The Genesis Flood,* p. 27.

[18] William M. Curtis, "Babel: The Origin of Diverse Languages and Races," Twin Cities Creation Conference, Northwestern College, Roseville, MN, 1992, p. 178.

[19] Ibid.

[20] Jonathon F. Henry, "Fate of the Ethnic Groups in the Table of Nations," Twin Cities Creation Conference, Northwestern College, Roseville, MN, 1992, p. 91.

[21] Ibid., pp. 91, 95.

[22] Ibid., p. 91.

[23] Ibid., pp. 92–93, 96.

[24] Ibid., p. 95.

[25] Ibid., pp. 97–98.

[26] Balsiger and Sellier, *In Search of Noah's Ark,* p. 148.

[27] Whitcomb and Morris, *The Genesis Flood,* p. 80.

[28] Frank L. Marsh, *Evolution, Creation and Science* (Washington, DC: Review and Herald Publishing, 1947), p. 291.

[29] Balsiger and Sellier, *In Search of Noah's Ark,* p. 149.

[30] Rachel L. Carson, *The Sea Around Us* (New York: Oxford University Press, 1951), pp. 91–92.

[31] Paul A. Moody, *Introduction to Evolution* (New York: Harper and Brothers, 1953), p. 262.

[32] Whitcomb and Morris, *The Genesis Flood,* p. 87.

7

THE MOUNTAIN OF PAIN

At the end of the hundred and fifty days the water had gone down, and on the seventeenth day of the seventh month *the ark came to rest on the mountains of Ararat* [emphasis added].

Genesis 8:3–4

There are many obstacles to overcome in the search for Noah's ark. I've climbed Ararat thirteen times now and I've climbed mountains all over the world but, let me tell you, Mount Ararat is just brutal. It's the worst I've ever climbed.

Actually from the south side, Mount Ararat looks like a nice volcanic cone, but on the opposite side there's this incredible canyon called the Ahora Gorge. Lined by vertical rock walls, the gorge is about one and one-half times the height of the Grand Canyon. I'm convinced the walls are unclimbable—due to the nature of the rock. I know I can't climb them.

Mount Ararat is a volcanic mountain and it has erupted many times since the Flood. On top of that, the summit is covered by a

17-square-mile glacier, which descends to about 14,000 feet. Also, finger glaciers come down to maybe 11,000 feet.

As that glacier moves, it erodes the volcanic layers and produces avalanches. Climbing through that loose, crumbly rock to the glacier is very difficult. We have had to face and overcome all kinds of problems—some of them deadly, such as avalanches, the weather, wild animals, attacking dogs, and snakes.

Once we get up on the glacier, the bottomless crevasses pose an even greater danger. Many a time we've almost died up on the glacier.

The mountain, being 17,000 feet high and capped by a glacier, presents incredible weather problems. On the glacier the winds always blow hard, and any evaporation in the area condenses on the summit.

Every afternoon there's a storm—either wind, rain, or snow—even in the summertime. The winds often blow more than 100 miles per hour! I had a friend who got caught in one of these storms, and he actually had to bolt himself to the ice to keep from being blown away!

The coldest night we ever experienced was in August of 1972. The temperature got down to minus 40 degrees, and the wind blew at about 80 miles per hour. During the day, the temperatures rose to just above freezing. The weather alone made that a very difficult climb.

Because it's a volcanic mountain, toxic volcanic gases and the sulfur fumes ooze out in places creating breathing problems and severe nausea. . . .

Many people also suffer at high elevations from what's called altitude sickness—or oxygen deprivation. We live up there sometimes for a week or more at a time, and it's very difficult to get your breath up there and feel normal in any sense of the word.

People who live near or on the mountain also pose a threat. We've been shot at a number of times—just by thieves mostly, but in recent years, terrorists have taken to the mountain and actually use Ararat as a staging ground for terrorism throughout the Middle East and against Turkey.

My groups have never encountered death, but we've had a lot of close calls and suffered a lot of injuries. A lot of people have died on that mountain searching for the ark. I know of one fellow that's buried in an avalanche up there, and I know of people trapped in crevasses whose bodies will never be recovered. There's just a lot of dangers that climbers face when they're on the upper slopes of the mountain.

Probably the worst thing that happened to my climbing group was when we were caught at the 14,000-foot level in an electrical storm. Before it was over, we were actually struck by lightning. Now, I'm convinced that God performed a miracle that day. No one was seriously hurt and we were able to complete our climb. We went up the mountain and spent about a week looking for Noah's ark.

There's just all kinds of dangers and problems faced by climbers who tackle Mount Ararat in their search for Noah's ark.

Dr. John Morris
geologist and ark expedition team director

Mount Ararat is a unique mountain and perilous in many ways. It is fiercely rugged, always changing, dangerous and yet alluring with an unmistakable, resplendent beauty that is difficult to describe. Among the many wonders of Ararat, a rainbow appears almost daily over the northern parts of the mountain.

Mount Ararat is one of the largest landmasses of any single mountain on earth, and its peak is the highest point in Turkey. Its formidable terrain, however, hides many hazards from even the most expert climbers, with severe—and often fatal—consequences.

The mountain stands alone, with the peak called Big Ararat rising majestically 16,984 feet and an adjacent mountain peak known as Little Ararat rising 12,806 feet from the plain of Bayazit, which is itself 3,000 feet above sea level. Rising high into the clouds above the plain in eastern Turkey, climbers fortunate enough to reach the summit can glimpse through the clouds far into three countries—Russia, Iran, and, of course, Turkey.

Because Ararat is near the borders of these countries, it is a strategic location. Throughout history, Ararat has been claimed and fought over many times—not only by different countries, but also by ethnic groups in the area. Regional fighting still takes place on the mountain today with frequent gun battles between Turkish soldiers, terrorists, thieves, and local Kurdish people who want their independence from Turkey.

At its base, Mount Ararat is about 25 miles in diameter. Its magnificent, solid ice cap—more than

200 feet thick in many places—covers 17 to 22 square miles of the upper slopes. Crevasses are formed when the ice and snow, slowly moving over the rough terrain, break into huge pieces. Some of these fissures fall over the Ahora Gorge. A misstep can send someone plummeting to his or her death hundreds or even thousands of feet below—swallowed up into the seemingly bottomless bowels of Ararat, never to be recovered.

Besides being an enormous area to search, the glaciers are slowly sliding and grinding the rocks of Ararat's upper slopes, creating avalanches that constantly change the shape of the mountain. A climber can easily set off an avalanche of rock or snow merely by talking to his companions. Even experienced climbers using maps and sophisticated equipment can get disoriented and lost. Ararat is an immense, inactive volcano that forever holds the bodies of many victims as proof of its lethal traps, creating many of local legends regarding the mountain.

THE MANY NAMES OF ARARAT

Mount Ararat has several names among the different ethnic groups that allude to the ark landing on Ararat. The Turks call it Aghri Dagh *(Ağri Daği)*, "the painful mountain." Its most common name means "the removal of the curse" or, in Hebrew, "the mountain of descent." The Armenians call the mountain *Masis,* which means "mother of the world." The ancient Armenian name was *Masis Leusar,* which means, "the mountain of the ark."

The Persians called Ararat *Kuhi-nuh,* "the mountain of Noah," or *Saad Dagh,* "the blessed mountain." *Urardhu* or *Urartü,* the Assyro-Babylonian name for the mountain as well as the area surrounding it and the peoples of Armenia, means "highlands," and the area was reportedly esteemed by the ancients as being the central part of the earth.[1]

Almost all of the names of the mountain and the towns surrounding it reflect the history of Noah's ark. *Arghuri* or *Ahora,* a town at the base of the Ahora Gorge, means "the planting of the vine," and this is presumably where Noah planted his vineyard. *Etchmiadzin,* where treasures from the ark were kept in the monastery, means "the place of descent." A village about 18 miles from Mount Ararat is called *Mahser,* which means "doomsday."

There is also an ancient city called *Thamanin* (*Tshaminim* or *Temanin*) on the Iranian side, which means "the region of eight persons." The Armenian town of Nakhichevan was once called *Apobaterion,* which means "the disembarking or landing place." Its present name, *Nakhichevan,* means "the first place of lodging."

The ancient city of *Erivan* (or *Yerevan*) near Ararat means "the first appearance," while the town of *Sharnakh* means "village of Noah." The village of *Tabrīz* (or *Ta Baris*) means "the ship," while *Korhan* means "the first town." Since many of these names are thousands of years old, it seems logical to assume that Noah's ark landed right where the Bible says it landed—*on the mountains of Ararat,* composed of two lone volcanic summits, Big Ararat and Little Ararat.

FACING THE DANGER

The late astronaut Colonel James Irwin, who walked on the Moon, climbed "the painful mountain" five times looking for Noah's ark. "There is a strangeness about Ararat," he said. "You don't notice it at first, because of the novelty of just being there and because you are looking for the prow of the ark behind every rock. But then you notice it: there are no trees. The entire immensity of Ararat is absolutely devoid of a single tree."[2]

Often the sound of thunder can be heard on the mountain, but it's not thunder; it's a chain reaction of echoes created as winds blowing more than 100 miles per hour send gigantic boulders crashing down the Ararat slopes. According to recent accounts, climbers have been killed by such boulders, which they could hear but not see as they stood in the mist of clouds that dropped like thick fog over the mountain.

Colonel Irwin was one such victim. He was hit in the head and almost killed by an unseen rock or ice block that came flying down the mountain, knocking him unconscious. He lost several teeth, was badly injured, and lost a lot of blood. He was, however, miraculously found and rescued after spending the night alone. We'll be looking more closely at Irwin's frightening experiences in a later chapter.

In his book *More Than an Ark on Ararat*, Irwin said,

> We faced risk of physical danger, for Ararat is a crumbling mountain. Every few minutes we could hear

rock slides and small avalanches. We slept in numbing cold, fell on loose rock, dodged tumbling boulders, grew exhausted from high-altitude climbing, had feet sore with blisters, had painfully cracked lips from sunburn, received various cuts and nicks, all in pursuit of a hidden and uncertain treasure.[3]

Ararat is an extinct volcano, and the north slope consists almost entirely of loose tailings of lava rock, which makes it much like walking on stacked bowling balls. There was no solid footing. Some rocks would roll away beneath us, starting small landslides. For hours almost every step would be on rocks that moved. This created extreme discomfort. Each step had to be calculated. You prepared yourself to slide, twist, and slip. Not only was it physically exhausting, the uncertainty of it all was mentally fatiguing.[4]

In addition to all of the other hazards on Mount Ararat, dangerous wild animals must be avoided at various altitudes. Near the base of the mountain, climbers encounter scorpions and deadly puff adder snakes. In the middle, vicious wolves and wild mad dogs prowl and will attack people, causing many explorers to carry guns for protection. On the higher parts of the mountain there are some bears that will generally leave climbers alone as long as they aren't disturbed or with their young.

Wild goats also populate the middle and upper reaches of the mountain, and while they are not dangerous in and of themselves, they trigger avalanches of crumbling volcanic rock and ash or snow in their efforts to get away from people.

The mountain claims lives on a regular basis. For example, Christopher Tease, a young college student from London, tried a solo climb in 1965. His parents sent search parties twice to try to find him, but his body was never recovered.

In 1985 two young women attempted to scale the mountain alone and were never seen again. The very next year, two Norwegians without permits attempted to climb the mountain. One went up one side with a guide, and the other one headed up in a different direction, alone. They were supposed to meet on the mountain, but the man and his guide were never seen again. The solitary climber was initially afraid to acknowledge his friend's disappearance since they were climbing without permits. Shocked and saddened, he went home alone.

John Libi, an experienced mountain climber who tackled Ararat eight different times in an effort to find the ark (the last time when he was seventy-three years old), saw two climbers killed. One, a Belgian, fell over 300 feet to his death. Libi himself fell off a cliff on Mount Ararat once, but was miraculously saved.

Altitude sickness was the most serious problem on Ararat for B. J. Corbin, a sociologist from Maryland and ark expeditioner. "I had the experience of flying on a helicopter that took us from 6,000 feet to 16,000 feet in about twenty minutes, and that's just too quick of a jump in altitude for your body," he says. "We were sick, nauseous, dizzy, and lost our appetites. We felt miserable and were ready to pass out. It was all we could do to put our tents up and then sleep."

Another hazard is the fog. The warm gases that vent from deep inside the volcano create fast-forming fog all over the mountain that can cause climbers to stumble into crevasses or lose their way.

Swiss climber Nicholas Van Arkle, on an expedition to Ararat in 1966, broke through a thin crust of snow and fell about 30 feet into a bottomless crevasse. He was saved by his rope and the quick-thinking Swiss climbers who were with him. Many other explorers haven't been as fortunate, and we will look at some of their stories in a later chapter.

Earthquakes are another natural phenomenon that can strike climbers without notice. In 1840 a devastating earthquake tore a huge chunk out of the mountain on the north side, completely burying the town of Ahora (also known as Arghuri) and the St. Jacob's Monastery. Underneath tons of rocks and dirt lie priceless treasures from Noah's ark in the monastery that will presumably never be seen again.

This incredible earthquake formed the almost two-mile deep Ahora Gorge that is not only deeper than the Grand Canyon but, according to many explorers, even more spectacular. The sheer cliffs of the gorge are two miles deep and a mile wide. Geologists say it was a more powerful earthquake than Mount St. Helens.

"That year, on July 2," says French explorer Fernand Navarra, describing the earthquake of 1840, "a little before sunset, the ground was shaken by undulating waves from the Great Ararat to the east. Fissures appeared on the sides of the mountain and gas fumes burst out, hurling stones. The ice cap was shattered. Witnesses heard a rumble for an hour within the mountain.

"The village of Ahora disappeared, also the

monastery of St. Jacob which had stood for eight centuries. Of the 2,000 and some inhabitants, only a hundred survived—those outside the village itself when the quake struck."[5]

According to geologist Dr. John Morris, the volcanic rock and granite scree contain enormous boulders, some of which are the size of Volkswagens. Others are smaller, but fly down the mountain at deadly speeds as the result of avalanches and rock slides. It is a constant struggle for climbers not only to watch where they are going but also to look up frequently to see if any rocks are flying through the air toward them.[6]

Thieves and terrorists live and hide on the mountain, and many ark explorers have been robbed—barely escaping with their lives. It is also quite possible that some of the missing climbers have not been victims of the mountain at all, but victims of terrorists and thieves.

One of the extremely few female Ararat climbers, Debbie Redmer, a registered nurse from Las Vegas, describes the terrorist situation faced by her and other climbers:

> Two sides of the mountain face hostile neighbors—Iraq and Iran—and even the lower elevations of the mountain are occupied by terrorist groups of one type or another.
>
> With the civil war in neighboring Iraq and the unpredictable situation following the breakup of the Soviet Union, the entire area is a hotbed of instability and a jeopardy to the outside climber. Also, Kurdish terrorists have been known to give expeditioners a great

deal of trouble—robbing them and even threatening them with death.

My experience with terrorists has been that it's a constant pending situation no matter where you are on the mountain. You're always aware that they could be watching you. Many times, we've heard footsteps coming into the campgrounds. We never really know if they're Turkish authorities or terrorists . . . it's a constant situation of fear.

On some occasions, climbers are even mistaken for terrorists. Many of the men that I've climbed with have been threatened at gunpoint by Turkish anti-terrorist squads thinking foreign climbers were terrorists.

They have robbers all over the mountain who come into your camp, and they don't care if they kill you or not. All they want is what you have—your camping equipment, your money—and your life is of no importance to them.

Following is an article from the Associated Press that appeared in numerous papers around the world in early September of 1992:

ANKARA, TURKEY—At least 43 people, including Kurdish guerrillas and civilians, were killed Saturday in three separate incidents linked to the Kurdish insurgency in eastern Turkey.

The semi-official Anatolia news agency quoted the governor of the Agri province as saying at least 20 Kurdish guerrillas were *killed in fierce fighting on Mt. Ararat* [emphasis added].

Gov. Ismet Metin told Anatolia that security forces could not get an accurate death toll because guerrillas took the bodies of their comrades.

Also Saturday, a group of guerrillas blocked a main highway in the southeastern province of Bingol and shot and killed seven travelers, Anatolia reported.

The illegal Kurdish Labor Party has been fighting for

self-rule in the southeastern part of the country since 1984. More than 4,500 people, including guerrillas, civilians and soldiers, have died in the fighting, which has escalated recently.

LEGAL ENTANGLEMENTS

The Turkish government has also made it increasingly difficult for ark expeditioners to climb Mount Ararat. Due to changing policies within a frequently changing government, it's not unusual for an expeditionary group to have all of its permits in order and either be on or even halfway up the mountain when they are escorted back down by Turkish soldiers— sometimes without even an explanation. It is, of course, extremely frustrating for scientists and explorers who have traveled up to halfway around the world to be stopped from climbing Ararat for no apparent reason. Specific examples of recent difficulties with Turkish permits and regulations will be covered in another chapter.

The Turkish Embassy in Washington, D.C., informed us that according to Turkish law number 2863,

As of May 13, 1988, foreign nationals can only be permitted to climb the tumulus [a possible alternative ark site advocated by a couple of Americans, as will be discussed in a later chapter] and Mount Ararat from the Dogubeyazit site, due to the danger of disrupting the area and for their own personal safety. Permission to scale the area must be obtained from the General Staff. The area is monitored from the air by the General Staff for both protection and rescue purposes.

In reality, this law means climbers are allowed to climb the south face of Mount Ararat but are prohibited from the north face, where all of the ark sightings have occurred.

Namik Tan, the First Secretary of the Turkish Embassy, says Ararat explorers must meet certain specific requirements to be granted a Mount Ararat "research permit." "They must meet an application deadline, justify their scholastic qualifications, and have contracted a professional Turkish guide. No visas are needed for U.S. citizens to visit Turkey, but to be on Mount Ararat, the research permit is required."

We learned that Turkish officials often deny Americans and other explorers research permits, and if they grant the permits, the officials frequently cancel them later, leaving expeditioners sitting in hotels at the base of Mount Ararat. To justify their actions, they cite bad climatic conditions, security considerations, attempted artifact smuggling, restrictions by local authorities, and attempts to research an area not covered by the permit (such as the north side of the mountain where the ark is located).

These reasons for research permit denials can be legitimate. However, even with valid permits things often function differently when in Turkey at Mount Ararat, as best illustrated by Bill Dodder, Colonel James Irwin's expedition administrator. "We had permission to fly around Mount Ararat, and Dutch National Television had permission to film. All of a sudden, we were arrested for what we were told was the failure to have a permit to film while flying."

One explorer explained all the problems this way: "It's almost like God doesn't want the ark discovered yet. How else could all of these frustrations and catastrophes dog the steps of so many expert mountaineers?"

WHY EXPLORERS PERSIST

But why do explorers and ark expeditioners keep going back to Ararat when they have to face such insurmountable odds? Eighty-one-year-old Eryl Cummings, the "father of Ark-aeologists," probably best summed it up in a 1986 interview with Dutch National Television when he said, "I've been on seventeen climbs on Mount Ararat. I know it's there. I've talked to seven people who've seen Noah's Ark. I've talked to people who have stood on it, looked in the windows, been all around it. There's no question of it being there, but you're talking about a mountain with an ice cap covering 22 square miles varying in thickness from 80 to 800 feet in thickness. It's not an easy job finding it."

"I did an interesting man-on-the-street interview," says ark expeditioner B. J. Corbin, "asking as many of the locals as I could around the base of Mount Ararat where they thought the ark was located. I found it really interesting that every local thought the ark was under the ice. That also verifies for me that the locals really do believe the ark is on Mount Ararat.

"In my opinion," says Corbin, "the only way the ark could have survived almost 5,000 years would be if it was buried partially or completely under the ice cap. Ice is a natural preserver that would keep the ark intact."

Another ark expeditioner we talked to is Bob Garbo. He's climbed Ararat four times and was the radar project technician on his most recent climb with the Charles Willis Tiger Team Expedition out of Fresno, California.

"I used radar to survey the ice cap on Ararat," he says "and determined its depth. There are at least 17 square miles of solid ice on Ararat year-round, and it's like a refrigerator freezer that is perpetually frozen. I've talked to glaciologists who study frozen artifacts at the South Pole, and they have indicated to me that a wooden boat can be preserved indefinitely in such surroundings.

"The ark needs to be resting in a caldera or a dome underneath the ice to survive," Garbe says. "If it's in an ice flow, it will be destroyed by the grinding action of the flowing glacier."

DISCOVERING ARARAT'S SECRETS

In their search for Noah's ark, Mount Ararat explorers have discovered some secrets about this foreboding mountain. The best time for exploring the mountain, they believe, is during the late summer months and in years when the melt back of snow is substantially above average.

"Mount Ararat is permanently covered year round with deep glacial ice and snow," says John Wanvig, an ark expeditioner and attorney by profession. "There are, of course, some seasonal changes that cause the ice and snow to melt back heavily in

August and September, increasing the chances of seeing the ark.

"However, there are warmer weather cycles that occur every few years which cause increased meltback of the snow-covered summit. It must also be remembered that Mount Ararat is a volcanic mountain and there are fissures and vents through which steam and gases from the core of the mountain are released. Geologically speaking, it's quite possible that the heat released to the surface through these vents contributes to some of the periodic cycles of meltback."

Others have also studied the meltback cycles of the mountain and come up with some provocative conclusions of their own. Mary Irwin, widow of astronaut and ark expeditioner Jim Irwin, has searched for the ark on Ararat also and explains what she has learned about meltback.

"Based on my own research of the meltback on Mount Ararat, it is not influenced by greater snows in the winter or warmer temperatures in the summer. Actually, it is influenced and depends a lot on whether the hot and powerful East winds come blowing off the desert in Iran. In fact, one local man told us that the way to stay out of these fierce winds is to stay on the trail that actually goes right up to Noah's ark."

This explanation may account for the view seen in some recently declassified Air Force black-and-white reconnaissance photos obtained by Colonel Irwin before he died. These photos showed Mount Ararat in an extreme state of meltback on June 17,

1949. It may also account for some of the World War II Air Force sightings.

"At these particular meltback times, in the area where the ark is believed to be located, on the Western Plateau or above the Ahora Gorge," Wanvig says, "it is likely that the ark is only visible or accessible during these infrequent meltback periods. At other times, an expedition looking for the ark could walk directly over the ice-bound ship and never even know that it was there."

Mount Ararat is a deadly puzzle with mazes and traps that lure the adventurous to scale its unstable slopes and trek over its crevasse-covered glaciers, often with tragic results. Ark explorers fortunate enough to even survive the treacherous climb frequently leave the mountain frustrated and discouraged. Why?

Maybe a clue can be found in this statement: "With no more than a half-dozen notable exceptions, all ark discoveries have been accidental and unplanned by 'novices with no special experience or qualification save curiosity and daring' who have stumbled upon the hiding place of Noah's old ship."[7]

Ararat entices and ensnares many, who pay dearly for a chance to see her exquisite treasures, but they are revealed to only a select few—usually those who aren't looking for the treasure in the first place. How ironic that the majestic Ararat is still carefully shrouding the 5,000-year-old mystery from some of the world's most experienced climbers using the most sophisticated equipment in the world.

What will it take to solve this mystery? Has the

ark truly been found on Mount Ararat? Will it ever be found again? After viewing the evidence, you can decide for yourself.

Notes

[1] Violet Cummings, *Noah's Ark: Fact or Fable?* (San Diego: Creation-Science Research Center, 1972), pp. 44–45.

[2] Jim Irwin, *More Than an Ark on Ararat* (Nashville: Broadman Press, 1985), p. 35.

[3] Ibid., p. 46.

[4] Ibid., p. 51.

[5] Fernand Navarra with Dave Balsiger, *Noah's Ark: I Touched It* (Plainfield, NJ: Logos International, 1974), p. 121.

[6] Violet Cummings, *Has Anybody Really Seen Noah's Ark?* (San Diego: Creation-Life Publishers, 1982), pp. 56–57.

[7] Ibid., p. 6.

8

ANCIENT SIGHTINGS OF NOAH'S ARK

The most beautiful thing we can experience
is the mysterious. It is the source of all true
art and science.

Albert Einstein

I have thought it unreasonable to refuse the
request of Jans Janszoon (Struys) who
besought me to testify in writing that he was
in my cell on the holy Mount Ararat,
subsequent to his climb of some thirty-five
miles.

This man cured me of a serious hernia,
and I am therefore greatly in his debt for the
conscientious treatment he gave me. In
return for his benevolence, I presented to
him a cross made of a piece of wood from
the true ark of Noah.

I myself entered that ark and with my own
hands cut from the wood of one of its
compartments that fragment from which that
cross is made.

I informed the same Jans Janszoon in
considerable detail as to the actual
construction of the ark, and also gave him a

piece of stone which I personally chipped from the rock on which the ark rests. All this I testify to be true—as true as I am in fact alive here in my sacred hermitage.

> Dated the 22nd of July, 1670,
> on Mount Ararat
> Domingo Alessandro of Rome[1]

This account, related by Dr. John Warwick Montgomery in his book *The Quest for Noah's Ark,* probably best describes the ancient sightings of Noah's ark. The seventeenth-century Dutch adventurer Jans Janszoon Struys wrote in his travel account of June 1670 that he was asked to visit a hermitage built on the side of Mount Ararat to treat a monk with a hernia. The monk was so pleased that he gave Struys a small wooden cross carved of wood taken from Noah's ark. The monk asked that the wood be taken to St. Peter's Church in Rome. Realizing the significance of the cross, Struys requested the written testimony confirming his visit.

The search for Noah's ark has always centered on "the mountains of Ararat" because that's where Genesis says it landed after the Flood. Eyewitness accounts support the biblical statement that the ark landed on Mount Ararat, located on the border separating Turkey, Iran, and the former Soviet Union.

ANCIENT LEGENDS

There is a fascinating ancient Armenian legend that says Mount Ararat is guarded by angels who watch over the ark in an effort to protect it and hide it.

The Armenian legend explains that after ungodly

descendants of Noah's son, Ham, attempted to climb the mountain to destroy the incriminating evidence of God's righteous judgment of a wicked world, God sent a great storm that obliterated the path to the ark and buried the massive ship under ice and snow. The legend says that the ark will remain protected and hidden from man until the "end of time," when it will be revealed again to prove that the Bible and the story of the Flood are true.[2]

In 1952 Akki Usta, an aged Kurdish historian living in the town of Igdir on Ararat, told French ark explorer Fernand Navarra of a similar legend related by the Kurdish people living in the area.

"Young men of France," he said, "you have come to explore Noah's mountain and you think to find the ark there. Well, this is what I have to say to you: You know the legend, the beautiful legend of the vessel which God the father brought to land on Ararat with its cargo of men and animals.

"And now listen to what I am going to say. The ark is still there! This I was told by the graybeards, and they were told it equally by those who were old during their youth. And all of us here believe it. All the people of Igdir, of Bayazid, of Erivan, to the last shepherd on the twin mountains, all believe it. And we shall hand on that belief to our children, with the bounden duty of passing it on to their descendants. . . . *The ark cannot be submitted to the outrage and sacrilege of the eyes of men!*"[3]

"The ark is still on top of the great sorrowful mountain," Akki Usta said on another occasion. "Everyone in my village believes this, everyone always has. But to reach it, the only way to reach it, is to be as pure as a young child, free of all evil."[4]

Other people who live near the base of the mountain believe that Mount Ararat is inhabited by evil spirits. For "evidence," they point out the number of climbers who are seen going up the mountain but never come back and the sheep that die mysteriously if taken too high, presumably from altitude sickness.

These beliefs help to explain why many nineteenth- and twentieth-century explorers have had trouble finding guides and porters to take them up the mountain. Many believe that the entire snow-covered area of the mountain is either sacred or evil, and man has no business scouring the upper slopes of Ararat trying to find the ark.

In 1856, Major Robert Stuart encountered the same superstitious attitude regarding the peak: "The Kurdish attendants came to a stop and refused to proceed any further, alleging in justification [their] ancestral traditions and the fear of treading on holy ground. They believe that to scale the mountain is impossible and that any attempt of the kind would be followed by the immediate displeasure of Heaven."[5]

However, since the time of Noah, literally hundreds of sightings of Noah's ark have been reported by the ancients. Many of their accounts are remarkably similar even though the eyewitnesses have never met.

RECORDED BY HISTORIANS

Other records from ancient historians reveal that the whereabouts of the ark were taken as fact, and pilgrimages to the ark to scrape off bits of the pitch or bitumen covering were widely known. The pitch scraped off the ark was put into amulets and used as good-luck charms.

Berossus, the Babylonian high priest and historian who lived during the third century B.C., said that in his day the remains of the ark could still be seen.

Around 30 B.C., Hieronymus, an Egyptian historian, and Nicholas of Damascus, the biographer of Herod the Great and the author of a universal history, both wrote about the ark.

Nicholas reported, in the first century A.D., that "there is in Armenia a great mountain called Baris, where many refugees found safety at the time of the Flood, and one man, transported on an ark, grounded on the summit, and relics of the timbers were long preserved."[6] Baris was another name for the present Mount Ararat.

Flavius Josephus, a well-known Jewish historian who wrote copious accounts of the Jews and the beginnings of Christianity in the first century A.D., reported in his *Antiquities of the Jews* a similar account to that given by Berossus:

> The ark landed on a mountaintop in Armenia. The Armenians call that spot the landing place, for it was there that the ark came safe to land, and they show the relics of it even today.
> This flood and the ark are mentioned by all who

have written histories of the barbarians, and among these is Berosus the Chaldean. . . .

Now I have for witness to what I have said all those that have written antiquities, both among the Greeks and the barbarians. For even Manetho, who wrote the Egyptian History, and Berosus who collected the Chaldean Monuments, and Mochus and Hestiaeus, and besides these Hieronymus the Egyptian, and those who composed the Phoenician History agree to what I say.[7]

Josephus, a contemporary of the Apostle Paul, who was a great intellectual and a Jewish Roman citizen, did not report in his writings that he had ever actually seen the ark himself, however. He merely carefully recorded and reported the sightings of others.

An interesting account of a visit to the ark by the East Roman emperor Heraclius early in the seventh century comes to us from Hussein El Macin of Baghdad, who claims that the emperor visited the remains of the ark after conquering the Persian city of Thamanin, near the base of Mount Ararat.[8]

In A.D. 678, after praying and asking God to let him see the ark, Saint Jacob fell asleep on Mount Ararat, and when he awoke, he found a piece of wood from the ark that he believes was given to him by God. With the wood he made a cross that he then took to the cathedral at Etchmiadzin.

Jacob was originally a monk, then Jacob of Medzipin, then Bishop of Nisbis, and finally deemed a saint. Etchmiadzin, located in Armenia, is said to have the oldest monastery in the world and is the seat of the Armenian patriarch who is the spiritual leader of all Armenians worldwide. We'll learn more about the wood at Etchmiadzin Cathedral in a later chapter.

Historians living during the Middle Ages also wrote about the ark. Isidore of Seville, who lived from A.D. 560 to A.D. 636, was the first Christian writer to undertake a compilation of universal knowledge in his acclaimed encyclopedia, *Etymologies*. One of the most learned men of his age, Isidore extended his influence for nearly a thousand years. His encyclopedia was the source for history and culture in the early Middle Ages. He wrote, "Ararat is a mountain in Armenia where the historians testify that the ark came to rest after the Flood. So even to this day wood remains of it are to be seen there."[9]

Jehan Haithon, a thirteenth-century Armenian prince who became a monk, is another who wrote about the ark. He said that in 1254 he saw the ark himself, and he wrote, "Upon the snows of Ararat a black speck is visible at all times—this is Noah's ark."[10]

In A.D. 1269, the famous explorer Marco Polo mentioned the ark on his way through Armenia to the Far East. In his book, *Travels of Marco Polo*, he said, "In the heart of Greater Armenia is a very high mountain, shaped like a cube, on which Noah's ark is said to have rested, whence it is called the Mountain of Noah's ark. On the summit, the snow lies so deep all the year round that no one can ever climb it; this snow never entirely melts, but new snow is forever falling on the old."[11]

In his play titled *The Four PP*, a playwright in the 1520s by the name of John Heywood mentions the fact that Armenia was considered to be the location of Noah's ark and a place of pilgrimage.[12]

The Dutch traveler Jan Janszoon Struys was also told by his monastic friend that "[because of the weather on the mountain] the ark is not decayed, and that it is after so many centuries as complete as the first day it came here."[13]

"The ark's presence on Ararat was a matter of such common opinion in the medieval period that merchants could use the expression 'under Noah's ark' as a synonym for Ararat without even mentioning the latter," says author Dr. Montgomery, in *The Quest for Noah's Ark.* This fact, he says, shows up in an ancient list of toll stations in the Armenian country.[14]

PILGRIMAGE TO THE ARK

The idea that climbing Mount Ararat would displease God probably originates from the misfortunes of those who tried to find the ark and met with fatal catastrophes. For a time, pilgrimages came to an end.

The ancient records of pilgrimages to the ark combined with other information indicate there may have been a distinct trail to the ark at one time that was either wiped out by the great earthquake of 1840 or, over time, has been covered up by rock slides, avalanches, or by the slow-moving summit glaciers.

Conceivably the climb to the ark was not as treacherous as it is today—before the earthquake in 1840 created the jagged cliffs of the Ahora Gorge. Also, if the present glacier gets thicker every year, it's possible that 1,000 to 2,000 years ago the glacier was either much smaller or didn't exist at all. Regardless of why the ark was relatively easy to see in the past, historical sightings indicate that Mount Ararat was widely accepted as the place where the ark landed. From the written and verbal accounts, the ark was seen by hundreds of people before the nineteenth century, and by many more during the past two centuries.

As we examine the incredible accounts of ark sightings in more recent times, we find even more fascinating evidence that the ark does indeed exist on Mount Ararat.

Notes

[1] John Warwick Montgomery, *The Quest for Noah's Ark* (Minneapolis: Bethany Fellowship, Inc.. 1972), pp. 99–100. Translated by Montgomery from Struys's account of his third voyage, chapter 18, in *Les Voyager . . . en Moscovie, en Tartarie, en Perse, aux Indes, & en plusiers autres Pays etrangers* (1684), II, pp. 146–162.

[2] Violet Cummings, *Has Anybody Really Seen Noah's Ark?* (San Diego: Creation-Life Publishers, 1982), p. 32.

[3] Ibid., p. 33.

[4] Dave Balsiger and Charles Sellier, *In Search of Noah's Ark* (Los Angeles: Sun Classic Books, 1976), p. 70.

[5] Cummings, *Has Anybody Really Seen Noah's Ark?* pp. 33–34.

[6] Charles Berlitz, *The Lost Ship of Noah* (New York: G. P. Putnam's Sons, 1987), p. 17.

[7] Flavius Josephus, *Antiquities of the Jews,* translated by William Whiston (Philadelphia: Henry T. Coates & Co.), book 1, chapter 3, sec. 5, cited by Tim LaHaye and John Morris in *The Ark on Ararat* (Nashville: Thomas Nelson, Inc., 1976), pp. 16–17.

[8] Tim LaHaye and John Morris, *The Ark on Ararat* (Nashville: Thomas Nelson, Inc., 1976), p. 22, as cited by Rev. S. Baring-

Gould, *Legends of the Patriarchs and Prophets* (New York: Hurst and Co.), p. 142.

[9]Montgomery, *The Quest for Noah's Ark*, pp. 75–76. Isidore's *Etymologies* translated by Montgomery from Vol. II of W. M. Lindsay's critical edition of the Latin text of Isidore's *Etymologies* (1911).

[10]LaHaye and Morris, *The Ark on Ararat*, p. 22. Jehan Haithon (13th century), as cited by Rev. S. Baring-Gould, *Legends of the Patriarchs and Prophets*, p. 142.

[11]Montgomery, *The Quest for Noah's Ark*, p. 11. From Marco Polo, *The Travels of Marco Polo*, ed. and trans. Ronald Latham (London: The Folio Society, 1968), p. 34.

[12]Cummings, *Has Anybody Really Seen Noah's Ark?* pp. 119–120.

[13]Richard C. Bright, *The Ark, A Reality?* (Humble, TX: Ranger Associates, Inc., 1984), p. 56. Cited by LaHaye and Morris, *The Ark on Ararat*, pp. 23–26, from A.J. Smith, *The Reported Discovery of Noah's Ark* (Orlando: Christ for the World Publishers, 1949), pp. 25–29.

[14]Montgomery, *The Quest for Noah's Ark*, p. 87.

9

SIGHTINGS AND DISCOVERIES IN THE 1800s

> A man of genius makes no mistakes. His errors are volitional and are the portals of discovery.
>
> *Ulysses*, James Joyce (1882–1941)

THE DARK, STONE HALLWAY WAS COLD WITH AN almost eerie silence. The nervous traveler stood alone in the long, narrow hallway of the old St. Jacob's Monastery at Ahora Village on the slopes of Mount Ararat. He was wondering if his visit—pilgrimage is what the monk had called it—was such a good idea after all.

Still, the lure of seeing treasures from Noah's ark rumored to be locked away there had compelled him to write several letters explaining his reasons, desires, and academic credentials, and then travel in 1829 to the monastery.

The trip had taken more than two months and now, instead of being thrilled with what might be one of the greatest discoveries of his life, he was uncomfortable to the point that he would have run out of the monastery and back into the fresh air if he'd only known how to find his way back to the front door.

St. Jacob's Monastery, built in 1088, was a dark, quiet labyrinth of hallways and small rooms made mostly out of smooth polished stones. It had a stale, musty smell and was obviously very old—eight centuries old according to his research. It had almost no windows that he could see and very little natural light. There were oil lamps on the walls, but they were spaced too far apart to really illuminate the place. They just created small halos of light surrounded by deep, mysterious shadows.

To the monks, the dark, dank silence of the monastery presumably felt serene and perfect for contemplation, but the gloom sent chills up and down the traveler's spine, and he couldn't wait to get out of there.

The monk who had met him at the door was uncommunicative, soft-spoken and solemn-looking, covered from head to toe in a dull, dark brown, hooded robe. Everything about him was dull, brown, and quiet. Only his eyes sparkled with the faintest glimmer of life. After the introductions, the traveler was led inside to wait for the monk who had corresponded with him for the past six months.

Within a few minutes, the monk appeared. He was short and round with dimples and a ruddy complexion. As uncommunicative as the first monk, he led the explorer down the hallway to the office of the Holy See. The monks all wore cloth slippers that were silent as they plodded through the halls of the monastery. The traveler's boots were the only shoes that had made any noise, and he felt self-conscious as he clumped along behind the short monk.

He had traveled thousands of miles for the sole purpose of seeing the rumored Noachian relics and a manuscript hidden among the stone walls of this monastery. He also knew that the Holy See could easily refuse his request, making the entire effort futile.

The rotund monk, who waddled more than he walked, went into the office alone, closing the heavy wooden door behind him without a sound, leaving the traveler in the hallway, alone again.

Standing there by the stone wall outside the Holy See's office, he felt odd and totally out of place. The time of waiting and wondering felt awkward—almost painful—and he could hear himself breathing heavily in the stuffy, oppressive silence.

Monks would suddenly appear in a pool of light and then pass him in the hallway without saying a word—just nodding a solemn greeting as they went by. If they had not been moving, one would have thought them dead, they seemed so lifeless. They were all covered with the same long, brown robes that almost made them blend in with the color of the stone walls. The soft rustling of their robes was the only sound they made in passing before they were swallowed up once again by the darkness.

The explorer peered nervously first in one direction, then in another so as to not be startled by a silent monk walking by. Waiting in the hallway seemed like an eternity before the thick wooden door of the Holy See's office creaked open.

"The Holy See will speak with you now," the monk smiled. "Come with me."

They went into a spartan room and bowed reverently in the Eastern style instead of shaking hands.

"I understand that you have come a long way to see the ancient relics of Noah's ark entrusted to us," the Holy See inquired softly. An old man with no hair visible on his head, he had piercing, intelligent eyes and a gray and white beard covering his gaunt, wrinkled face. He appeared serious, yet kind; thin but not feeble.

"Yes, your Holiness. I have traveled thousands of miles to see what God has entrusted to you from Noah's ark."

The Holy See nodded. "Well, the brothers have assured me that your motives are pure, and we will grant your request." With that he turned and went back to his desk. The visitor and the monk bowed, and then the monk led his guest from the room, silently closing the door behind them.

The monk took him through an impossible maze of narrow hallways to a tiny chapel containing a couple of wooden benches, a wooden altar, and two ornate chests. The monk told him to sit on one of the benches and he would show him the holy artifacts. So begins the 1829 story of the search for the ark by the Russian-born German physician Dr. J. J. Friedrich W. Parrot.

EXPLORER ACHIEVES
AMAZING GOALS

Dr. Parrot, professor at the University of Dorpat in Russia, was the first modern ark explorer to leave a record of his Ararat adventures with the publication of his book, *Journey to Ararat.*

The physician achieved three amazing goals in 1829 when he conquered Mount Ararat. He visited the Armenian Etchmiadzin Cathedral where he saw a cross made from the wood of Noah's ark, he visited the St. Jacob's Monastery at Ahora where ancient ark relics and manuscripts were kept, and he scaled the treacherous mountain, reaching the summit in late September. The Parrot Glacier on the northwest side of the grueling mountain is named after him.

At the Etchmiadzin Cathedral, located in what until recently was Soviet Armenia, Dr. Parrot was the first Westerner to ever view a piece of wood said to be from Noah's ark. He described it this way: "A fragment of the Ark of Noah [hangs] by a little chain: it is a small, dark-coloured, quadrangular piece of wood, in good preservation, and carved upon one surface."[1]

From the time of Parrot's account, we hear very little of the relic until it is shown again to the American traveler and Los Angeles radio commentator, Carveth Wells, in 1932. Wells captured the occasion by taking a picture of Archbishop Mesrob, acting head of Etchmiadzin Cathedral, holding the large ornate casket containing the wooden cross.

"I opened the last casket, which looked very much

like an ordinary icon from the outside, but on opening the two doors of the casket, instead of finding the usual painting of Jesus, there was a piece of reddish-colored petrified wood, measuring about 12 inches by 9 and about an inch thick," says Wells, describing the moment in his book. "It was obviously petrified wood, as the grain was clearly visible."[2]

In 1989 Texan Bill Crouse, editor of the *Ararat Report,* a newsletter that chronicles modern-day ark expeditions, visited the Etchmiadzin Cathedral. This cathedral is still the current seat of the Armenian Apostolic faith, and it is said that the stones used in the building of the cathedral came from Mount Ararat 40 miles away.

Crouse reports,

> They say the ark relic was brought to Armenia by Saint Jacob in A.D. 318, and finally found its way to the Etchmiadzin Cathedral in A.D. 678, where it has been kept locked in an elaborate silver case since 1698.
>
> I was only the second Westerner this century allowed to view and examine the bejeweled cross up close. The relic looked like petrified wood. It was grayish brown with some dark markings. To me, its size was about 8 inches by 5 inches—it seemed smaller than Wells's estimate.
>
> When I noticed one of the corners was broken off, I was told that in the eighteenth century a piece was sent as a gift to Catherine the Great of Russia.

Dr. Parrot left Etchmiadzin and proceeded to St. Jacob's Monastery at the 2,000-foot level of Mount Ararat. Here at the monastery in the village of Ahora, he viewed ancient Noachian relics and a manuscript. Although he never said what he actually saw, scholars surmise he probably saw household items and pottery from the ark. The manuscript could have been the ship's log or the story of Noah and the Flood written by priestly scribes. However, Dr. Parrot did tell us the small facility included a chapel, a walled enclosure, a garden, an orchard, and a small residence area.[3]

Dr. Parrot's recorded adventures gave the world valuable information about the St. Jacob Monastery and the village of Ahora, once located on the slopes of Mount Ararat. Eleven years after his visit, the village of Ahora was destroyed by the devastating earthquake of 1840, a cataclysmic disaster somewhat akin to the Mount St. Helens eruption in 1980. Explorer James Bryce wrote about the destruction in 1840 that killed 2,000 people:

> There formerly stood a pleasant little Armenian village of some 200 houses, named Arghuri, or Aghurri. . . . Not far above the village . . . stood the little monastery of St. Jacob, eight centuries old. Towards sunset in the evening of the 20th of June, 1840, the sudden shock of an earthquake, accompanied by a subterranean roar, and followed by a terrific blast of wind, threw down the houses of Arghuri, and at the same moment detached enormous masses of rock with their superjacent ice from the cliffs that surround the chasm.
>
> A shower of falling rocks overwhelmed in an instant the village, the monastery, and a Kurdish encampment on the pastures above. Not a soul survived to tell the tale. . . .
>
> The little monastery, where Parrot lived so happily among the few old monks . . . is gone forever.[4]

Dr. Parrot's group left St. Jacob's Monastery and proceeded to the Ararat summit, where he describes what he saw:

> I pressed forward round a projecting mound of snow, and behold! Before my eyes, now intoxicated with joy, lay the extreme cone, the highest pinnacle of Ararat. Still, a last effort was required of us to ascend a tract of ice by means of steps, and that accomplished, we stood on the top of Ararat.
>
> [The summit] formed of eternal ice, without rock or stone to interrupt its continuity, it was the austere, silvery head of Old Ararat. Towards the east, this summit extended more uniformly than elsewhere, and in this direction it was connected by means of a flattish depression, covered in like manner with perpetual ice, with a second and somewhat lower summit . . . only 397 yards, or less than a quarter of a mile [away].
>
> The gentle depression between the two eminences presents a plain of snow moderately inclined towards the south, over which it would be easy to go from the one to the other, and which may be supposed to be the very spot on which Noah's ark rested, if the summit itself be assumed as the scene of that event. . . .[5]

In Violet Cummings's book *Noah's Ark: Fact or Fable?* there is an amusing account taken from Dr. Parrot's book:

> [Dr. Parrot's] first attempt to scale the peak met with minor disaster when he and his climbing companion lost their footing and rolled a considerable distance down the mountainside. When they arrived back at camp, at the Armenian monastery . . . covered with bruises and sore, they took "special care" not to let a moan escape them while among the Armenians, since they would certainly have taken the tumble as an evidence of divine

punishment for their rash attempt to reach the top, "access to which," explains Parrot, "has been forbidden by a divine decree."[6]

Dr. Parrot never did see the ark himself, but he wrote, "They are all firmly persuaded that the ark remains to this day on the top of Mount Ararat, and that in order to ensure its preservation no human being is allowed to approach it."[7]

FURTHER EXPEDITIONS

At the summit, Dr. Parrot is reported to have planted a cross to mark his accomplishment. After he returned home, news of his climb inspired scores of others to attempt to conquer Mount Ararat, many with the goal of finding—or disproving the existence of—Noah's ark.

In 1835 Karl Behrens reached the summit and confirmed seeing the cross planted by Dr. Parrot, but he also failed to locate the ark. His ascent was attested to by the Imperial Russian Geographical Society.

Dr. Hermann von Abich, a German geologist and professor of mineralogy also from the University of Dorpat, finally reached the summit on July 29, 1845, after three frustrating and unsuccessful attempts. The eastern summit is named after him as well as two of the mountain's glaciers—Abich I and Abich II.

Dr. Abich apparently wasn't looking for the ark at first but rather climbed Ararat to see whether or not the stars and the other planets were visible during the day from extremely high mountaintops.[8]

In 1850 a Russian Army officer, Colonel Khodzko, reached the summit with a well-organized team of sixty persons. Their goal was to systematically search the mountain until the ark was found. However, due to severe weather, they were forced to leave the summit and abandon their plans for an extensive search.

According to Ararat explorer Fernand Navarra, Napoleon III sent an expedition to Mount Ararat sometime between 1852 and 1870 specifically to search for the ark. A Frenchman reported to Navarra that his grandfather had participated in that expedition and that a piece of wood had been recovered. However, no one knows where the wood is today.[9]

In 1856 British Major Robert Stuart led an expedition of four other British climbers that successfully reached the summit of Mount Ararat and created quite a sensation with the local Kurds. The group's original goal was apparently just to reach the summit, but the accounts of several members of the expedition show how they also became intrigued with the idea of finding the ark. These accounts give us some fascinating insights into the post-earthquake mountain and the beliefs of the local Kurds, which have changed very little in the past century.

ARK LEGEND PART OF KURDISH FAITH

Major Stuart wrote, "The Kurdish tribes who dwell on the slopes and at the base of Aghri Dagh, and whose forefathers have been there since the earliest dawn of history, the native Christians of Georgia and Armenia—all indeed who preserve the traditions of the land—are familiar with the story of the Deluge. Their account of that great event varies but slightly from that which has been transmitted to us by Moses, and they hold it as part of their faith that Noah's ark rested on Aghri Dagh, that the hull still remains on the summit, deeply buried out of sight. . . ."[10]

The Kurds firmly believed that the summit was the "second cradle of the human race" and that it was not only impossible to reach the summit, but that any attempt to do so would be followed by serious repercussions and, as Major Stuart put it, "the immediate displeasure of Heaven."

Another member of the Stuart expedition, John Evans, wrote, "the Koords were quite superstitious about the mountain, saying that it was a holy mountain, and no one was allowed to set his foot on it; that several attempts had been made, but that the parties had either given up the attempt, or that their bones had been found afterward at the foot of the mountain. . . ."[11]

According to Major Stuart, "The Kurdish attendants came to a stop and refused to proceed any further alleging in justification [their] ancestral traditions and the fear of treading on hallowed ground. Their superstitious companions abandoned them without further ceremony, leaving the foolhardy climbers to spend the night as best they could, alone in the lee of the rocks, while they retired to a safer position below!"[12]

When Major Stuart's party reached the summit,

they could be seen by the Kurdish chief waiting below, who reportedly said, "Mashallah! God is great. We have always thought, and our fathers before us thought, that God had made that holy mountain inaccessible to man. Many have tried to ascend it, but no one ever succeeded until you came. [He presumably wasn't aware of the successful climbs of two previous groups.] Allah be praised!"

Violet Cummings reports,

As the members of Stuart's party returned from their strenuous climb, "They found horses awaiting them at the nearest possible spot. The Kurdish messengers held their stirrups with profound reverence as they mounted, and as they approached the upper encampment, its occupants, old, young, and middle aged, turned out to look at these strange English Beys, who, as they had all seen with their own eyes, had scaled the forbidden mountain. . . .

Until a late hour the door of the tent was blocked up by Kurds, old and young, who were anxious to see with their eyes and hear with their ears the wonderful Beys of the mountain, for they no longer looked upon them as ordinary men, but as beings of a superior order, who could not be affected by the religious restrictions imposed upon themselves, and who were not subject to the physical infirmities of other men."[13]

INCREDIBLE DISCOVERY

In the late 1870s, Viscount James Bryce, a respected British statesman and author, conducted extensive field and library research and became thoroughly convinced of the historical accuracy of the Bible. Persuaded that the ark was still on Mount Ararat, he set out to disprove the prevailing winds of atheism that Charles Darwin had set in motion at that time.

In 1876 Bryce successfully climbed the mountain, reaching the summit of Mount Ararat alone after his guides left him at the ice cap. He then wrote an intriguing and well-researched book about his experiences called *Transcaucasia and Ararat* as well as an article for the *Journal of the Royal Geographical Society* in London titled "The Ascent of Mount Ararat in 1876."

The highlight of Bryce's trip was not conquering the summit but rather being the first person in modern times to discover hand-tooled lumber on Ararat. Following is an excerpt from his book regarding his wood find:

> Mounting steadily along the same ridge, I saw at a height of over 13,000 feet, lying on the loose blocks, a piece of wood about four feet long and five inches thick, evidently cut by some tool, and so far above the limit of trees that it could by no possibility be a natural fragment of one. . . .
>
> Whether it was really gopher wood, of which material the ark was built, I will not undertake to say, but am willing to submit to the inspection of the curious the bit which I cut off with my ice-axe and brought away. Anyhow, it will be hard to prove that it is not gopher wood.
>
> And if there are any remains of the ark on Ararat at all . . . this wood suits all the requirements of the case. In fact . . . the argument is exceptionally strong.[14]

It's impossible to say whether or not the wood that Bryce found came from Noah's ark, as no scientific dating tests were available in his time—but it is a distinct possibility given the circumstantial evidence.

AMAZING NINETEENTH-CENTURY SIGHTINGS

Probably the most significant nineteenth-century eyewitness sighting of the ark occurred somewhere between 1850 and 1880. It's the story of Haji Yearam, an Armenian who lived his final days in America. His story was told in 1952 by Pastor Harold H. Williams of Logansport, Indiana. Here are excerpts of this most amazing story, published by Violet Cummings in her book, *Noah's Ark: Fact or Fable?*

Haji Yearam's parents and family lived at the foot of Greater Mount Ararat in Armenia. According to their traditions, they were descended directly from those who had come out of the ark, but who had never migrated from that country. Haji's forebears had always remained near the mount where the ark came to rest in a little valley surrounded by some small peaks. . . .

For several hundreds of years after the flood, his forebears had made yearly pilgrimages up to the ark to make sacrifices and to worship there. They had a good trail and steps to the steep places. Finally the enemies of God undertook to go to Ararat and destroy the ark, but as they neared the location there came a terrible storm that washed away the trail, and lightning blasted the rocks. From that time on, even the pilgrimages ceased, because they feared to betray the way to the ungodly, and they feared God's wrath.

When Haji was a large boy, but not yet a man fully grown, there came to his home some strangers. There were three vile men who did not believe in the Bible and did not believe in the existence of a personal God. They were scientists. They were on this expedition specifically to prove the legend of Noah's ark to be a fraud and a fake.

They hired the father of young Haji Yearam as their official guide. They hired the boy to assist his father as guide.

It was an unusually hot summer, so the snow and glaciers had melted more than usual. After extreme hardship and peril the party came to the little valley way up on Greater Ararat, not on the very top but a little way down from the top. This little valley is surrounded by a number of small peaks. There the ark came to rest in a little lake, and the peaks protected it from the tidal waves that rushed back and forth as the flood subsided. On one side of the valley the water from the melting snows and glacier spills over in a little river that runs down the mountain. As they reached this spot, there they found the prow of a mighty ship protruding out of the ice.

They went inside the ark and did considerable exploring. The whole structure was covered with a varnish or lacquer that was very thick and strong, both outside and inside the ship. The ship was built more like a great and mighty house on the hull of a ship, but without any windows. There was a great doorway of immense size, but the door was missing.

The scientists were appalled and dumbfounded and went into a rage at finding what they had hoped to prove non-existent. They were so angry and mad that they said they would destroy the ship, but the wood was more like stone than any wood we have now. They did not have the tools or means to wreck so mighty a ship and had to give up. They did tear out some timbers and tried to burn the wood, but it was so hard it was almost impossible to burn it.

They held a council, and then took a solemn and fearful death oath. Any man present who would ever breathe a word about what they had found would be tortured and murdered.

They told their guide and his son that they would keep tabs on them and that if they ever told anyone and they found it out they would surely be tortured and murdered. For fear of their lives, Haji and his father had never told what they found except to their best trusted and closest relatives.[15]

According to Pastor Williams, Haji's story was confirmed by an elderly scientist on his deathbed in London. His report continues:

One evening (I am pretty sure it was in 1918) I sat reading the daily paper in our apartment in Brockton. Suddenly I saw in a very small print a short story of a dying man's confession. It was a news item one column wide and, as I remembered it, not more than two inches deep. It stated that an elderly scientist on his deathbed in London was afraid to die before making a terrible confession. It gave briefly the very date and facts that Haji Yearam had related to us in his story.

Haji Yearam had died in my parents' home in Oakland, California, about the same time that the old scientist had died in London. We had never for a moment doubted Haji's story, but when this scientist on his deathbed on the other side of the world confessed the same story in every detail, we knew positively that the story was true in every detail.[16]

In 1883 a surprising turn of events affected every subsequent expedition searching for the ark of Noah.

On May 2 another devastating earthquake encompassed Mount Ararat, causing destructive avalanches of rocks and ice that once again buried

According to the Bible, Noah's ark landed "on the mountains of Ararat," composed of two lone volcanic summits—Mount Ararat (Big Ararat) and Little Ararat, as seen in this rare summertime aerial photograph. The mountains stand alone, with Big Ararat (background) rising majestically 16, 984 feet and Little Ararat rising 12,806 feet from the plain of Bayazit, which is itself 3,000 feet above sea level.   COURTESY OF JOHN MORRIS

Based on the purported 1902 sighting of Noah's ark by George Hagopian, artist-illustrator Dr. Elfred Lee drew this picture to match Hagopian's description of the ancient vessel. Other purported ark eyewitnesses have also confirmed that this is an accurate depiction. According to the Bible, the three-deck ark was 450 feet long, 75 feet wide and 45 feet high. A row of windows beneath a roof catwalk extended the length of the ark.   COURTESY OF DR. ELFRED LEE

Researcher Robert Ripley of "Ripley's Believe It of Not" fame is dwarfed as he poses for a picture beside what he claimed to be the anchors from Noah's ark in Kairouan, Tunisia. Ripley says these anchors were used in tying the ark to Mount Ararat. No one has yet been able to disprove his claim or offer any alternative explanation for the anchors.

This large bronze Noah's ark coin was struck 1,700 years ago at Apameia Kibotos in Asia Minor (modern Turkey) near the mountains of Ararat. The profile of Emperor Trebonianus Gallus appears on the front while three scenes from the Flood story are depicted on the reverse side. In the center of the coin, the head and shoulders of Noah and his wife protrude from the ark as it floats on water and shelters them from the rain. The second scene above the lid shows a dove with the olive spray in its beak symbolizing the subsidence of the waters. The third episode shows Noah and his wife with arms upraised in an attitude of prayer for their salvation. The side of the ark is inscribed with three Greek letters meaning "Noah."

Evidence that the nearly 17,000-foot Mount Ararat was once underwater during what many geologists believe was Noah's global flood is the abundance of pillow lava. Volcanic pillow lava forms only underwater, when water rapidly chills the lava, creating circular formations resembling pillows. Pillow lava like the huge block in the photograph has been found as high as 14,000 feet and would probably be found on the summit if Ararat was not ice-covered.

COURTESY OF JOHN MCINTOSH

This small iron pot reveals ancient biblical man had smelting and manufacturing abilities. The iron pot was reportedly found in 1912 encased in a block of coal at the Municipal Electric Plant in Thomas, Oklahoma. The pot, with an affidavit from the pot finder, is now on display at the Miles Musical Museum in Eureka Springs, Arkansas. Some scientists believe the pot was from the biblical time of Tubal-Cain and buried sedimentarily in the world-wide flood of Noah's day.

COURTESY OF MILES MUSICAL MUSEUM

In 1959 a strange shiplike object was noted in this Turkish Army aerial photograph taken about 17 miles south of Mount Ararat. Explorers David Fasold and Ron Wyatt claim this formation is the remains of Noah's ark, although examination of the site by several scientists have concluded it is nothing more than a rare geologic formation. Also, in this same immediate region near Little Ararat, Fasold and Wyatt fail to mention or explain numerous other similar boat-shaped formations. Is one to conclude that Noah had a fleet of arks, contrary to the biblical account?

COURTESY OF TURKISH AIR FORCE

A ground view of the Fasold-Wyatt Noah's ark site reveals a natural land formation left after water erosion. Dr. Ron Charles, an archaeological historian, explains the site as composed of two formations—the upper Fasold-Wyatt Ark site and a lower formation connecting on the right. After three on-site inspections, Dr. Charles concluded the site was once a Mongol reconnaissance fort built by Mongol conqueror Tamerlane in the late 1300s. The upper tier would have been used for observation, supplies, and officer's quarters, while the lower tier was quarters for the mercenary army.   COURTESY OF B. J. CORBIN

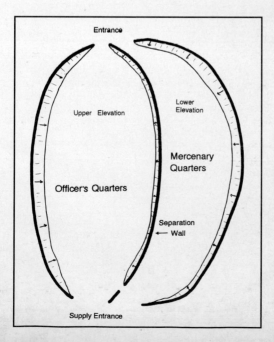

Entrance

Upper Elevation

Lower Elevation

Mercenary Quarters

Officer's Quarters

Separation
← Wall

Supply Entrance

This bejeweled cross said to have been made from the grayish-brown wood of Noah's ark was brought to Armenia by St. Jacob in 318 A.D. It found its way to the Etchmiadzin Cathedral about 40 miles from Mt. Ararat in 678 A.D., where it has been kept locked in an elaborate silver case since 1698. This picture taken in 1989 was only the second occasion this century in which a Westerner was allowed to see or photograph this ancient relic.

COURTESY OF BILL CROUSE

On July 6, 1955, Fernand Navarra posed atop the crevasse where he recovered a piece of wood believed to be from Noah's ark. This moment was the apex of his three expeditions to Mount Ararat to recover wood from the ark. Also, in 1969 Navarra led the SEARCH Foundation expedition to the site of his 1955 wood find. They again discovered hewn wood in a small glacial pond adjacent ot the 1955 crevasse location.

COURTESY OF RAPHAEL NAVARRA

Fernand Navarra holds a piece of wood recovered from Mount Ararat that is believed to be from Noah's ark. Although greatly deteriorated, the wood is both hand-hewn and squared. The bottom photo shows a piece of wood recovered by Navarra during the 1969 SEARCH Foundation expedition. It is encased in a special container to prevent further deterioration.
COURTESY OF RAPHAEL NAVARRA AND DAVID W. BALSIGER

The French SPOT Satellite was utilized to specifically pinpoint the exact location of the ark on Mount Ararat. SPOT satellite photos were taken of Mount Ararat from 500 miles up in September of 1989. The SPOT picture enchanced by computer is of an S-shaped 1,500-foot-long crevasse above the Ahora Gorge that is about 90 feet wide. The "+" marker indicates where there is a defined object approximately 80 feet wide, with 90 feet of length extending out of the snow over a rocky ledge. An additional 200 feet of the object is under the snow protruding downward from the marker.
COURTESY OF SPOT IMAGERY CORPORATION, MIKE HOLMAN

Phantom arks have fooled several expeditioneers searching for Noah's ark on Mount Ararat. In 1989 one ark expedition leader photographed this arklike object and even announced the discovery to the worldwide news media. Later helicopter observations in the same year and a ground expedition in 1990 confirmed that it was a rock formation.   COURTESY OF JOHN MORRIS

In 1986 astronaut Colonel James Irwin returned to Mount Ararat having obtained a permit to fly a light plane around the mountain. A Dutch National Television crew headed by Jan Van der Bosch went with Colonel Irwin and shot a documentary. This amazing photograph was taken of what Dutch National Television believes is a portion of the ark protruding out of the icy snow. Unfortunately, Colonel Irwin died of a heart attack before he could mount a ground expedition to confirm whether this was really a portion of Noah's ark.

COURTESY OF DUTCH NATIONAL TELEVISION

"Believe It of Not" columnist Robert Ripley, who has never been proved wrong, says he found the authentic tomb of Noah in the Lebanon Mountains of the Holy Land near rhe ancient city of Damascus. It is a very sacred spot, as shown by the gifts of clothing and shawls brought to the tomb. Ripley is seated in the foreground.

COURTESY OF RIPLEY ENTERTAIN- MENT INC., COPYRIGHT © 1993

villages on the slopes of the mountain. While not as severe as the 1840 earthquake, it did shake the mountain to its very foundations and the devastation was reported around the world.

Later that year, the Turkish government sent an expedition of commissioners to survey the mountain to determine the extent of the damage of this earthquake-prone region.

Captain Gascoyne, an Englishman and attaché of the British Embassy in Constantinople (now called Istanbul), went with the Turkish surveying team. The explorers actually stumbled upon the ark and, once informed of the historical significance of the find by Mr. Gascoyne, the surveying team took detailed measurements and notes on the great, wooden ship. Part of the ark was protruding from a glacier, but they were unable to determine the exact length because much of it was still completely submerged in glacial ice. The surveyors were able to go inside.

The local people also told the surveying team that the ship had been partially exposed for the previous six years and that it had been the topic of much discussion by those living near the mountain.

Elated with their historic find, the Turkish commissioners informed the world's press and were totally unprepared for and shocked at the response. The original press release from Constantinople has never been found, but the article supposedly closest to the original story was located in the British *Prophetic Messenger,* published in the summer of 1883. The following is an excerpt from the article:

We have received from our correspondent in Trebizond news of the return of the Commissioners appointed by the Turkish Government to inquire into the reported destruction of Mosul, Ashak, and Bayazid by avalanches, and to render relief to the distressed villages in the glens of the Ararat ranges, who had suffered so severely from the unusual inclemency of the season.

The expedition was fortunate in making a discovery that cannot fail to be of interest to the whole civilized world, for among the vastnesses of one of the glens of Mount Ararat, they came upon a gigantic structure of very dark wood, embedded at the foot of one of the glaciers, with one end protruding, and which they believe to be none other than the old ark in which Noah and his family navigated the waters of the Deluge. The place where the discovery is made is about five days' journey from Trebizond, in the Department of Van, in Armenia, about four leagues from the Persian frontier. . . .

At last they were rewarded by the sight of a huge dark mass, protruding 20 or 30 feet from the glacier, on the left side of the ravine. They found it was formed of wood not grown in these elevated districts, not nearer than the hot valleys of the Euphrates, where it is known by the natives as "izim," said to be the gopher wood of the Scriptures. It was in a good state of preservation, being painted on the outside with a dark brown pigment, and constructed of great strength. . . .

The projected portion seemed about 40 or 50 feet in height, but to what length it penetrated into the glacier they could not estimate.

Effecting an entrance through one of the broken corners, the explorers found it filled for the greater part with ice, the interior being partitioned off into compartments about 12 or 15 feet high, into three of which only they were able to make their way, owing to the mass of frozen substance with which these were filled, and also because of their fear of the structure collapsing with the overhanging mass of the huge glacier. . . .[17]

WIDESPREAD RIDICULE

Rather than inspiring scores of scientists, archaeologists, and journalists to journey to see the ark for themselves, the report received widespread ridicule and disbelief of the sort usually reserved today for tales of alien abductions and UFOs. Anyone who dared to express any belief in the report was humiliated for his or her naïveté.

Following is a brief excerpt from the August 10, 1883, edition of the *New York Herald:*

> Now let the heathen rage and the free-thinkers call on their respective beer cellars to hide them, for has not Noah's ark been discovered. . . . If arks were the fashion 4,400 years ago, why may not dozens of them have drifted from their moorings during the great November freshet of 2616 B.C. and gone ashore on Mount Ararat?[18]

And from the August 13, 1883, issue of the *New York World* comes the following ridicule:

> At this point archaeology could afford to rest at any ordinary period of the world and we should expect the luckiest finders to form a syndicate and open a bazaar for the sale of relics.
>
> We must not forget that the planting of the Cardiff Giant was not so much to make money as to establish the missing link. The Noah's Ark syndicate are only following the tactics of the antiquary who recently offered to sell an original manuscript of the Mosaic Law signed by Moses to the British Museum.

With these principles in view, the reader must not be surprised to learn by the latest dispatches from our representative . . . that the engineers have broken through the third compartment of the ark, and in the true spirit of the age have discovered the original log kept by Noah and his sons.[19]

Embarrassed and irritated by the reaction of the world's press, the Turkish government did not follow up the amazing find with another expedition, and apparently the snows that year covered the ark and hid it once again from view.

PRINCE NOURI'S NOTABLE DISCOVERY

The next notable discovery of the ark was by Prince John Joseph Nouri, whose full name and title as listed in one account are as follows: His Pontifical Eminence, the Most Venerable Prelate, Monseignior, the Zamorrin Nouri, John Joseph, Prince of Nouri, DD., LL.D. (by Divine Providence), Chaldean Patriarchal Archdeacon of Babylon and Jerusalem, Grand Apostolic Ambassador of Malabar, India, and Persia. The discoverer of Noah's Ark, and the Golden Mountains of the Moon [who was soon to be coronated as] Patriarch of the Chaldean (Nestorian) Church.

John Joseph was also called the "Sacred Crown's Supreme Representative-General of the Holy Orthodox Patriarchal Imperiality" as well as "The First Universal Exploring Traveler" of a million miles.[20]

Another publication in 1894 listed his titles as follows: The Rev. Dr. John Joseph Nouri, DD.,

LL.D., Chaldean Archdeacon of Babylon and Jerusalem, Pontifical Delegate General of Malabar and Ex-grand Secretary of the Metropolitan Archdiocese of India and Persia.[21]

The prince, who spoke ten languages, claimed to have climbed Ararat three times (presumably without lugging all of his titles and crowns) and to have finally found the ark on his third climb on April 25, 1887, when he was in his early twenties. His account gave support to the 1883 account of the Turkish surveying team.

Prince Nouri's account of finding Noah's ark was published in the *Zion's Watch Tower* of August 15, 1894:

> The bow and stern were clearly in view, but the center was buried in snow, and one end of it had fallen off and decayed.
>
> It stood more than 100 feet high and was over 300 yards long [an estimate; without any ability to measure the vessel, Nouri has overestimated the size compared to biblical dimensions]. The wood was peculiar, dark reddish in color, almost iron colored in fact, and seemed very thick. I think the cold has preserved the wood. I am very positive that we saw the real ark, though it is over 4,000 years old!
>
> Though within rifle shot, they could not reach it, the slope from the bench on which it rested being a glare of ice and snow, and they could not remain till the midsummer thaw.[22]

To no avail, he tried desperately to find help and financial support to recover the ark before it froze over again or before it fell deeper into a crevasse. His dream was to take the ark to the Chicago Exhibition, the 1893 World's Fair. But his dream, obviously, never came true. He died suddenly of pneumonia a few years after the World's Fair without leaving a map or any written record of the ark's location.

Flamboyant Prince Nouri's report wrapped up the expeditions and ark sightings of the nineteenth century—a most significant century for studiers of Noah's ark. The conquest of Mount Ararat's summit was achieved by many climbers during that century. Hand-tooled wood believed to be from the ark was recovered at the 13,000-foot elevation. Also, the first official recognition by the Turkish government of the discovery of Noah's ark occurred during this century. Finally, the attempt by disbelieving scientists to destroy the ark made the 1800s a particularly intriguing era.

WERE STORIES OF
SIGHTINGS CREDIBLE?

The question which must be asked about ancient and even modern Noah's ark sightings is, are the claims and stories about actually seeing the ark on Mount Ararat really credible? We went to Richard Bright, who has been on six expeditions to Mount Ararat and is a commercial airline pilot and the author of *The Ark, A Reality?* He has done an extensive comparison of ark sightings.

> I have studied virtually every historical sighting account of the ark on Mount Ararat. They are pretty close to always being consistent in what is being described by eyewitnesses.

Over the past 200 years many accounts of these sightings have gone into considerable detail. I have compared in detail thirty-two of these sightings and have found there's tremendous consistency between eyewitnesses even though they never knew each other, and may have seen the ark many, many years from each other.

For instance, there are four reports of the ark with the door off. There are seven reports of one end broken off, and eighteen reports of it sticking out of the ice and snow. There are nine reports of a melt-water pond, eight reports of a ledge, and ten reports of a ravine, valley, gully, or some such place which the ark sitting on a ledge could be in. There are three reports of a very difficult or hazardous climb to reach the ship.

There are at least two reports of the ark leaning against a rock or ridge, and two reports of it sitting in a north-south direction. There are three reports of a stream down the mountain and two reports of the ark having openings around the top.

We can choose to believe that all of these reports are based upon lies, *or* based on the information presented, we can choose to believe the ark or a large wooden barge is on Mount Ararat—if just one of the reports is true.

From all the eyewitness reports, Bright says in his book, it's possible to reconstruct the ark site at about 13,000 to 14,000 feet and show what modern-day searchers will find regarding the condition of the ark:

The ark is located on a ledge, in some sort of a ravine, leaning against a rock or ridge, and is in the ice and snow. When there is melting, the melt-waters form a small pond, that when full to its banks overflow and run down the hill. The ends of the ark point generally in a north-south direction, with at least the exposed end broken, or broken off, and the door is missing.[23]

The nineteenth century unveiled incredible evidence of the existence of Noah's ark on Mount Ararat. But the twentieth century is proving to be even more rewarding in its disclosures. Not only has the scientific knowledge and space technology of our time confirmed the ancient sightings, but the hidden secrets of this historic vessel have been unlocked as well.

Notes

[1] Friedrich Parrot, *Journey to Ararat* (New York: Harper and Brothers Publishers, 1846), p. 113.

[2] Carveth Wells, *Kapoot* (New York: Robert M. McBride and Company, 1934), p. 228.

[3] Tim LaHaye and John Morris, *The Ark on Ararat* (Nashville: Thomas Nelson Publishers, 1976), p. 30.

[4] John Warwick Montgomery, *The Quest for Noah's Ark* (Minneapolis: Bethany Fellowship, 1972), p. 140. Cited from Sir James Bryce, *Transcaucasia and Ararat* (1877), pp. 239–241.

[5] John Warwick Montgomery, *The Quest for Noah's Ark,* pp. 137–138. Cited from Friedrich Parrot, *Journey to Ararat* (1846), p. 176.

[6] Violet M. Cummings, *Noah's Ark: Fact or Fable?* (San Diego: Creation-Science Research Center, 1972), p. 52.

[7] Charles Berlitz, *The Lost Ship of Noah* (New York: G. P. Putnam's Sons, 1987), pp. 20–21.

[8] Ibid., p. 21.

[9] Cummings, *Noah's Ark: Fact or Fable?* p. 196.

[10] Montgomery, p. 166. Cited in Proceedings of the Royal Geographical Society (1877), pp. 77–92.

[11] Cummings, *Noah's Ark: Fact or Fable?* p. 54.

[12] Ibid., p. 52.

[13] Ibid., p. 53.

[14] LaHaye and Morris, *The Ark on Ararat,* pp. 53–54. Cited from James Bryce, *Transcaucasia and Ararat* (1877), pp. 264–265.

[15] Cummings, *Noah's Ark: Fact or Fable?* pp. 189–192.

[16] Ibid., pp. 192–193.

[17] LaHaye and Morris, *The Ark on Ararat,* pp. 56–57.

[18] Ibid., pp. 59–60.

[19] Ibid., pp. 61–62.

[20] Cummings, *Noah's Ark: Fact or Fable?* pp. 119–120, 122.

[21] Richard Bright, *The Ark, A Reality?* (Humble, TX: Ranger Associates, 1984), p. 57.

[22] Ibid., p. 58.

[23] Ibid., pp. 405–406.

10

GROUND AND AERIAL
SIGHTINGS IN THE EARLY 1900s

Every man without passions has within him
no principle of action, nor motive to act.
> Claude Adrien Helvetius (1715–1771)

My grandfather was the minister of the big
Armenian Orthodox Church in Van (near Lake
Van), and he always told me stories about
the holy ship on the holy mountain.

And then one day my uncle said,
"Georgie, I'm going to take you to see the
holy ark." We packed supplies on his
donkey, and together we started our trek
toward Mount Ararat.

My feet were getting sore, and the donkey
kept wanting to go in the wrong direction,
but we continued climbing until we got about
halfway up. Then Uncle took both supplies
and me on his back, and we climbed and
climbed.

It took us almost eight days from the time
we left Van to the moment we got to the
place on the holy mountain where both my
grandfather and my uncle had said the holy
ship had come to rest.

I guess my uncle took me there that year because it was a year without much snow— a "smooth year" we called it. There's one of those about every twenty years.

And then we got to the ark. It was getting dark and misty around us. My uncle dropped his pack, and together we began to haul stones to the side of the ship. Within a short time we had stacked a high pile of rocks against the side of the ship.

"Georgie, come here," he said, grabbing me by my arm. "You are going on top of the holy ark." He lifted me up and put me on his shoulders, and together we climbed the pile of rocks. When he had reached the top, his hands grabbed my ankles and he began to push me up.

"Reach for the top, Georgie," he yelled. "Grab the edge and pull yourself up!"

I stood up straight and looked all over the ship. It was long. The height was about 40 feet.

"Look inside the ark," my uncle called up to me. "Look for the holes. Look for the big one. Look inside and tell me what you see."

I shivered from the cold and from fear and glanced around me. Yes, there was the hole, big and gaping. I peeked into the blackness of the hole, but saw nothing. Then I knelt down and kissed the holy ark.

When we were there, the top of the ark was covered with a very thin coat of fresh fallen snow. But when I brushed some of it away I could see a green moss growing right on top. When I pulled a piece off . . . it was made of wood. The grain was right there. This green moss made the ark feel soft and moldy.

On the roof, besides one large hole, I

remember small holes running all the way from the front to the back. I don't know exactly how many, but there must have been at least fifty of them running down the middle with small intervals in between. My uncle told me these holes were for air.

That roof was flat with the exception of that narrow raised section running all the way from the bow to the stern with all those holes in it.

I remember, my uncle took his gun and shot into the side of the ark, but the bullet wouldn't penetrate. Uncle then pulled his long hunting knife from his belt, and with the heavy handle he chipped a piece from the side of the ark. Then we went down the mountainside and returned to Van.

Ten-year-old George Hagopian's account of his 1902 visit to Noah's ark[1]

ARTIST SKETCHES ARK FROM DESCRIPTION

George Hagopian was an eighty-year-old Armenian when he related this account to artist-illustrator Dr. Elfred Lee and ark researcher-explorer Eryl Cummings in Easton, Maryland, in 1970. Following several additional interviews with Hagopian, Dr. Lee was able to sketch the very first likeness of Noah's ark, including where the windows were placed. Dr. Lee's illustration of the ancient vessel has since been published in biblical reference books throughout the world.

Hagopian again went back to the ark in 1904 while on a pilgrimage for "holy" flowers. He gave

Dr. Lee additional details regarding the ark's features:

> I saw the ark a second time. I think it was in 1904. We were on the mountain looking for holy flowers, and I went back to the ark and it still looked the same. Nothing had changed. I didn't get to the top that time, but I stayed at the side, and really got a good look at it.
>
> It was resting on a steep ledge of bluish-green rock about 3,000 feet wide.
>
> Another thing I noticed was that I didn't see any nails at all. It seemed that the whole ship was made of one piece of petrified wood.
>
> There was definitely no door in the side of the ship that I could see. No opening of any kind. There may have been one in the part I couldn't see, but that I don't know. That side was practically inaccessible. I could only see my side and part of the bow.
>
> The sides were slanting outward to the top and the front was flat. I didn't see any real curves. It was unlike any other boat I have ever seen. It looked more like a flat-bottomed barge.[2]

Paul Meier, a renowned medical doctor and psychiatrist, author and co-founder of the sixty-seven Minirth-Meier New Life Clinics across the United States, is an expert in analyzing the behavioral patterns of people. Dr. Meier was asked to analyze the audio tapes and video interviews of George Hagopian and two of the ark eyewitnesses discussed in Chapter 14. He is particularly well-suited for the task, having been the medical officer on a 1985 ark-Ararat expedition led by John McIntosh from California. He reports,

As a psychiatrist, I've authored forty books on personality types and traits, and human behavior, and can determine whether or not people are telling the truth and whether or not they are in touch with reality. By studying audio and video tapes for several hours over several days, I was able to make an analysis of George Hagopian's eyewitness account as well as those of other eyewitnesses.

I found George Hagopian to be a very interesting Armenian in his seventies who actually grew up and lived in the Mount Ararat area. He claims that he and his friends made treks up the mountain to Noah's ark. These types of things have been reported by a number of Armenians who live in the United States, Russia, and in other parts of the world. [Seeing the ark] was a tradition of the Armenian culture.

When George got up there, his father told him, "You are a holy man now." He traveled to the ark when he was only ten years old and then again when he was thirteen years old. Now, his description of the ark and some of the details were not accurate, but he was describing them from a ten-year-old's perspective and a thirteen-year-old's perspective.

George said that the ark seemed like it was 1,000 feet long and we know from the Bible and reconnaissance photos that it's only about 450 feet long. His descriptions of the width and height were much closer. He said that the cliff it was up against was 3,000 feet high and 3,000 feet wide and we know that that was a gross exaggeration, but again, he was a young, ten-year-old child and a thirteen-year-old child when he saw the ark.

When asked about windows, he said, "No, I didn't see any windows, but I saw fifty holes along the top." Well, that's exactly what others have described—a series of windows on a top piece along the top of the ark. He mentioned that it was on a northeast corner of the mountain.

I found George Hagopian to have a very normal

personality. He has broken English so it's hard to understand him at times, but he did not brag about himself. He did not brag about his exploits. He seemed very humble. He had a lot of what we call obsessive-compulsive features. He was a perfectionist in his description of the details. He had some normal, healthy, human emotions and concern for the interviewer. I found Mr. Hagopian, in spite of some of the discrepancies from his childlike perspective when he climbed the ark, to be extremely credible and I believe his account.

GOAT PATH LED TO ARK

Another Armenian to see the ark in the early 1900s was Jacob Chuchian, who lived in the village of Or-tulu on the southwest side of Ararat. Chuchian saw the ark a number of times between the ages of nine and nineteen. Information concerning Jacob's visit to the ark comes from his son, Arthur, who is an engineer at Channel Two television in St. Louis, Missouri.

In a 1975 interview with Rev. Stuart Brassie, Arthur related what his father Jacob told him regarding the path to the ark and what his father reportedly saw at the site.

To reach the site where the ark is, one must follow a narrow goat trail, approximately 4 feet wide, which starts out of nowhere and runs for about three miles. It is an obvious, worn trail and ends at a solid mountain wall overlooking the ark, which is positioned about 100 feet below the trail.

The ark rests in a large body of water about three to four times the size of the boat, and except for one time when the front third of the boat was plainly visible, the boat was completely covered by a shimmering, very clear covering of ice, so that only the huge, but clear outline, of the ark could be seen.

The boat has a reddish brown wood appearance and is similar to a houseboat with a flat deck surface. The ark rests on a type of cleft or ledge and is accessible only by the goat's trail. The ledge on which the ark rests drops off very rapidly from the front side, and is surrounded on the other three sides by walls of rock.[3]

Chuchian's account of how one reaches the ark is almost identical to other mid-twentieth-century sightings in which the guides were Armenian. These Armenians all say that by staying on the Great Trail, climbers avoid the tremendous winds in reaching the ark site, which they indicate is about two thirds of the way up the mountain. They also claim that around the turn of the century, the Armenian people used to take entire villages by groups up to visit the ark. They said the climb was not that difficult.

In 1982 astronaut James Irwin and veteran ark hunter Eryl Cummings used a map drawn with the help of Arthur Chuchian. They located the old goat trail and followed it for a time, but it branched off in several directions at various places. Armenians knew which path to take to the ark because of a special insignia marking the path. Unable to locate the insignia, Irwin's group abandoned the effort in favor of other approaches.

TURKISH SOLDIERS SEE ARK

Many others in this century have also reported seeing the ark. In 1916 six Turkish soldiers, returning home after serving in World War I in the Baghdad area (approximately 450 miles south of Mount Ararat), claimed that they had climbed Mount Ararat and had seen the ark. Since none of the men could read or write, they told their story to a learned friend, Duran Ayranci of Adana, Turkey. In 1946 the men asked him to write a letter to the American Embassy in Turkey offering their services as guides to any Americans looking for the ark.

The letter affirmed, "We saw Noah's ark leaning against the mountain. I measured the length of the boat. It was 150 paces long. It had three stories . . ."

Little is known about these men because none of them were still alive by the time researchers became aware of their letter and story in 1966—twenty years later! All researchers now know is what they've been able to learn from Mr. Ayranci, the man who wrote the letter and knew the soldiers, but unfortunately did not know the route to the ark.[4]

RUSSIAN PILOTS SIGHT ARK

Also in 1916, another report surfaced about a Russian pilot who allegedly saw the ark while flying around Ararat testing a high-altitude engine. The story of Vladimir Roskovitsky's sighting of the ark was vividly described in a 1940 issue of *The New Eden* magazine. It generated thousands of inquiries before the editor admitted that the article was 99 percent fiction. However, it was based on the single fact that a Russian aviator had seen a boatlike structure on Mount Ararat.

If the Roskovitsky account was false, what do we know about the real Russian aviator who actually saw the ark? The answer came on October 6, 1945, in a detailed article in the White Russian publication, *Rosseya*. Russian General Alexander Jacob Elshin and Colonel Alexander A. Koor not only confirmed that there was a Russian aviator sighting but also an expedition sent by the Russian czar to investigate the wooden boat on Mount Ararat.

Colonel Koor, an officer in the czar's White Russian Army, was a friend of some of the solders involved in the aerial expedition that spotted the ark on Mount Ararat. Ark researcher Eryl Cummings obtained the following communication from Colonel Koor in 1946:

> Here are some data which should help our research, from the official records of the Russian Caucasian Army, 1914–1917, by General E. B. Mavlovsky. In 1916, the 3-D Caucasian Aviation Detachment, under the command of 1st Lt. Zabolotsky, served air duty over the region at Mount Ararat, Lake Van and Lake Urmia. This aviation detachment served the 4th Caucasian Corps, and the Army Aviation Inspector was Captain Koorbatoff. I hope 1st Lt. Zabolotsky is the man you are looking for, for he, from an airplane, sighted the ark and started the investigation. Captain Koorbatoff was his supervisor. . . .
>
> I understand that the discovery of Noah's ark was in the end of 1916, with the scouting parties having to wait until the summer of 1917.
>
> About July or August 1921, I and Lt. [Peter Nicolovich] Leslin met 1st Lt. [Paul Vasilivich] Rujansky in Harbin. During one of our conversations, 1st Lt. Rujansky told me about the details because he was wounded and sent to Russia, but he knew because his

brother, Boris Vasilivich Rujansky, Sergeant of the Military Railroad Battalion, was a member of the investigating party which was sent to Mount Ararat to corroborate the discovery of Noah's ark.

Lt. Leslin admitted he had also heard about the discovery of Noah's ark, not as a rumor, but as news, from the Senior Adjutant of his division, who had told him that Noah's ark was found in the saddle of two peaks of Mount Ararat. This is all I heard from these two officers, and I am sure both told me the truth.[5]

"I personally talked to Colonel Koor," says Dr. Elfred Lee, "and he told me Noah's ark was very much like George Hagopian described it. He also confirmed that the czar's expedition did indeed take photographs and measurements of the ark."

In 1976 the authors of this book located Mrs. Gladys Evans of El Cajon, California, who remembers that three of the White Russian airmen who had flown over the ark in 1916 and had been on the 1917 foot-reconnaissance expedition spent a week in her father's San Bernardino, California, home as houseguests in the fall of 1940. Mrs. Evans vividly remembers some of the details described by the airmen to her father and brother.

They told how the ark was "half in and half out of a lake like a log floating in water. It was an immense thing, and it had cages—some with metal on them. It had a catwalk on top and the door was off. The door was nearby and had apparently been struck by lightning because it was partly burnt. The ark was pitched within and without with some kind of lacquer. It was just as good as the day it was built." The wood reminded them of oleander.

When they first saw the ark from the air, they

thought it was a submarine, but couldn't figure out why someone would be building it on a mountain. On the later reconnaissance expedition, these three airmen actually got inside the ark where they took pictures and measurements. The film was turned over to the Russian government.[6]

The Russian airmen who stayed at the home of Mrs. Evans's father were not the same airmen who first spotted the ark while testing their airplane. Mrs. Evans says these airmen also flew around the site, but the original discoverers were other Russian airmen, whose names, mentioned at the time, have since been forgotten by Mrs. Evans.

CZAR SENDS EXPEDITION TO ARARAT

In the summer of 1917, the czar sent two research divisions with a total of 150 infantrymen, army engineers, and scientists on a ground expedition to find the ark. It took them a month to reach the site due to all of the difficulties they experienced—including incredibly harsh weather.

The hardships were worth it, however, when they finally reached their goal. "As the huge ship at last loomed before them, an awed silence descended, and 'without a word of command everyone took off his hat, looking reverently toward the ark; everybody knew, feeling it in his heart and soul,' that they were in the actual presence of the ark. Many 'crossed themselves and whispered a prayer,' said an eyewitness account. It was like being in a church, and the hands of the archaeologist trembled as he snapped the shutter of the camera and took a picture of the old boat as if she were 'on parade.' "[7]

The Russian investigators took measurements and found that the ark was about 500 feet long, about 83 feet wide at the widest place, and about 50 feet high.[8] These measurements correspond more closely to the 20-inch cubit rather than the 18-inch cubit most frequently cited by Bible scholars.

The results of the ground investigation and photographs of Noah's ark were sent back to Czar Nicholas II, who many say never received them due to the outbreak of the Bolshevik Communist Revolution in 1917.

"The results of the investigation have either never been found or never been reported. A rumor exists that the results of the investigation and the pictures of the ark came to the attention of Leon Trotsky, who either destroyed them or placed them in a file destined to be kept permanently secret. According to the same rumor, the special courier's silence on the matter was also permanently secured by his execution."[9]

The authors of this book made an exhaustive effort to locate the 1917 czarist expedition photographs and report on Noah's ark. A Moscow radio commentator was hired to go through the Kremlin archives and museums looking for these items. Christie's and Sotheby's auction houses in London were contacted and asked to review the czarist family collections to determine if these items might be hidden among the czarist papers and artifacts. Weeks of searching did not produce the report or photos, but did prove that both reached the czar at his palace.

Minnesota resident Alvin Holderbecker, nephew of a czarist expedition eyewitness, reports the following:

> My aunt Eva worked in the czar's palace as a housemaid during World War I when she was about nineteen or twenty years old. Her father was a medical officer in the White Russian Army and a highly respected friend of the czar and his family. He was the chief medical officer on the expedition that found Noah's ark. When he came back from the expedition, he showed my aunt Eva the photographs and reports.
>
> Then, the Bolsheviks took over and confiscated all of the photographs and reports and killed as many of the men from the expedition as they could find. My aunt Eva was the only one from her family who escaped. She was sent by the czar to Kaiser Wilhelm in Germany.
>
> My aunt, having seen the pictures, told me the ark was three decks high, and on top of the roof there was a catwalk that was about knee-high with openings underneath to provide ventilation or light.
>
> She said that the czar and his family were not killed, but rather a rumor they started to hide their escape. She said they actually escaped into Poland, and my aunt Eva escaped from Germany to Canada, and then later came into the United States.

"There's been controversy surrounding the czarist expedition that took place in 1917," says Megan Butler, managing editor of Regnery Gateway Publishers in Washington, D.C. "Our author of *Anastasia: The Last Expedition* spent twenty years researching Anastasia, the last surviving member of the Russian royal family.

"During one of his personal interviews with her, he was shocked when she started talking about the expedition her father, the czar, had commissioned to go to Ararat to measure and photograph Noah's ark. She told him that she'd actually seen the photographs and report from the expedition. She then told him that she wore a cross made of wood from Noah's ark."

"I talked to Alexi Nicholi Romanov, the son of Czar Nicholas Romanov," says Noah's ark archivist Dr. Elfred Lee, "and he told me that when he was a boy in the palace, there was much talk about the discovery of Noah's ark. He said there was much excitement about the photographs and the measurements. But he said when the Revolution broke out, there was a lot of confusion, and 'we don't know what happened to everything. We were in fear of our lives.' "

RADIO CELEBRITY SMUGGLES PIECE OF ARK

As stated in an earlier chapter, Carveth Wells, a well-known radio personality from KFI Radio in Los Angeles, set out in 1933 to find Noah's ark on Mount Ararat. He visited the Etchmiadzin Cathedral, where he viewed the cross made of wood from Noah's ark. He was allegedly prevented from climbing Ararat on the Russian side, but apparently slipped across the border, visited the ark, and brought back a piece of reddish-colored wood.

One of Carveth Wells's friends wrote Eryl Cummings the following note: "I am very interested in the ark and about thirty years ago, Carveth Wells was at the ark and smuggled a piece of it out, and I examined it and it is of very hard wood. The piece he brought out was by bribing a government inspector. The piece was about 2 feet long and 8 inches wide and 1½ inch thick."[10]

AMERICAN FLYERS SPOT ARK

Many sightings over the years have been by pilots who either specifically went looking for the ark or just happened to see the great ship while flying over or around Mount Ararat. During World War II, American flyers flew hundreds of flights over Mount Ararat in an effort to keep the Russian Army supplied with war materials. These flights took off from Allied bases in Tunisia en route to the Soviet Air Base in Erivan.

Reports frequently surfaced about American, Australian, and Russian airmen seeing the ark locked in Ararat's icy snow. One of these sightings was reported in the military *Stars and Stripes* newspaper.

"Since the early 1800s, there have been dozens of newspaper articles concerning the ark on Mount Ararat," says Cliff Moody, Noah's ark researcher from Sacramento, California. "The *Stars and Stripes* alone published forty-nine articles dealing with Noah's ark from September 1949, through August 1984. Unfortunately, the particular European issue containing actual photos of the ark has not yet been located."

However, Vence Will, now a pastor in Springfield,

Missouri, saw the photographs while serving in the Air Force as a TEC Sergeant during World War II:

> In World War II, I was stationed in North Africa with the signal installation battalion that was attached to the Army Air Force. We put up electronic beacons that airplanes would fly on. These beacons stretched from North Africa and India on up into Europe. At the time, I was working in Tunisia, Algeria and in Italy.
>
> One time, I was in the airport in Naples, Italy, with a buddy of mine and we went over to the officer's mess to have a cup of coffee. Our guys had been flying supplies over Turkey to the back part of Russia, and one of the pilots had taken some pictures. Three officers were looking at the pictures of Mount Ararat and a boatlike object on it, and we looked too.
>
> Some of them thought that it was Noah's ark. Two of the pictures were hazy, but one of them was clear. A section of the ark was sticking out of the snow 40 to 50 feet without anything underneath it. The wood was darker than the rocks around it. The ark itself was in pretty good shape. I couldn't see any holes on the top. There was a hole on the right side where you could see the different levels and structural beams. I could see two decks through the hole.
>
> As we looked at these photos, there was no question in the minds of these flyers that this was Noah's ark. I'm convinced that I was looking at Noah's ark, and a similar picture was put into the *Stars and Stripes* in about 1944. It was a front-page photo that looked just like the one I saw in the officer's mess.

Another interesting World War II sighting of the ark involved Lester Walton of Spring Valley, California. He was in the Army Air Force, assigned to testing a new Fairchild camera that was supposed to give better resolution of bomb sites during bombing missions. They were flying in a seven-plane squadron of B-24s from their base in North Africa to a target in eastern Europe when they flew over Mount Ararat and accidentally photographed Noah's ark.

"The on-board cameras were designed to take movies of the bombing mission. When we flew over Mount Ararat, a structure was seen and the speculation was that it was the ark," remembers Walton. "The pilot of the plane banked sharply to position the camera to get a good shot, and then proceeded on to our objective."

Walton recalls a major canyon on the north side of the mountain. He remembers "a box-shaped structure protruding out from the ice or rock debris. The north end of the structure was higher than the south end and the entire things was tilted about thirty degrees. It was darker than the surrounding rock.

"At the time, an expeditionary effort was proposed to document the object, but was ruled out due to the lingering instability of the area," says Walton. "Soon, word came that the documentation would be carried out by the National Geographic Society as soon as hostilities cooled." Mr. Walton never heard the results of any such expedition.

ARK PHOTOS DISAPPEAR MYSTERIOUSLY

Many passengers aboard aircraft also claim to have seen Noah's ark. George Jefferson Greene was an American oil and pipeline engineer working in the Middle East in the early 1950s. In the late summer of 1953, he was on a helicopter flying over the north-eastern flanks of Mount Ararat on business when he was suddenly shocked to see a wooden ship protruding from the ice and rocks below.

Greene directed the pilot to fly as close to the ship as possible, and he took pictures with the superb photographic equipment he had on board that belonged to his employer. Some of the incredible photos were shot from just 90 feet away. He was thrilled with his unbelievable archaeological discovery and couldn't wait to see the proof in his priceless photographs.[11]

He showed the developed eight-by-ten-inch black-and-white photos to friends both in the Middle East and in the United States in an apparently futile attempt to find financial backing for an expedition to recover his historic find. Incredibly, even with clear photographs that were seen by a number of people, he was unable to generate any interest in the project.

Disheartened by the lack of interest, he went to British Guyana, where he hoped to make a fortune in a placer mining operation. On December 27, 1962, George Greene was murdered, and his body was found floating in the hotel pool.

Frank Neff, a friend of Greene's, was one of the many people in Texas who had seen the photos of the ark on Mount Ararat. When he found out that researchers were looking for copies of the photos, he remarked that he thought Greene had kept duplicates in a manila envelope in a storage unit he had rented there in Texas. Ark researcher Eryl Cummings went to the storage unit with Neff only to find that it had been broken into and ransacked just ten days before.

"As he opened the door [of the storage unit], Cummings stared in dismay. The contents of the once well-organized shelves had been unceremoniously dumped into a great scattered heap in the middle of the floor.

"For what had the vandals been searching? Had a certain large—and vitally important—manila envelope been among the items the robbers had carried away?"[12]

The copies of the photos were never found, but Eryl Cummings tracked down a total of thirty individuals who readily recalled seeing Greene's high-quality photos of the ark. With so many witnesses, the fact that the explicit, eight-by-ten-inch black-and-white photos existed cannot be questioned. But where are they now?

"He was probably murdered for his gold," says Dr. Elfred Lee, ark researcher-illustrator, whose friend tracked down the final demise of Greene. "The contents of his briefcase were stolen, which included both the gold and the six precious photographs."

Did the murderer or murderers want the gold that he supposedly had in his briefcase, or did they want his maps and photos of the ark? Was the robbery of the gold just a "bonus" for the killer's main objective?

FIGHTER PILOTS DESCRIBE ARK

In the late 1950s, a number of American pilots based in Adana, Turkey, with the 428th Tactical Flight Squadron under the command of the NATO Military Assistance Pact, reported seeing an enormous ship on Mount Ararat, but none of them were able to take any photographs because of their close proximity to the Russian border.

One fighter pilot, Captain Gregor Schwinghammer (then a Second Lieutenant) saw the ark from his F-100 cockpit. "In 1959 we were flying fighters over Mount Ararat when we spotted what looked like a large, rectangular, barge-like structure sticking out of the side of the mountain. It was in kind of a horseshoe-like depression and it definitely appeared to be man-made. I didn't think of Noah's ark at the time because, frankly, I wasn't aware of a biblical story placing Noah's ark on Mount Ararat."

Lieutenant Colonel Ben Bowthorp, the deputy base commander at the time Captain Schwinghammer saw the ark, told author Charles Berlitz, "It was about two thirds of the way up the mountain, made of wood, and it looked like a boat or a wooden boat-shaped wall. I don't know who first said it was Noah's ark. Most of us felt it could be."[13]

SECRET PHOTO MISSION OVER ARARAT

In 1974 Dr. Walter Brown, a retired U.S. Air Force colonel now living in Phoenix, Arizona, was summoned to the Central Intelligence Agency headquarters in Langley, Virginia. There he was debriefed by the highest CIA officials on all he knew about Noah's ark on Mount Ararat. The CIA indicated they were making a study of the ark, but did not disclose the reason behind the study.

It's believed that the Brown CIA debriefing had something to do with a mysterious top-secret photographing of the ark by the Air Force in the same year. Al Sipple (real name being withheld to protect pilot's identity) flew on that secret Air Force mission and provides these details:

Something happened in 1974 when I was in the service. Another pilot and I were assigned a mission from the higher ups to fly a highly secret mission over Mount Ararat to photograph something that they thought might be a Soviet-made defense installation.

I had experience in aerial photography, so I was taken along on an F-4 fighter to take pictures of the object. We flew over it at a low altitude—less than 1,000 feet from the surface of the mountain while I took pictures.

The film was turned over to the Air Force and classified "Top Secret." I don't know what they did with it, but I can tell you what I saw with my own eyes. It was a dark, black foreign object about two thirds of the way up the mountain near a gorge. It was oblong and partially buried in ice, overhanging a cliff. To me, it certainly looked like a boatlike object—definitely man-made. It also appeared as though it didn't belong on the mountain. It was just totally out of place.

U-2 PILOTS PHOTOGRAPHED ARK

This would not have been the only secret mission flown over Ararat for the U.S. military and the CIA.

It's been reported that pictures of Noah's ark were taken by U-2 pilots before the unexpectedly sudden ending of the U-2 program when American Gary Powers was shot down by the Soviet Union.

Apache Jim Wilson of Oden, Arkansas, had a client whose son was a U-2 pilot. The father was a Bible believer, so his son had obtained from secret military files a couple photos of the ark on Ararat. The father is now dead and his sons told Wilson they destroyed the photos on their father's death because they didn't want classified photos in their possession. However, Wilson saw the photos in 1973 and describes what he saw in the pictures.

> The object looked as though it was broken into two pieces—the ends were jagged. The pieces were separated, being some distance apart and partially covered with ice and snow. The parts sticking out of the snow looked to be 20 to 50 feet long. I saw six to eight windows on the top. I don't know where it was on the mountain, but the enlarged pictures were very clear.

Also in the early 1960s, the Air Force was dropping freight for the CIA in eastern Turkey and doing aerial electronic eavesdropping on the Soviets. In preparation for this book, one of the Air Force technicians aboard the DC-3s on secret Air Force–CIA flights agreed to talk—providing we didn't mention his name.

> We flew over Ararat at a low altitude several times and I saw Noah's ark. It was near the gorge and half sunk in ice, [lying] in a north-south direction with the lower side tilted slightly to the west. It was large and long—like a

narrow barge. It had blunt ends that were kind of rounded. You could see it was made of wood; it stood out as plain as day. There was no doubt what it was in my mind.

These are just two of the accounts of dozens of pilots who say they have seen Noah's ark while flying over Mount Ararat.

ARK SIGHTED FROM AIR FORCE ONE

Probably the most interesting aerial sighting of the ark during the late 1970s involved a U.S. president and a UPI White House photographer. Ronald Bennett, now living in La Jolla, California, is the UPI White House photographer who saw Noah's ark while flying aboard Air Force One (AF One Plane 2700) with then-President Jimmy Carter.

The Bennett sighting took place on a flight that departed from Washington, D.C., going to Warsaw, Poland, on December 29, 1977, and then on to Tehran (or Teheran), Iran, on December 31, for a New Year's Eve party being hosted by the shah of Iran at his winter palace. It was en route to Tehran that Bennett and other journalists aboard Air Force One saw Noah's ark on Mount Ararat. Bennett says,

During the terms of four U.S. presidents—from Nixon through Reagan—I was the UPI photojournalist covering the White House. I always flew aboard Air Force One, reporting the activities of the president. On this particular occasion, with then-President Jimmy Carter, we were en route from Poland to Teheran to attend a New Year's Day celebration given by the shah.

During the flight, while we were flying over eastern Turkey, our attention was called to the window. It was a dramatic moment as Soviet Mig fighter jets were escorting us wing-on-wing. At the same time, someone also told us that if we looked down we would see Noah's ark. We looked and there was a mountain with snow and glaciers on it.

There, maybe halfway up the mountain, clearly visible, was a large, dark boat. It was partially covered with snow or ice. I'm convinced, based on what I saw there, that it was Noah's Ark. It's my opinion that the president probably had Air Force One routed over Mount Ararat and most likely saw the ark too.

Carter has not confirmed whether he also saw the ark.

The ark of Noah has also been photographed by U.S. and foreign spy satellites—but more about that in a later chapter.

The ark has been seen by literally hundreds of people in this century alone—many just by accident. It's been seen by people from every walk of life and from many different cultures. It's been viewed by peasants and possibly even a U.S. president, and by people who were totally unaware of the biblical story.

Just think how bizarre the sight of Noah's ark must be to many people—a wooden ship, almost the size of a modern aircraft carrier, near the top of a mountain? It's almost impossible to believe—except for the people who have seen it.

Notes

[1] Elfred Lee, George Hagopian interview, July, 1990, in Easton, MD.

[2] Ibid.

[3] Interview with Arthur Chuchian conducted in St. Louis, MO, on June 24, 1975, by Rev. Stuart Brassie and Thomas Sass of the Arkfact Research Association.

[4] Tim LaHaye and John Morris, *The Ark on Ararat* (Nashville: Thomas Nelson Publishers, 1976), pp. 90–91.

[5] Ibid., pp. 84–85. Cited material from Violet M. Cummings, *Noah's Ark: Fact or Fable?* (San Diego: Creation-Science Research Center, 1972), pp. 143–145.

[6] Dave Balsiger and Charles E. Sellier, *In Search of Noah's Ark* (Los Angeles: Sun Classic Books, 1976), pp. 108–109. Cited interview with Gladys Evans in February, 1976, El Cajon, CA.

[7] Cummings, *Noah's Ark: Fact or Fable?* p. 136.

[8] Ibid.

[9] Charles Berlitz, *The Lost Ship of Noah* (New York: G. P. Putnam's Sons, 1987), p. 33.

[10] LaHaye and Morris, *The Ark on Ararat,* p. 97.

[11] Cummings, *Noah's Ark: Fact or Fable?* p. 215; and LaHaye and Morris, *The Ark on Ararat,* pp. 135–137.

[12] Cummings, *Noah's Ark: Fact or Fable?* p. 222.

[13] Berlitz, *The Lost Ship of Noah,* p. 45.

11

THE NAVARRA EXPEDITION AND OTHER GROUND EXPEDITIONS

There was never any doubt in my mind . . .
that it could only be the Ark.
                    French Explorer Fernand Navarra

In 1937 I served in the French military forces
in the Middle East. During my days off, I
took long walks in the hills above Damascus,
accompanied by an Armenian friend, Alim.
One day, hiking farther than usual, we
started climbing up Mount Hermon. About
1,300 feet from the top, Alim sank to his
knees exhausted. I trudged on by myself
until I reached the top, an altitude of over
9,000 feet. There I stayed for half an hour
viewing the sea of haze and clouds
stretching before me under the blue sky and
a burning sun. On my way down, I rejoined
my companion, and as we walked, he began
to tell me his own life story.

"I was born in 1907 on the island in Lake
Van," he said. "As a child, I lived there
happy with my mother, father, and sister,
until 1920. Then my parents moved to
Damascus. Before I left Armenia, I went to

visit my grandfather in the town of Bayazid at the foot of Mount Ararat. The old man assured me that Noah's ark was still on the mountain. 'When I was young,' he told me, 'I once tried to reach it. But I wasn't strong enough in the high altitude and had to give up. I never found it.'

"I promised granddad that I would try, too," continued Alim. "But you are the one who should go, Navarra. Mountain climbing does not wear you out the way it does me. I am sure you would bring back a fragment of the ark."

The idea intrigued me, and I determined to give it a try. But not till fifteen years later did I have my first opportunity to tackle the mountain.

It was 1952 before I was able to take my first expedition, which included a friend, two motion-picture cameramen, and a retired staff officer who had studied at the French Museum of Natural History.

It was the middle of August before we began our ascent, plagued by mosquitoes, 120-degree temperatures, and thunderstorms. Our goal was to reach the summit and then look at a lower elevation for the ark.

We followed our guide along a goat trail, then through névés [fields of snow at the head of a glacier], pastures, and rocky terrain. The mosquitoes disappeared at the higher elevations, but clouds with intermittent showers and hail, up to 13,450 feet, hindered our climb over and around numerous blocks of lava.

We set up camp on a plateau covered with such blocks, but with sufficient open

surface for the tents. The tents were just up
when a blizzard struck, covering the blue
basalt with white.

The mules had suffered, and so had their
packs. Every case had been dented or
ripped. Milk, ham, chocolate, and alcohol
fuel made a horrible mixture. We succeeded
in preparing cocoa, which was not quite
what it should have been, but at least was
hot. Afterward, we went to sleep, listening to
the snow-muffled night noises. The next day
we hoped to reach our goal.

We were up before dawn. Clouds heavy
with snow were gathering and a strong icy
wind whipped our faces. The snow that had
fallen during the night was wet, and our
footprints filled with water that froze
immediately.

Our guide, Hazam Calatin, walked in front.
The path wound between two névés and a
sharp ridge strewn with boulders.

Moving forward was difficult. We had to
scale the blocks, and the slope was steep.
After this chaos, the ridge grew even sharper
with rocks on which we cut ourselves when
we fell.

By 9 A.M. we reached 15,400 feet. A half-
hour later, the altimeter read 15,850 feet.
Here we stopped, and Calatin refused to go
any further. We decided to continue the
ascent alone.

It was not good at such a height to make
prolonged halts. We realized this when we
set forth again. Our cooled joints rebelled
when we started to move. Breathing was
difficult. The rarefied air, the lower pressure,
made us gasp. We had the feeling that the
mountain was defending itself. Just lifting an

arm was painful, and throwing a pickaxe forward to catch a block seemed impossible.

We wanted to lie down and sleep and put an end to following these stations of the cross, with frequent falls. Under our feet nothing was solid, neither rocks nor ice. We were not walking, but clawing, our bodies stuck to the ground, trying to adhere to the moving wall.

Bruised, with scum on our lips, we finally reached a terrace of hard ice. We broke off pieces, which we sucked, hoping to quench our thirst, but this ice did not melt, and worse yet, it was salty.

A sharp wind kept us awake. Above our heads, a cover of dark clouds gathered; underneath us, a sea of lighter clouds. Between the two, as between two shrouds, we were rowing in a moonlike scene, hallucinating, wondering if we were losing our minds. . . .

The altimeter read 16,934 feet. A few steps more and the team would reach the summit of Noah's mountain. But the most important part of all was yet to be accomplished. Now I wanted to find the remains of the ark.

After returning to Bayazid for fresh supplies, we set out for this new adventure.

On August 17, at two o'clock in the afternoon, I was alone on the cap of ice, which in this place was clear of snow. I felt no fatigue, but a great anxiety. In the sky, an eagle circled, carried by the wind.

I crossed an arm of the glacier and climbed to the top of the moraine. On one side, I could see a mountain of ice lined with crevasses, on the other, sheer wall. At the bottom, I saw a dark mass.

This mass was clearly outlined, its lines straight and curved. The general shape, I thought, resembled that of a ship . . . at least fragments of one.

My mind was perfectly clear, and those who knew me had usually given me credit for having common sense.

At that altitude, in that desert of ice, what could it be? The ruins of a building, church, refuge, or house never mentioned in any account, or tradition, never seen by any of these who came to this place? The wreckage of an airplane? No one ever used beams of that size to build a fuselage.

Those remains, I thought, must be what's left of the ark. Perhaps this is the flat bottom of the biblical vessel, the top structures of which must have been scattered.

The structure was really there, but out of reach, and I lacked the necessary equipment to go down to the site. All I could do was to locate it as accurately as possible and rejoin my companions, promising myself that I would come back again.

Our expedition had been a success from an alpinist's point of view, for we had scaled the fabled mountain. But as regards the discovery of the ark, it was an apparent failure. We brought back neither fragment nor photograph.

In July 1953, I made a second attempt, accompanied by a Turkish photographer. I found my way fairly easily, climbing to within a hundred yards of the site of the timbers. But boulders, perched precariously above, rolled down at the sound of my voice. Photographer Alaedin Seker had already stopped his climb, and I was on my own.

I was able to get about twenty yards closer, when I suddenly felt faint. My head felt as if it was caught in a vise and about to burst. I could not coordinate my movements, and could think of only one thing—to go back down! I sat down and shut my eyes. For ten minutes, I felt numb. I left and, twenty yards lower, found my companion, pale, curled up between two rocks, visibly as bad off as I was. I warmed him up and cheered him as well as I could, but we were both so exhausted that during the three hours of our descent to camp, we did not utter a word.

My own interest kept on growing, becoming an obsession. Night and day, I recalled the dusty Turkish roads, the glaciers, the moraines of disintegrated rocks, and the big shadow of the ark. At night, I dreamed of extraordinary ways by which I could pull off a fragment of the wreck and triumphantly bring it back.

Months went by. In September 1954, I learned that the American, John Libi, had come within thirty yards of the ark, and that he planned another expedition in 1955. Then, I made up my mind: I would go a third time.

The Libi story reinforced my conviction that the glaciers had receded. What had not been possible in 1952 and 1953 might be possible in 1955. If the winter was mild, my chances of reaching the Ark would be better.

To explore Mount Ararat, a forbidden military zone, I needed to obtain a pass, which the Turkish authorities were reluctant to give. They most likely would refuse if I applied before leaving France. Yet, requesting a permit in Turkey, as we had done in 1952 and 1953, posed the risk of being told every day for a month or two: "Come back tomorrow." And I had no time to lose.

My knowledge of the area enabled me to plan an itinerary along Lake Van, avoiding the main roads which are more closely watched. But even after having taken this precaution, I might meet up with a police patrol. Any foreigner in a border area is suspected of spying. However, a family on vacation would hardly arouse suspicion. That is why I decided to take my wife and three sons—Fernand, thirteen; Raphael, eleven; and Jose, nine. We set our departure for June 1955.

It was in late June the road to Mount Ararat opened up before us! Now, I decided, we would go to Karakose, fifty miles from Mount Ararat. There, my wife would stay in a hotel with Fernand and Jose, while Raphael and I attempted the ascent.

On July 5, at 7:30 A.M., we stood at the bottom of the mountain of ice which separated us from the site where the ark rested.

We had to climb that mass, heavy as we were with our other ladder, ropes, pickaxes, hatchet, wide-blade knives, crampons, cameras.

We attached our crampons, roped ourselves together, and began to climb. I stopped at times to film this awesome fairy-like scene. In some places, the ice was a light blue; in others, it resembled transparent lace.

When a gust of icy snow fell on us, we took shelter behind a wall of ice. It was rather precarious; the temperature had suddenly dropped twenty degrees—to zero— and we were frozen. Raphael was wrapped so completely that I could see only a red nose and big eyes shining with pleasure.

"This is a real mountain," he said, his voice muffled.

I thought it was about time he realized this.

When we set forth again after the storm, we still had to cross a maze bordered with deep crevasses. Two hours later, we had climbed the last thirty yards, reaching the top at noon.

The first problem was solved. Now for the second one. The other side ended in a sheer wall, and we could not see what lay at its foot. If I walked too close to the edge, I feared the ice would break under my feet. How could we have a look into this hollow without falling into it?

Raphael found the solution. "Take a good hold of me with the rope. I'll get close to the edge and try to see what's at the bottom."

I hesitated a moment, then agreed. I braced myself carefully and propped my back against the rock. He leaned over.

"A little bit more," he called. "More—a bit more—"

I played out a little more rope.

"There, I can see now. Yes, the boat is there, papa. I can see it distinctly."

I almost fainted with joy, but this was no time to let Raphael go! I gave him the camera, and he took the scene in movies.

Still, the problem was to reach the basin bottom. We had to lower ourselves down a bank about as high as the one we had just climbed.

We took from our sacks tools to cut wood from the ark. Just then, the snow started falling heavily. Fortunately, a few steps away, there was a little hollow where we took refuge. It was a real ice cave, almost square, five yards deep and two yards high—a perfect shelter for a few minutes.

An hour passed, and still the snow fell thickly. To go out was impossible. As the cold grew more intense, I decided to make a small fire with "canned heat." To get one tablet to burn, I had to strike eight matches, for oxygen was scarce. Finally, I succeeded in lighting a small flame on a shovel. It warmed us up a little, but half our supply of the fuel was used. Fearing we might have to stay there longer than we had planned, I put aside the rest of the tablets.

We were really imprisoned. We could not keep on with the search, nor could we return to camp. At three in the afternoon, the sky was almost as dark as night. We could only hope that the whimsical temper of Mount Ararat would change, and the weather would clear up soon.

After emptying his knapsack, Raphael sat on it to avoid direct contact with the ice. Our eyes were getting accustomed to the near obscurity, and we examined our abode more closely. It was hollowed out like the inside of an igloo.

Still, we sat enclosed in a refrigerator, and I began to think about spending the night there. Even if the snow had stopped falling and the weather had cleared, we could not have returned to camp in less than two hours. The snow, hiding the crevasses, would have turned them into death traps.

At six in the evening, the curtain of snow

lightened, but night had come for good. Until then, we had not had time to get weary. We told each other stories, and Raphael talked a lot. Finally, he got sleepy. I crouched on the rock, which seemed slightly warmer for our presence there. I had Raphael slide into the knapsack, then took him on my lap and hugged him in my arms until 11 P.M. I often looked at my faithful watch, which, like me, was on its third trip up the face of Ararat.

My principal concern was not to get frozen. I had heard about the sense of well-being one feels when freezing. I felt comfortable, and that worried me; wasn't this the first symptom of the freezing process? All of a sudden, I heard myself scream, "Rub my arm! I'm freezing!"

Waking up with a start, Raphael murmured, "I am cold, too."

He grasped my arm and made it turn like a windmill's sail. The pain reassured me. I was only stiff. But we had had such a close call that we broke out into a sweat in spite of the temperature.

Until morning, we exercised every half hour. At dawn, the cold grew more intense. I burned our last tablets of alcohol to warm us up and to prevent the cameras from freezing. We'd been in the ice cave for thirteen hours.

About 5 A.M., Raphael went out, took a few steps in the snow, and threw some snowballs. "Come out—it's warm." His voice sounded cheerful.

I joined him. The snow lay soft and white under the clear sky. We lost no time in gathering our equipment, attaching crampons, and heading toward the crevasse in foot-deep snow.

Once on the edge of the crevasse, I

lowered the equipment on a rope. Then I secured the ladder and climbed down myself, assuring Raphael I would not be long.

Passing through the corridor, I found the sloping terrace and started clearing off the snow to uncover the dark strips I had seen the day before.

Soon the strips appeared, but—this was the worst disappointment of my life. These shapes were not wood, but frozen moraine dust! It was easy to be fooled; from a distance, the mass looked like a ship's carcass. I cleared off the snow along another fifty yards. Everywhere it was the same.

At that moment Raphael's voice, distorted by the echo, came to me.

"Well, papa, have you cut off a piece of wood?"

"No, it isn't wood, it's only moraine dust."

"Have you tried to dig in?"

In my dismay, I had not thought of it! Attacking the ice shell with my pickaxe, I could feel something hard. When I had dug a hole one and one half feet square by eight inches deep, I broke through a vaulted ceiling, and cleared off as much icy dust as possible.

There, immersed in water, I saw a black piece of wood!

My throat felt tight. I felt like crying and kneeling there to thank God. After the cruelest disappointment, the greatest joy! I checked my tears of happiness to shout to Raphael, "I've found wood!"

"Hurry up and come back—I'm cold," he responded.

I tried to pull out the whole beam, but couldn't. It must have been very long, and perhaps still attached to other parts of the ship's framework. I could only cut along the grain until I split off a piece about 5 feet long. Obviously, it had been hand-hewn. The wood, once out of the water, proved surprisingly heavy. Its density was remarkable after its long stay in the water, and the fibers had not distended as much as one might expect.

I took snapshots and movies, then carried my wooden prize to the foot of the ladder. I attached it to the rope and left it there, for I wanted to give Raphael the joy of hauling it up himself. At last I climbed up the ladder.

Back on the edge of the crevasse, I took movies of Raphael hoisting up this ancient piece of wreckage.

It was 7 A.M., July 6th, 1955.[1]

So goes the account of how French explorer Fernand Navarra and his son found the ark in 1955.

WAS NAVARRA'S WOOD ACTUALLY FROM THE ARK?

Navarra was sure the wood was from the ark. "There was never any doubt in my mind. I had done so much research and had so many documents that proved that it could only be the ark."

He had to cut the wood into pieces to keep the weight of it across his knapsack from making him lose his balance on their descent. "I regretted having to cut up such a venerable relic, but felt better about it later on when I split it up in smaller pieces to submit to various experts."[2]

Then, in 1969, the famous French explorer agreed to join the Scientific Exploration and Archaeological Research team known as SEARCH. Navarra would prove for the first time since 1955 that he could lead an expedition back to the same glacial ice pack on Ararat . . . and, it was hoped, recover more wood.

After retracing his way up the treacherous mountain, the SEARCH team struggled to locate wood in the same crevasses where Navarra had found it. But the crevasses were not melted as deep as they were in 1955. No wood could be found in them.

Navarra then decided to probe the bottom of a small pond adjacent to the ice pack. Since the team's probing poles would not reach to the bottom, he began to probe a small runoff stream from the pond.

At 11:15 A.M. on July 31, 1969, Navarra and the SEARCH team struck paydirt—five pieces of wood resembling planking, the longest piece nearly 17 inches long.[3]

Navarra, being the only person bringing back wood from Mount Ararat in modern times and declaring it to be from Noah's ark, created quite a stir in both scientific and religious circles. Critics also raised three significant questions: Was the wood actually from Noah's ark? What kind of wood was this that came from a totally treeless mountain? Did the wood date old enough to be from Noah's ark?

Dr. Richard Bliss, former adjunct science professor at the University of Wisconsin and presently Science Department head at a California graduate science institution in San Diego, examined the Navarra wood and the age-dating reports acquired by Navarra. He reported,

> The Navarra wood sample is a structural beam and impregnated with bituminous pitch. It has mortise and tenon joints. And it's definitely hand-hewn and squared. These observable features square with the biblical account and pre-dynastic ship building methods.
>
> The corroded and cracked surface indicates deterioration by freezing and thawing as well as water soaking. The wood will no longer float on water because of its gain in density. The elongated cells in the specimen most likely resulted from glacial pressure on the wood.
>
> The heartwood of 50 centimeters [indicated in the wood] means Navarra's sample came from a tree about 5 feet in diameter with a height of about 150 feet. Also, the particular *Quercus* variety is a white oak and grows only in the Mediterranean region where Noah is believed to have built the ark.[4]

Although much has been learned about the Navarra wood sample, additional testing has raised some peculiar findings. The late astronaut James Irwin had a sample of the Navarra wood tested in 1985 at the University of Georgia in its Center for Applied Isotope Studies. Dr. John Noakes reported these findings back to Colonel Irwin:

> A second portion of wood was submitted to pretreatment cleaning prior to dating. The dark bituminous-like coating turned out not to be just surface coating but distributed throughout the wood. This was very surprising as we have only encountered this before in dealing with pressure pretreated woods.
>
> The bituminous-like material associated with the

wood sample was very much of an intrigue to us. How a modern-age coating material could be associated with a wood sample at least 1,500 years old is a perplexing problem to explain. Still further of a mystery is how this material could be impregnated so deeply within the wood fibers without the use of present-day technology.[5]

[The answer may be earlier in this book, where Dr. Don Shockey explained that "gopherwood" was the term for a treating and sealing process rather than for a species of wood.]

HOW OLD WAS NAVARRA'S WOOD?

Just how old was the wood brought back by Navarra? In 1956—prior to the popularity of carbon-14 testing—Navarra had four different archaeological tests conducted on the wood. His test methods determined the degree of lignite, or coal, formation, gain in wood density, cell modification, and the degree of fossilization.

The following explanation provides a better understanding of the tests used by Navarra in dating his 1955 wood sample.[6]

The degree of lignite formation is assessed to determine the present stage of conversion of wood to coal. A very thin section of the wood is mounted on a slide and examined by using a petrographic microscope that measures the angle of reflection of the X rays off the wood.

Another method to determine degree of lignite formation is to treat the wood sample with alcohol or organic solvents to destroy the cell material, leaving only the coal or carbon. If it dissolves very little cell material, the sample is highly coalified; and if it dissolves a lot of cell material, it is only slightly coalified.

The degree of fossilization is assessed by determining the amount of water salts contained in a wood sample. This test is performed by treating the wood samples with acids or alcohols, then examining the specimen under microscope for traces of calcium carbonate or silica. The fuller the cells are with these minerals, the greater the degree of fossilization.

The gain in wood density tells us how compact the wood is and whether the wood will float or sink in water. To determine the gain in density, the sample is weighed in the air using a Metler analytical balance. Compression or contraction can cause a sample to sink. Also, a piece of wood that has undergone any degree of fossilization will show a gain in wood density.

Cell-modification tests determine the degree of cell collapse and cell-wall chemical change. Wood cells may become elongated or may combine with each other. This modification can be charted for age.

A slide of the wood sample is examined under a microscope for cell changes. The key factor in this test is the interpretation of what is seen through the microscope; that is, determining what caused the cells to change shape, to combine with other cells, or to collapse.

The Navarra tests were conducted at the National Museum of Natural History in Paris, the National Center of Scientific Research in Paris, the Forestry Institute of Research in Madrid, the Center for Forestry Research and Analysis in Paris, the Department of Anthropology & Prehistoric Studies at the University of Bordeaux, and at the Cairo Museum in Egypt.

All the tests performed by these distinguished institutions placed the age of the wood at around 5,000 years old, give or take 500 years. But what did American ark illustrator Dr. Elfred Lee discover when he had both the 1955 and 1969 Navarra wood samples dated by Dr. Willard Libby's carbon-14 process? The results of the carbon-14 tests conducted at the University of Pennsylvania obtained dates ranging between 1,250 and 1,700 years old. Similar results were obtained on the 1955 sample at the University of California, with the Center for Applied Isotope Studies in Athens, Georgia, setting the carbon-14 dates at 862 and 1,557 years old—far short of the 5,000 years given by the biblical account, and a rather extreme fluctuation between tests on the same piece of wood.

Although many have assumed that carbon-14 dating is always the final word in age dating, the method is plagued with some serious flaws, as stated in the McGraw-Hill publication, *Encyclopedia of Science and Technology:*

A measurement of the carbon-14 content of an organic sample will provide an accurate determination of the sample's age if it is assumed that (1) the production of carbon-14 by cosmic rays has remained essentially constant long enough to establish a steady state in the carbon-14/carbon-12 ratio in the atmosphere, (2) there has been a complete and rapid mixing of carbon-14 throughout the various carbon reservoirs, (3) the carbon isotope ratio in the sample has not been altered except by carbon-14 decay, and (4) the total amount of carbon in any reservoir has not been altered. In addition, the half-life of carbon-14 must be known with sufficient accuracy, and it must be possible to measure natural levels of carbon-14 to appropriate levels of accuracy and precision. Studies have shown that the primary assumptions on which the method rests have been violated both systematically and to varying degrees for particular sample types.[7]

Dr. Melvin A. Cook, former professor of metallurgy at the University of Utah and the 1968 Nitro-Nobel Gold Medal winner for his invention of slurry explosives, says carbon-14 results indicating an extremely young age on Navarra's wood are "inaccurate because the assumptions on which carbon-14 is based are not applicable to this piece of wood." He explains,

Living mollusks are sometimes found deficient in carbon-14 to such an extent as to appear to have been dead as long as 3,000 years. This is due to carbonate-ion exchange in salt water in contact with old calcite and dolomite deposits. These mollusks are in an environment of old carbonates, and during their life cycle, they assimilate those carbonates that have no radiocarbon in them, rather than [being] in steady state with the atmosphere.

The reverse (dates that are too low) will also happen by involving carbonate-ion exchange in freshwater lakes, which become high in alkalinity and thus tend to absorb carbon dioxide from the air to form new calcites and dolomites—which explains the discrepancies in dating of bristlecone pine.

The bristlecone pine is always dated by tree-ring dates as older—as much as 2,000 or 3,000 years older—than the date obtained by radiocarbon dating. It's due to the contamination of the bristlecone pine with newer material . . . diffusion of new carbon into the cells of the bristlecone pine.

We can't really use the carbon-14 dating method to date the Navarra wood. It can't be used unless we know exactly the conditions that the wood has been under during its existence.

That's a volcanic mountain, and the wood has been taken from water subjected to the gasses and the solutions from volcanism. It also shows fossilization, which means there has been an ion exchange within the wood.

All it would take for this test to be completely off would be to have excess carbonate-ion exchange, and the carbonate-ion in this case would be from freshwater deposits where the wood was found submerged. Carbon-14 dating would make it appear younger than it really is. And I think this is probably the explanation of the fact that the dating on this wood is only 1,300 to 1,700 years.

Also, just contamination of the wood sample alone would make it impossible to really date it by the radiocarbon method. The sample has undergone a lot of different environments that would promote the possibility of ion exchange.[8]

Dr. Libby, the inventor of the carbon-14 procedure, says the Navarra wood cannot be accurately dated using his method. According to Dr. Elfred Lee, "A group of our men talked to Dr. Libby, and he stated that his method is unreliable, especially during certain time periods. This wood brought back from this mountain, he said, has been soaking in meltwater at a very high altitude and bombarded by carbon of a more recent vintage, and the date would be thrown off. He said we should try another dating method."

With carbon-14 not being a suitable method for dating Navarra's wood, the four tests performed by Navarra and widely used by archaeologists remains the best evidence that the wood is 5,000 years old and probably from Noah's ark. We'll leave the final conclusion up to you.

MAN IN A BOX

Another mid-twentieth-century ark account nearly as dramatic as the Navarra wood recovery on Ararat unfolded in the life of David Duckworth, now a security guard in Farmington, New Mexico. This unsolved mystery started in 1968, as Duckworth relates the story in his own words.

I was working at the Smithsonian Institution in Washington, D.C., in 1968 as a volunteer in the vertebrate paleontology section. When I went to get some acetone to clean up a specimen I was working on one day, I noticed my immediate supervisor with a visiting scientist named Dr. Robert Geist. They were both bending over a magnification tripod viewer looking at some photographs. I wandered over there and just asked what they were doing. They told me to take a look myself, so I did.

What I saw was a composition picture of like four photographs put together to make one whole picture. In the picture, there was an oblong object resembling a ship that wasn't under the ice and snow but was semi-covered with it. This object appeared to be broken in the middle with several feet separating the two halves, and one end definitely appeared to be smashed.

I asked my supervisor some more questions and he said the photos had been taken on a mountain named Ararat in Turkey and that the photos had been taken from a balloon suspended by cables with an airborne camera package. You could see the shadow of the balloon on some of the pictures.

He said the film that I was looking at was a composite of infrared photographs. So I looked at it and browsed through the pile of pictures next to it. Some of them were just taken from different angles at different altitudes and some showed people on the ground looking at the ship.

There were also some pieces of fossilized wood. It was heavy wood, like stone, but it was wood. You could see where it had been chopped and drilled—where it had been worked and the remains of wooden-like pegs in it.

Then, the next day, a friend of mine and I took a shortcut to the cafeteria. You can either cut through the underground loading docks or through the visitor's center, and we cut through the loading docks. Anyhow, there were some boxes and crates on the loading dock. My friend mentioned that they were from Ararat and they were going into his section, which was physical anthropology.

One of these, a box, was an oblong, sacrophagus-like thing that I was told later was made out of alabaster. It had a sliding panel on one end that slid down into grooves and locked with stone pins on the side. It was on a pallet, and it was lashed down and everything.

Later on, this same fellow told me that they found the body of some fairly important personage from the Bible in it covered with resin. They said they had reason to believe—and I don't know why—but reason to believe it was Noah.

Now, there never was a gag order or anything from the Smithsonian like, "Don't discuss this with anyone under penalty of law." It was just an understood thing at the time that, "What you see here, what you say here, what you hear here, you leave here," and that was the understood thing.

So I didn't tell anyone except my parents about it. I

told them because they had some interest in Noah's ark after a pilot friend of theirs said he saw something in the ice over there during the Korean War years.

Frankly, I didn't think much more about it until I came out to Farmington, New Mexico, where a fellow named Eryl Cummings called me about his book, *Noah's Ark: Fact or Fable?* I said, "Fable? Well, that's a strange title for the book since I'd seen it [the ark] four years before."

That's really about all I remember.

In Cummings's second book, *Has Anybody Really Seen Noah's Ark?*, Duckworth comments, "It [the ark] *does* exist, and it *did* happen. If the government itself is covering it up . . . the people will be mad, or if the museum is covering it up, then the people and the government will be mad at them."

Duckworth said he later again questioned his friend about who was really in the coffin box. "Noah," was the friend's response. "They found him in the wreck, preserved, and a tablet with him."

When Duckworth asked Dr. Geist about the "man in the box," he was told it was "none of his concern. If the religious fanatics ever found out who was in that box it would really cause trouble." Duckworth, being nineteen at the time, asked no further questions.

Whether the body aboard the ark was Noah would be open to debate as there is an allegedly authentic tomb of Noah in the Lebanon Mountains near the ancient city of Damascus. Another possibility is that the body may have been that of Adam. One of the books of the Apocrypha—those books early church fathers decided not to include in the

Protestant Bible read today—indicates that Adam's body was taken aboard the ark for preservation from the Flood.

COVER UP?

To check out Duckworth's story, Cummings's daughter, Phyllis Watson, contacted S. Dillon Ripley, secretary of the Smithsonian Institution, who had this to say in a letter dated December 12, 1976:

> I want to assure you that the Smithsonian Institution has never been involved in a search for the remains of Noah's ark in any manner. None of our staff has participated in such an expedition, nor have we solely or jointly been involved in supporting or financing such a project, nor have any artifacts recovered from such an enterprise been seen by our staff. . . .

Still further emphasizing Secretary Ripley's firm insistence that "the Smithsonian Institution has never been involved in such a search" was an almost identical statement by Dr. Henry Setzer, curator of mammals at the Smithsonian. He said that he had even gone so far as to question "the Research Committee of the National Geographic Society" on the subject and had, in turn, been assured that "the Society has never mounted an expedition to search for the ark, nor had they even contributed toward such an expedition."

In spite of these official denials, it was later learned through Ralph Crawford, president and founder of the SEARCH organization, that the National Geographic Society had, after all, contributed to "an expedition to search for the ark"; that, in fact, in 1969, they had "contributed" to an expedition they themselves had not "mounted" by supplying "thousands upon thousands of dollars' worth of free (and the finest type of) film" to the Navarra-SEARCH expedition to Ararat to search for the ark!

Rene Noorbergen, a hard-hitting veteran newsman, war correspondent, and author of *The Ark File,* at that time was the public relations director of SEARCH, and he confirmed Crawford's statement. "The National Geographic," he said, "had reserved first rights to the photographs in the event of a possible discovery. . . ."

Also, Noorbergen related that he met a "man at a legal meeting who mentioned to him that he had been involved in an expedition to Mount Ararat in 1968, at which time they had, among other activities, shot infrared photographs of an object they believed to be Noah's ark. 'Can't talk about it any further though,' the spokesman apologized. 'I've already said too much.' "

"During the course of Noorbergen's personal sleuthing (as reported to Cummings in April 1972), he had learned of a man who had 'sat in' on some kind of meeting in 1970 in which these two institutions (Smithsonian Institution and National Geographic Society) allegedly discussed a 'joint expedition' and its discovery—and decided *not to reveal it*!"[9]

Additional corroborating information came from two chaplains in the U.S. Air Force in Turkey and three other officers. Sometime during autumn of 1964, a group reportedly "identifying themselves as members of a National Geographic expedition returning from Mount Ararat" stopped at the U.S. Air Force base in Trabzon, Turkey. This significant event is carefully recounted in a letter dated November 12, 1973, from Chaplain (Lt. Col.) Roger H. Pearson, in response to a letter from Dr. Charles Willis, an ark expeditioner from Fresno, California.

Excerpts from Chaplain Pearson's letter are as follows:

> Sometime in late 1964 a group of people stopped at Trabzon [Turkey] and asked for overnight lodging. They drove a Land Rover and I believe there were four individuals in the group. I could be mistaken, but my recollection is that one of them was a woman, the wife of one of the men in the party. They identified themselves as members of a National Geographic expedition from Mount Ararat. . . . When I asked him almost jokingly if they had discovered the ark, he said, "Chaplain, you wouldn't believe what we found!" He went on to explain that he couldn't talk about what they had found, but gave the impression that they had made a discovery of tremendous significance. I was impressed so much that for about a year I kept checking issues of *National Geographic* for information. When I saw nothing about it, I assumed they hadn't discovered anything, and stopped looking for an article about it. . . .[10]

In another letter noted by Cummings from Chaplain (Capt.) Clair Shaffer to Dr. Willis dated September 4, 1973, he writes:

> A team had stopped and spent the night at our base [Samsun, Turkey]. This was a National Geographic expedition which had been to eastern Turkey and to

Mount Ararat and was on their way home. When asked the expected question, "Did you find the ark?" they answered, "We cannot answer that question now, but may we say that we have made the greatest discovery in the history of man!"

Three other substantiating letters were received by Dr. Willis, reinforcing statements of both Pearson and Shaffer that a group identifying themselves as affiliated with the National Geographic Society did stop at both Trabzon and Samsun en route from Mount Ararat, where they admittedly had been interested in a search for the ark.[11]

So, the plot thickens . . . Who is lying about the National Geographic Society and Smithsonian involvement in an ark expedition—and why?

We do know from the last chapter that military man Lester Walton was informed in 1946 by the "higher ups" that the National Geographic Society was going to undertake an expedition to investigate the boatlike object photographed by them while testing the Fairchild bombsite camera. According to the testimonies of eyewitnesses, the National Geographic Society conducted expeditions to Mount Ararat in 1958, 1964, and 1968, and the Smithsonian *was* involved in the analysis of the Ararat findings.

Navarra's wood finds in the 1950s spawned a surge of interest and a renewed search for the ark in the 1960s and 1970s.

DISCOVERY BY AIR

In 1961 Dr. Lawrence Hewitt of California and Wilbur Bishop set out to study the glacial activity of the mountain from the air, observe melting patterns and, it was hoped, actually make the momentous discovery of the ark.[12]

Hewitt and Bishop believed that the ark was near the summit of the 17,000-foot mountain, and only later did they realize that during their aerial search they may have actually spotted the ark at a lower elevation—without realizing it at the time!

Bishop and Hewitt, photographing the summit from the air, happened to swoop down the northern face over the Ahora Gorge area. Out of range of the area that they were interested in, they temporarily rested their cameras while the pilot turned the plane around and regained altitude. Both of the men commented on a strange shiplike object protruding from a glacial finger, high in a crag, in the upper reaches of the Cehennem Dere Cir on the western face of the Ahora Gorge. They were only a few hundred feet away and noticed the appearance of ribs. But neither of them believed that this was where the ark might be, and so, even though they thought it odd, no particular significance was attached to it, and no pictures were taken.

Several years later, when informed that the research indicated that the Cehennem Dere was the most likely area, both men sheepishly recalled the incident but unfortunately could not recall the exact location of the huge canyon. A frantic restudy of all of their photographs revealed no clue.[13]

AMAZING DISCOVERIES

In recent years, it's been determined rather conclusively that the ark is not located in the Cehennem Dere of Mount Ararat but that the canyon cited by Hewitt and Bishop, near the Ahora Gorge on the north side of Ararat, is in the target area. However, ark expeditioner Ray Anderson, a retired aerospace engineer and photo analyst living in Bell Buckle, Tennessee, made some amazing discoveries while studying Dr. Hewitt's slides of Mount Ararat taken over several expeditions:

I found one slide that had a very interesting object in it. When I looked at this particular object under the microscope, it appeared to me that it could be the north end of the long piece located in the horseshoe above the Ahora Gorge at about 15,500 feet.

Now the ark is broken in two—we have conclusive evidence on that from many witnesses. During an earthquake, the south end of the Ark, about 100 feet or more of it, slid down the slope and lodged in a crevasse at about the 14,500-foot elevation.

So I examined this lower, shorter object which is only shown in one picture of the many hundreds that I have examined, and under the microscope, I could quite clearly see what appeared to be a section of the roof of what we call the superstructure.

I then examined the slides of the upper north end. You can see a rectangular shape of the north end with decks faintly exposed.

I took this slide and used a millimeter micrometer to determine the size of the object. I measured the width and height and came up with 75 feet wide by roughly 45 feet high. Using the same procedure, I found this long piece to be approximately 350 feet in length. Now eyewitnesses have estimated the shorter piece to be approximately 100 feet in length.

You have 350 feet in the long, north-end piece and 100 feet in the short, south-end piece, equaling 450 feet in total length.

Coincidentally, if you go to the Bible and check the measurements that Noah was instructed to use, he should have built the Ark to be 450 feet long, 75 feet wide, and 45 feet high—that's precisely what we got from the measurements of these two pieces.

Interest in finding the ark had reached an almost feverish pitch in the 1970s, and groups from around the world with and without official permission tackled Mount Ararat in search of the ark. The expeditions ranged from groups of highly qualified scientists to bizarre religious fanatics clumsily combing the mountain for clues. But little was achieved on any of the expeditions.

The 1980s ushered in a decade of Ararat exploration that saw many high-tech innovations brought into the ark search and a considerable amount of public attention when astronaut James B. Irwin joined the search. Colonel Irwin led his first expedition to Ararat in 1982, which ended in a nearly fatal fall to be discussed in a later chapter.

MOST SIGNIFICANT EXPEDITIONS

Although during any given summer, about a half dozen groups attemp Ararat expeditions, the following is a recap of the most significant expeditions and their achievements:

• **1986**—Colonel Irwin returned to Ararat on his fifth expedition, having obtained a much sought after permit to fly a light plane over the mountain. His expedition ended suddenly when his team was put under house arrest for allegedly spying. However, before the arrest, a Dutch National Television crew headed by Jan Van den Bosch went with Irwin and shot a documentary while Irwin's team shot twenty-two rolls of film of the Ahora Gorge area in their search for the ark. One of these Dutch TV photos will be discussed later as possibly a photo of Noah's ark.

• **1987**—Colonel Irwin of the High Flight team and geologist Dr. John Morris of the Project Ararat team, hoped to fly both a helicopter and a fixed-wing aircraft in and around the Ahora Gorge. Again, the Dutch Television crew was along to document the event. However, the Turkish governor of Dogubayazit forbade them to fly over the gorge and suggested that the team publicly promote an alternative location fifteen miles away called the Durupinar site as the "real" location of Noah's ark—more about this so-called Durupinar-Wyatt-Fasold site in a later chapter.

Both Irwin and Morris eventually received permission to fly around the southwestern side of the mountain, but not over the massive Ahora Gorge, which is larger than the Grand Canyon.

• **1988**—This was a year of unprecedented and significant activity by new ark expeditioners. Colonel Irwin did not participate this year, but San Diego commodities trader Larry Williams and former police officer Bob Cornuke represented him, making four flights to photograph obscure areas of the Ahora Gorge.

Newcomers, helicopter pilot Chuck Aaron and Florida businessman Al Jenny, flew their helicopter up and down the Gorge, ascending to 16,500 feet and descending to 11,000 feet. They then flew around the mountain at about 14,500 feet with all cameras in action. They returned with historic photographs and video footage—and the conclusion that the ark was not inside the Ahora Gorge as some had suspected.

Dr. Charles Willis, a prison physician-psychiatrist from Fresno, California, whose most famous client is Charles Manson, fielded the sixteen-member Snow Tiger Team to study the ice cap of the eastern plateau of Mount Ararat. This was Willis's fourth Ararat expedition, having used ice drills and chain saws in 1983 and 1986 to cut large trenches in the plateau ice cap, where he had believed the ark to be hidden. With the use of ice-penetrating radar, the Snow Tiger Team was able to determine that the eastern plateau was merely an 80-foot-deep ice-filled saddle depression—without Noah's ark encased in it! They came to the conclusion that the ark would have landed at a lower elevation.

• **1989**—Immanuel Expeditions, headed by helicopter pilot Chuck Aaron of West Chicago, announced to Turkish media on September 21 that it had found and photographed the ark. The story was carried on Turner's Cable News Network and by the major wire services. Aaron, displaying video footage and still photographs of an "ark object" located on the west side of Ararat at 14,500 feet, was quoted in both UPI and AP stories that he was "one hundred percent certain" that what they had photographed from the helicopter were the remains of Noah's ark.

Aaron's premature press announcement caused him disappointment and embarrassment as a second flying trip around the site revealed it was only a phenomenon of nature that assumed a very arklike shape.

Nobody can accuse Chuck Aaron of giving up easily, and to this day, he holds out hope that this still might be the ark, even though his patron, Bob VanKampen, says, "We flew within 15 feet of it and it's not Noah's ark!" Also, Swedish medical doctor-explorer Gunnar Smars, Jr., was within 100 to 200 feet of the same site in 1972 and went back again on another ground expedition in 1990. He confirms that this site, known as "the ice cave," is not Noah's ark.

Lost in the drama of allegedly finding the ark, Aaron also made a daring landing near the Ararat summit and attempted to do sonar imaging of the western plateau, but was only partially successful, having determined that the ice was up to 700 feet deep.

Also during 1989, Scott Van Dyke of the Houston-based Mount Ararat Research Foundation succeeded in hiring a professional Turkish mapping company to completely map the Mount Ararat area with a high-resolution camera. Four types of film were used, including infrared. In all, 910 overlapping photos (in stereo pairs) were made, covering approximately 50 square miles and all of the mountain above 10,000 feet. Van Dyke says the resolution is so good that sheep on the mountain are clearly visible. They say it will take years to analyze all the photos—with anticipation of maybe finding a clue of the ark under the icy surface.

Dr. Don Shockey's expedition from Albuquerque, New Mexico, returned again to follow up on an ark location pinpointed by satellite on the north side of Ararat above the Ahora Gorge in the Abich II glacier area. It was on this trip that Shockey's guide obtained a clear photo of a snow-covered object with sharply marked symmetrical lines at the site where military satellite imagery indicates there is a wooden structure.

• **1990**—The Don Shockey expedition spent well into the six figures using a Russian-made M18 helicopter, which was flown in from Istanbul complete with six crew members and space for up to twenty-four passengers. Numerous flights were made to get aerial video footage and still photographs of the site pinpointed by satellite and photographed from 300 yards away by Dr. Arslan in 1989. An attempt to reach the site by ground failed when the three members of the ground team came down with severe mountain sickness.

However, Dr. Shockey, an Albuquerque optometrist, cultural anthropologist, author, and founder of the FIBER Education Foundation, provided insights into what his expedition has been trying to investigate on Mount Ararat:

We've been given new information about the possible real locations of the ark on Mount Ararat. Through a meeting with a government official who analyzes satellite information, he gave us some information on two objects located in the ice cap high on the northeast side of Mount Ararat. He told us the depth, how far apart they were, and the size. He described it as rectangular, with one piece being about 1,000 feet below the other.

In 1989 I went to Turkey on my second trip to Mount Ararat. We hired two Turkish guides and climbed the mountain. Since Americans weren't allowed to go around to the north side we sent them. I marked for them a map exactly where the satellite information said to look.

The Turks went, and one of them [Dr. Ahmet Arslan], took a photograph from a distance and came back all excited and said, "It's a coop. It looks like a chicken coop. There's something man-made there and I think it's the ark."

• **1991**—The Kurdish insurgency and the Desert Storm operations kept ark searchers home with the exception of Chuck Aaron, who in July made ten quick flights around the mountain in a fixed-wing aircraft. No new discoveries were made.

• **1992**—Heavy fighting between Turkish soldiers trying to put down Kurdish insurgents and terrorists kept ark climbers and aerial observers away from Mount Ararat. The Ararat slopes were the site of several deadly confrontations between Turkish soldiers and terrorists.

• **1993**—A nine-member Search for Truth Expedition headed by California science teacher John McIntosh and airline pilot Dick Bright made another attempt to search Mount Ararat. They were granted a permit in Ankara to fly a helicopter around Ararat. However, their permit was later canceled by the regional governor of Kars, headquartered fifty miles from Mount Ararat. The governor cited a secret military operation that was taking place on Mount Ararat as the reason for canceling their permit.

Within a couple of hours, after the expeditioners departed their hotel, PKK guerrillas attacked the hotel and killed two Turkish policemen that were involved in security measures for the hotel and the expeditioners.

Also in 1993, twenty-three-year-old New Zealander Paul Thomsen, who was looking for the ark on Ararat, was captured by the PKK and held for five weeks. The PKK was also holding other Ararat climbers—two Italians, two Germans, and two Swiss —as hostages in an attempt to persuade the Turkish military not to bomb their strongholds for fear of killing the foreign hostages.

• **1994**—No ark-Ararat expeditions were attempted due to the heavy shelling and bombing on Ararat slopes.

This treacherous and deadly mountain called Ararat, and Agri Dagh, "the painful mountain," has exacted a heavy price from almost every expedition that has set out to search for its hidden treasures. In the next chapter, we'll tell you the personal, harrowing stories of expeditioners who survived terrorist attacks and near-death experiences with the mountain itself.

Notes

[1] Fernand Navarra with Dave Balsiger, *Noah's Ark: I Touched It* (Plainfield, NJ: Logos International, 1974), pp. xiii, xiv, 31–39, 40–63. Reprinted by special permission.

[2] Dave Balsiger and Charles E. Sellier, *In Search of Noah's Ark* (Los Angeles: Sun Classic Books, 1976), p. 176. Cited interview with Fernand Navarra by Robert Guenette of Sun Classic Pictures, February 9, 1976.

[3] Balsiger and Sellier, *In Search of Noah's Ark*, p. 177.

[4] Ibid., pp. 180, 185. Cited interview with Richard Bliss, March 1976.

[5] Letter to James Irwin of the High Flight Foundation from John Noakes of the Center for Applied Isotope Studies, University of Georgia, Athens, GA, February 12, 1985.

[6]Balsiger and Sellier, *In Search of Noah's Ark,* pp. 182–183.

[7]R. E. Taylor and R. A. Muller, "Radiocarbon Dating," *Encyclopedia of Science and Technology* (New York: McGraw-Hill, 1987), p. 124.

[8]Melvin A. Cook interviews, Salt Lake City, UT, February, 1976, and June 16, 1992. The 1976 interview cited in Balsiger and Sellier, *In Search of Noah's Ark,* pp. 188–189.

[9]Violet Cummings, *Has Anybody Really Seen Noah's Ark?* (San Diego: Creation-Life Publishers, 1982), pp. 201–203.

[10]Ibid., pp. 206–207.

[11]Tim LaHaye and John Morris, *The Ark on Ararat* (Nashville, TN: Thomas Nelson Publishers, 1976), p. 147.

[12]Ibid., pp. 147–148.

[13]Ibid., pp. 147–148.

12

TERRORISTS, DEMONS, AND MIRACLES

> Wisdom consists in being able to distinguish among dangers and making a choice of the least harmful.
>
> Machiavelli

We were on an expedition to Mount Ararat several years ago and even though you can have permits to be on the mountain, it doesn't protect you from local terrorist groups.

On this particular day, we had climbed up to the 13,500-foot level on the south face of the mountain and proceeded to set up camp for the night. It was pretty close to midnight when suddenly, we heard a lot of noise. I couldn't understand what they were saying but it was pretty clear they wanted us out of our tents. When we came out, we were unprepared for what we saw. Eight armed Kurdish terrorists had taken over the camp. They had lights strapped to their heads so when they were looking at us we couldn't see them very well. Their faces were also hidden with scarves and they each held an AK-47—pointed right at us.

The other people in our group were being ordered out of their tents, too. They hauled out everything we had and pulled aside our cameras and any other valuables they wanted to keep. Then they proceeded to torch everything they didn't want. Thousands of dollars worth of scientific equipment and climbing gear—gone up in smoke in minutes.

They had everybody in our group move back into a line. At that instant, it didn't really dawn on me what was taking place—until I looked up. Several of the terrorists were arguing heatedly among themselves while the others leveled their weapons at us. It looked pretty much like this was going to be the end of the line.

I can tell you this, there was a lot of praying going on right about then. We pretty much thought, "Well, this is it."

Then, the one who looked like the leader yelled something at us and motioned for us to leave. Believe me, we didn't wait around for them to tell us twice. We went down the mountain fast, and we were very happy to get out of there.

I guess you'd have to say that we were pretty lucky, too. Those guys were a very tough group.

After everything was reported, the Turkish military sent about 500 soldiers onto the mountain. One terrorist escaped. Another one was captured. The rest were shot and killed in a gun battle with the soldiers.

Expeditioner John McIntosh,
describing an August 1985 terrorist attack

THE PERILS OF HUMAN TREACHERY

The physical rigors of climbing Mount Ararat are not the only hazards the searchers of Noah's ark face on the mysterious mountain. These heroic explorers frequently encounter an even greater peril—human treachery.

Nomads, bandits, insurgents, and terrorists often assault the brave searchers. "It's wise to beware of anyone on the mountain carrying a gun," suggests one expeditioner. John Morris, in his book *Adventures on Ararat,* tells how his expedition was assaulted by bandits, robbed at gunpoint, and hit by lightning—all on one trip! Even local guides have betrayed the trust of the explorers and abandoned them.

Of all these dangers, perhaps betrayal by paid guides is the least expected. For reasons of their own —superstition or ancestral beliefs, exhaustion, injury, or a myriad of other reasons—many have abandoned the climbers to fend for themselves on the hostile slopes. Some guides have even extorted more money out of the explorers before deserting them halfway up the mountain.

As the expeditioners relate their harrowing stories of survival, this treachery adds its own mystique to the historic site.

In 1856 Major Robert Stuart wrote about his experience with Kurdish guides.

The Kurdish attendants came to a stop and refused to proceed any further, alleging in justification [their] ancestral traditions and the fear of treading on holy ground. . . . [The Kurds also] hold it as part of their faith . . . that any attempt of the kind would be followed by the immediate displeasure of Heaven.[1]

On one of Eryl Cummings's ascents of Mount Ararat, his two Kurdish guides stopped at 12,500 feet and put down their packs. Cummings couldn't understand what they were saying, but the message was clear—they were not going any higher.

The guides had already been well paid for their work, but they wanted more money. Since Cummings still needed their help, he reluctantly gave in to their demands. Some 300 feet higher, however, the Kurds again set down their packs, this time for good.

According to Kurdish tradition, the uppermost parts of the mountain are inhabited by evil *djinn*— demonic spirits. No amount of money or persuasion will get some guides to go past a certain point on Mount Ararat. Many explorers do not discover this until it's too late.

Not only was Cummings unsuccessful in getting his guides to continue the climb, they fervently tried to convince him to give up the effort, too.

With wild gesticulations, rolling eyes and excited chatter in their native tongue, they indicated the steepness of the ridge ahead, the sheer dropoffs on either side, and even attempted to physically turn their foolhardy companion [Cummings] around and start him back down the mountain toward the camp.[2]

Finally, he continued up the mountain alone. On his return, the guides were shocked and delighted when they saw that he had survived the uppermost parts of the mountain alone. They rushed to his aid, carrying his packs back down to the base camp.

In July of 1952, Fernand Navarra attempted to scale the mountain but ran into difficulties with his guides, too. He recorded the encounter this way:

> As the party progressed they were regaled with tales of former "pious pilgrimages" to the ark, but were once more assured that they could never negotiate the steep cliffs ahead. "You can't go that way," warned a young shepherd, "because there's magic there." And at an elevation of 10,000 feet their native escort abandoned them with significant glances, and refused to go a step farther into the "magic zone."[3]

Most of the Kurdish locals, who are neither Christian nor strong Islamic followers, hold a number of beliefs regarding ancient superstitions and evil spirits. Also, memories of mountain-related tragedies prevent them from climbing the mountain or guiding explorers much above the snowline.

THE JOHN LIBI EXPEDITIONS

American explorers also continued to encounter the hardships of Mount Ararat. Consider the case of John Libi from San Francisco. His is a typical case of a man against the mountain, with man losing the battle again and again. An extremely capable and experienced mountain climber, fluent in Turkish and several other languages, knowledgeable leader and dedicated adventurer, Libi tried eight times in fifteen years to find the ark. He nearly lost his life several times on the mountain as his expeditions met with failure.

• **1954**—Thinking that the ark was near the summit, Libi engineered two ascents. On one of the climbs, Libi was attacked and chased by two huge bears near the ice cap. The additional exertion required to outrun them, coupled with rarefied air and the cold, caused Libi to develop a serious illness and fever, from which it took a month to recuperate. On the second climb, late in the summer, the weather turned bad even though it had been quite favorable, and further explorations were impractical.

• **1955**—Libi returned with his team of explorers, but due to unexpected political turmoil, permission to climb the mountain was rescinded.

• **1958**—This time leading a group of forty men, Libi, sixty-two years old, fell 30 feet to a rock ledge, and had to be carried off the mountain and hospitalized in a nearby town.

• **1960**—The weather on Ararat won another battle, for again Libi required hospitalization, this time in Ankara, the capital of Turkey, for pneumonia.

• **1962**—On May 9, while boarding a train in Italy en route to Ararat, Libi was robbed of all the expedition's finances.

• **1965**—A horrible July thunderstorm and blizzard separated the team of ten into three groups. One group finally returned to camp suffering from advanced stages of fatigue and exposure after wandering on the mountain slopes in search of safety for three days. The storm washed away the entire food supply, and the dejected group returned to the States.

• **1967**—In Libi's estimation, the worst weather he had ever seen on Mount Ararat virtually attacked them. Great quantities of snow and extreme cold forced them off the mountain. The weather claimed the life of a Belgian climber who had joined Libi's party. The freshly fallen snow and a recent earthquake had loosened the footing, and the youth slipped over the edge of a huge cliff to his death.

• **1969**—Libi, defying his seventy-three years, and in spite of the fact that in 1967 he swore that he would not return, reached the summit and the spot where he believed the ark to be. There he found a layer of waterborne fossils, but no ark.[4]

NARROW ESCAPE

Dr. Charles Berlitz, linguist, explorer, and author of *The Lost Ship of Noah,* ran into a unique problem on his ark expedition:

> I was staying in a town near Ararat, and the day of my permitted exploration for the ark was unfortunately the same day some people had been shot down in the streets in a demonstration against the government.
>
> I had noticed a lot of commotion on the streets because of the shoot-out between the people and the police, and I got caught up in the crowds. Not knowing what was going on, I went on through the area but I didn't have my documents or passport with me.
>
> When the Turkish authorities realized I was an American, they demanded to know what I was doing among the crowd after the riots. I was arrested and taken to a prison by police with some very unfriendly black guard dogs.
>
> Fortunately, after two days in prison, I managed to convince them to take me back to the hotel so I could

get some of my belongings. It was late at night when we arrived at the hotel, and the guards stayed downstairs. I left most of my things in my room, but grabbed my passport and slipped out a back entrance.

I jumped on a bus to Mecca, but when we arrived at the nearest airport I got off and bought a ticket to Ankara. I suppose the gendarmes are still looking for me. I owe my survival in part to Turkish culture, because if there hadn't been a bus on its way to Mecca, I wouldn't have been able to get out of Turkey!

Based on my own experience, my advice to travelers is to keep your passport with you at all times and above all, stay away from crowds—especially if they are taking part in any manifestations against the government.

NEAR-FATAL MISTAKE

In 1982 astronaut Colonel James Irwin's High Flight Foundation put together an expedition to do a systematic search of Mount Ararat for the ark. In his book, *More Than an Ark on Ararat,* Irwin wrote,

> We were a band of committed Christians who had sacrificed money, time, and effort in trying to find the greatest archaeological treasure of all history, the ark of Noah.
>
> We slept in numbing cold, fell on loose rock, dodged tumbling boulders, grew exhausted from high-altitude climbing, had feet sore with blisters, had painfully cracked lips from sunburn, received various cuts and nicks, all in pursuit of a hidden and uncertain treasure. Even knowing the risks, no doubt many of you readers would have joined us on this adventure if you had been given the opportunity.[5]

During this expedition, Irwin made a mistake that almost cost him his life. The following excerpts from

his book, reprinted here by permission of the publisher, describe his accident and the possibly miraculous event that helped to save his life:

One morning I had hoped to reach the summit with a
small group of climbers, but I was moving too slowly.
Disappointed with my performance and wanting to
conserve my strength, I left the group. I headed back
down to base camp in order to coordinate our move off
the mountain, which had been planned for the next day.

I set out for the rocky ridge down Ark Rock, but
around noon saw a shortcut down a snowfield.

It was slippery, so I sat down to put on my crampons,
and that's the last thing I remember until near dusk. I
must have been struck from behind by a falling rock.

The next thing I knew I was at the bottom of the
snowfield in a pile of sharp rocks, and I was a bloody
mess. I had broken five teeth, had several jagged gashes
on the top of my head, a deep cut over my right eye and
on the bridge of my nose, a sprained neck, a badly
sprained ankle, sore ribs, and numerous other cuts and
gashes on my face, hands, and legs.

I tried to stand, but was so weak from the loss of
blood that my legs simply wouldn't support me.
Fortunately, I had my sleeping bag in my backpack,
which was miraculously still on my back. It was almost
dark at this point. I was shivering in the cold. I climbed
into my sleeping bag, knowing I'd have to spend the
night alone on the mountain.

I realized I was still in a dangerous spot, for rocks
were continually cascading down. I dragged myself
behind a big rock that would be a shield for me. Soon
after doing that, a huge boulder came crashing down the
mountain, bounced off my shield rock, and barely
grazed my sleeping bag.

In traveling alone, I'd broken the very rule I'd given
to the others. The Turkish commando was to be

alongside me at all times, but I told him to go on ahead with the two who had climbed the summit.

The base camp at Lake Kop and the high camp at the 14,000-foot level had walkie-talkie contact. The high camp reported that I'd left at mid-morning, and they wondered if I'd gotten into camp safely. The base camp naturally hadn't seen me, so the alert was out that I was missing.

It was almost dark. There would be no way they could find me in the vast wilderness of Ararat at night. It would be hard enough in the daylight!

They made plans before going to bed that the high camp would send its members down in three different routes, and that three more groups would start out in different directions from base camp. They would all select the most probable route I may have taken, but none knew about my shortcut, which was not on any of the routes they'd chosen.

In the middle of that night one of the Americans awakened in base camp at 2:00 A.M. The wind was blowing at the flaps of his tent. It was bitterly cold. He was one who had linked arms and prayed earlier that I'd be found.

As he prayed again, he felt an indescribably strong impulse to go to a certain ridge on the north slope and look for me there. It was a place he'd been earlier in the week. He determined to find that spot with his search party the next morning. He went back to sleep until 5:00 A.M.

Try to imagine the immensity of Mount Ararat. It is the highest mountain in Turkey at 16,945 feet and is purported to have one of the largest landmasses of any single mountain in the world.

There are glaciers, canyons, snowfields, ridges, mass jumbles of broken rocks, crevices, crumbling cliffs, and streams. To find a man, especially if he is unconscious and lying in one of the tens of thousands of crevices on the mountain, would be nearly impossible.

And remember, I had not followed one of the

normal routes. Instead, I had taken a shortcut across a treacherously steep snowfield.

When I awakened the next morning, I knew I was still in danger of falling rocks. I tried to move but couldn't stand up.

All six groups started out very early that morning— the three from the top and the three from the bottom. Of the three groups that started out from base camp, two were comprised of two Turks each. The third group had two Turks and the one American who was going to hike toward that certain ridge where he thought he would find me.

They began the search and covered the immense mountain as well as they could. Interestingly enough, only the American called my name. As he went through the canyons, across the bottom of Parrot Glacier, and up the ridge that led to Ark Rock, he kept calling, "Jim . . . Jim . . . Jim." This proved to be absolutely essential to my eventual rescue.

It had been two hours since the groups started out, the ones from the high camp carefully picking their way down through the ice fields and crumbling rock from the top, and the ones from base camp climbing as swiftly as they could up into the 12,000- and 13,000-foot level. It was rough going from both directions. They not only had to watch their footing on the treacherous rocks, but they were also looking for an injured or dead man.

The American from the base camp reached the base of Parrot Glacier . . . nearing the ridge he felt directed to.

When he came up onto that jagged ridge, he was right where he had envisioned it the night before. He could see far into Russia and over into Iran.

The chilly morning wind hit his face. He saw nothing but the expanse of Ararat, ridge after ridge of crumbling north-slope canyons.

Once again he called my name.

I heard him!

I was no more than fifty yards away!

I answered weakly, hoping he would hear.

I shouted again. Setting off a smoke signal device which alerted the other search parties, he started off toward me, though he still couldn't see exactly where I was.

I feel God answered the prayers of that small group the night before . . . and led this search party to within fifty yards of where I was lying in a broken heap. Given the vastness of Ararat, I can think of no other answer.[6]

MIRACULOUS ESCAPE

Chuck Aaron is an ark expeditioner and helicopter pilot who has been to the mountain eight times and conducted many helicopter surveys of Mount Ararat. He tells of both aerial and ground problems encountered by his expedition group.

As a helicopter pilot, one of the greatest difficulties is getting the permits to fly around the mountain. I've piloted more than 100 flights around Mount Ararat to photograph and explore it from the air.

Wind currents from 70 to 150 miles an hour are not uncommon. In filming a mountain like this one, the idea is to get as close as possible yet not get caught in any unknown wind currents that would smash you into the side of the mountain.

During an expedition in which Aaron was surveying the western plateau of the Ararat summit using ice-penetrating radar, he, too, experienced a close call with terrorists and a miraculous escape. His story is told by Paul Thomsen in *The Mystery of the Ark* and is reprinted here by permission of the publisher:

For three exhausting days, they systematically worked across the caldera, and now they closed in on the final section where the ark could be trapped. The radio crackled to life, with the gravely voice of the gendarme commandant. Chuck Aaron hurried to the tent and picked up the radio. Puffing, he more gasped than spoke, "This is caldera. Go ahead, base."

"This is an urgent message. You must get off the mountain of Ararat immediately. We have just received word that a pack of PKK terrorists are moving up the north face of the mountain. Our informer has told us that they intend to surprise and attack your outpost. These men want no hostages—they are killers, your lives are in jeopardy, you must leave immediately. Do you understand? Over."

Gripping the transmitter, Chuck looked up and waved at Bob Garbo and B. J. Corbin working the radar equipment 200 meters out. "Roger, base, I read you loud and clear. We are to prepare to leave immediately. We'll get our essential gear ready. By the time Yavuz gets here in the helicopter, we'll be prepared to leave. Over."

"Ah, roger, I have a message for you from the helicopter pilot. Let me read it to you. 'To Expedition Leader Aaron: I'll meet you at the 8,000-foot level. Get yourself off the mountain. Signed, Yavuz.' This means he doesn't want to fly the helicopter above the limits of its capability, and I cannot force him to do so.

"You'll have to climb down to 8,000 feet. Remember, come down the south face—the bandits are coming up the north face. May Allah be with you." Click!

Lowering the radio, Chuck shook his head in disbelief as the other men huffed up.

"That was the Commandant. He said we've got to leave immediately. Terrorists are coming up the north face, and they're comin' after us!"

"We better get crackin' and have Yavuz fly up here fast," said Bob, scanning the sky that was beginning to drop huge snowflakes.

"You haven't heard the best part. Yavuz is chicken to fly up and land!"

"What?" said both men at once, looking in shock at Chuck.

"Yeah, he left us a note—said, 'Get yourself off the mountain. Signed, Yavuz.' "

"Let's take stock, guys. It's late in the day—at best, we have two, maybe three, hours of light. We've got no weapons but a flare gun. The bandits are coming up the north face; it's 9,000 feet straight down the south face. And there's bad weather moving in."

"I suggest we do some heavy, fast prayin'," said Bob. Nodding agreement, all three men bowed their heads. "Lord, we are three guys in deep trouble. Please help guide us to safety."

As the men scrambled to pack essentials, B. J. looked up, "Hang on, it may be too late—look at that!" All three men straightened and stared through the falling snow as a lone, gray figure approached in the distance. Chuck fumbled for his binoculars.

"Is it a friendly or a bandit?" said Bob, squinting into the snow.

"I'm not sure, but the guy appears to be alone and he isn't carryin' a machine gun." The three men stood and watched the stranger silently come toward them through the softly falling snow. As he drew closer, he stopped, then raised a bare hand, the international sign for peace.

Silently walking past the men, he motioned them with a calloused hand to follow as he paced toward the caldera ledge a hundred meters out. Reaching the dropoff, he squatted on his haunches. The three cautious men with backpacks and ice axes came up and stood behind him. Looking down into the abyss, the stranger's eyes swung to his left following the 60-degree ice wall that led 500 feet over to a finger point of black volcanic rock. The rock formed a wedge that descended toward the valley somewhere below in the swirling snow. Twisting his head, he held out a hand and motioned for

Chuck's ice ax. Chuck hesitantly handed it to him handle first.

Taking the ax, the stranger reached down and chipped out a notch. Then, twisting his face to the wall, he swung his lanky leg out over the ledge, slipped his tennis shoe into the notch and put his left hand on the inward-slanting ice wall. At waist-high, he cut a second notch, smaller than the first. Again standing, he looked back, smiled slightly, and nodded for the men to follow.

"Wait a minute, this guy actually wants us to follow him in a traverse across the ice wall to the rocks. I mean, some guy appears out of nowhere in a tweed suit, tennis shoes, no socks, says nothin', and then, with his bare hands and an ice ax, proceeds to chip out holds and shinny across a sheer, 9,000-foot dropoff—we've no ice crampons, no rope, no clamps. And further, we don't even know if he's a terrorist or what. Man, this is absolutely wild!" exclaimed B. J.

"You bet your life, it's wild," said Chuck over the rising wind, "but the way I figure it, we're running outta time, weather and light. We really don't have much of a choice—it's either sit here and face the terrorists, or follow 'Tennis Shoes' across the ice wall. Something in my gut says we've gotta trust this guy." Chuck twisted to face the wall, then swung a leg out over the ledge, feeling with his foot for the first notch.

In a left-to-right, step-by-step traverse across the ice face, for forty-five minutes they hugged the wall, clinging to life in five-inch toeholds.

"Don't look down," yelled Chuck as Bob hugged the wall, clinging precariously while his foot thrashed, searching for the toehold. Finding it, he equalized his weight. Then pumping out jets of steamy breath, he looked at Chuck, his cheek hugging the ice.

One by one, the exhausted climbers reached the rocky haven. Collapsing against the boulders, the men sat elbows on knees. With heads down and chests heaving, they sucked great gulps of the rare air. After a moment, the tall stranger, still standing, motioned them to follow. Rising slowly, the men followed his lead down through the maze of rocks and crevasses. For an hour, they stumbled on; then, too exhausted to continue, Chuck held up his hand and flopped back in the recesses of black volcanic rock.

"Mister, I don't know who you are, but we can't go a step further. We're gonna break out the sleeping bags right here and bed down," Chuck said. Reaching over, he broke the strap on his backpack. With his heart pounding hard, he continued. "We've gotta be safe now. There's no way those terrorists can traverse that ice wall in the dark."

The stranger turned from looking down the mountain; his dark eyes fixed on Chuck. Silently, he bent over, placing the ice ax against a boulder. Then standing straight, he lifted a bare hand, took a step back into the swirling snow, and disappeared into the darkness.

B. J. echoed the thoughts of the other two exhausted men as they crawled into their down sleeping bags. "That was just a miracle—no other way to explain it!"[7]

They finally made it to the 8,000-foot level where they were met by their helicopter. They then went to the commandant's office at the base of the mountain to brief the commandant.

Tilting back on the hind legs of his chair, the commandant of the gendarme studied the ten-inch knife he twisted between his hands. After listening intently for thirty minutes to their account, he looked past the knife and spoke slowly and deliberately to the expedition team seated in front of his huge cedar desk.

"The flashlights you saw coming up the mountain last night were my commandos. They must have passed you about midnight, because an hour later they scaled the ice wall. Once on top, they snuck up on your camp, surprising four terrorists.

Leaning forward, he jabbed the knife into the desktop with a thud and growled, "A firefight broke out, and my men killed all four of them. Later, they continued on to the summit and are now sweeping the north face for any additional bandits."

Yanking the knife out, he leaned back and said with a shrug, "As for your special guide in the tweed suit, I have no idea who he was. I assure you, he was not one of my men."

Pointing his knife at Chuck, he raised his eyebrows, "Remember, Mr. Aaron, what I told you about the savage mountain. Mysterious things happen up there. But the one thing you can count on for sure—expect the unexpected."[8]

MAGIC MOUNTAIN

There is something magical about that mountain— something those explorers who have been on the brink of disaster or death cannot explain in natural or scientific terms. Was it the power of prayer that turned the course of events for them? Or was it an angel who rescued them from certain doom? We cannot say exactly what it was, other than to agree with them when they say "it was a miracle" that saved their lives, giving them yet another opportunity to search for Noah's ark.

In light of all the unsuccessful expeditions, however, we are still left with the question, is Noah's ark truly on Mount Ararat? Some vigorously claim they have found evidence of the ark at two locations many miles from Mount Ararat. As you examine the evidence for other sites, decide for yourself. Can we believe their accounts? Or must we continue to climb the mystical mountain of Ararat until we find the elusive ancient ship?

Notes

[1] Violet Cummings, *Has Anybody Really Seen Noah's Ark?* (San Diego: Creation-Life Publishers, 1982), pp. 33–34.

[2] Ibid., p. 52.

[3] Violet Cummings, *Noah's Ark: Fact or Fable?* (San Diego: Creation-Science Research Center, 1972), p. 178.

[4] Tim LaHaye and John Morris, *The Ark on Ararat* (Nashville: Thomas Nelson Publishers, 1976), pp. 139–142.

[5] James Irwin, *More Than an Ark on Ararat* (Nashville: Broadman Press, 1985), p. 46.

[6] Ibid., pp. 63–73.

[7] Paul Thomsen, *The Mystery of the Ark* (Brentwood, TN: Wolgemuth and Hyatt Publishers, 1991), pp. 35–47.

[8] Ibid., pp. 50–51.

13

ALTERNATIVE NOAH'S ARK SITES

It is not who is right but what is right that is
of importance.

Thomas Henry Huxley

COLUMBUS, OHIO, 14 NOV (AP) Sevket
Kurtis has filtered stereographic airphotos in
Turkey, from which maps can be produced,
and he has made a curious discovery.

The "discovery" has not yet been verified.
However, Kurtis assumes that the curious
form of the discovered object could be the
ark of Noah, which is described in the Bible
and the Koran.

The airphotos were taken a year ago on
behalf of the Geodetic Institute of Turkey.
But the curious object was just recently
discovered in one of the photos. The "ark"
was not recognizable with the unaided eye. It
was discovered when in Ankara, Captain
Ilhan Durupinar used a stereoplanograph in
order to prepare maps. With this instrument
this object was discovered, which could not
have been created by nature itself but by
human hands.

Kurtis reports that Captain Durupinar has
worked on thousands of square miles in this

method for the preparation of maps, but has never seen a similar object in stereographic airphotos.

The size corresponds with the description of the ark in the Bible and in the Koran. The object has the form of a boat, is 450 feet long and 160 feet wide . . .

Kurtis said that the object, which could be the ark, is sunk in a field of lava. Through heat the ark might be preserved like Herculaneum and Pompeii. If it is really Noah's ark, then it must be 7,000 years old.

Dr. Arthur Brandenberger of the Geodetic Institute of Ohio State University said after he had seen the stereophotos he also is convinced that this discovery cannot be a "product of nature" but possibly a "petrified boat." He added that if it were really Noah's ark it would be a sensational discovery. . . .

The Staats Zeitungf Und Herald,
Woodside, NJ, November 15, 1959

The most recent chapter in the long history of the search of Noah's ark began in a Turkish military laboratory in September of last year.

During a routine examination of aerial photos made during a geodetic survey, Capt. Ilhan Durupinar stopped short, stared in stunned disbelief at one negative that was remarkably different from the thousands of others he'd studied.

Clearly outlined in the photo was something shaped like a large ship, apparently embedded in a stream of lava.

Bubbling over with excitement, he called other officers. All were convinced that 6,000 feet up in the Ararat range was a ship of

gigantic dimensions, and immediate orders
were issued to work out its measurements.

Among the experts who studied the photo
was Dr. Arthur Brandenberger, a professor at
Ohio State University and one of the world's
top experts in the field of photogrammetry
and geodesy. "There's a ship on Ararat," he
declared positively, "and someone had
better find out how it got there."

Toronto Star Weekly,
July 23, 1960

DOGUBEYAZIT—At the Uzengili village,
which is near the Dogubeyazlt district, is
located the boat-shaped formation.
Scientists from the U.S.A. have confirmed
that it is Noah's ark. The governor has
announced that it is now a national park and
open for tourists.

At Uzengili village, which is 15 kilometers
from Dogubeyazit, Turkish scientists, Mr.
Ronald Eldon Wyatt, and his team from the
U.S.A. made a research of the area. They
took samples of the soil. Test results
revealed that the soil has iron and fossil boat
structures. Scientists confirmed that Noah's
ark is at the Uzengili village.

Mr. Sevket Ekinci, Governor of Agri; Mr.
Cengiz Gokce, Head Official of the District of
Dogubeyazit; Mr. Osman Baydar, President
of the Municipality; some Turkish scientists,
and Mr. Wyatt participated in the ceremony
opening the area for tourists.

Mr. Sevket Ekinci said, "Turkey is a
country of great interest for tourists. The
Holy Bible and the Koran also say that
Noah's ark is in this area."

Mr. Ekinci added, "It is my pleasure that I
am opening this area which is getting great

attention for Noah's ark and I appreciate all
the scientists for discovering Noah's ark. We
are laying a foundation for a welcome center
for Turkish and foreign tourists. Thank you."

Hurriyet, Turkish newspaper,
June 21, 1987[1]

HOT DEBATE

The dedication of the site as Noah's Ark National
Park began one of the most controversial and hotly
debated chapters in the story of the search for the
ark.

"The government officials were delighted with the
prospects of the influx of tourists and of more money
with which to improve the lives of their people," says
Ron Wyatt of Nashville, Tennessee, an anesthetist by
profession and a self-styled ark hunter. "The locals
were happy with the good jobs made available
through the construction of the new super highway
leading to the visitor's center soon to be built overlooking the remains of Noah's ark."[2]

But is this boatlike formation known as the
Durupinar site really Noah's ark? Although we'll examine the Ron Wyatt claims and counterclaims later
in this chapter, some experts cite the Koran—the
Moslem holy book—as being the authoritative
source as to where the ark landed. According to the
Koran, the surviving boat landed on the Mountain of
Al-Judi, a 7,000-foot peak that is some 200 miles
south of Mount Ararat in southern Turkey. Today
the mountain is called Cudi Dagh and is within eye-
sight of the Syrian and Iraqi borders. The Tigris

River flows at its base, and it overlooks the Mesopotamian plain.

Dr. Charles D. Willis, a medical doctor and psychiatrist who has led several expeditions to Mount Ararat, now argues for the ark landing on Mount Al-Judi. "Since we radared all over to the Eastern Plateau peak of Mount Ararat in 1988 and found nothing, it led me to reevaluate whether or not Ararat is the correct mountain—which I think it is not. The correct mountain is Mount Al-Judi with its two peaks within the ancient kingdom of Urartu inside Turkey. Here the parameters are clearly met historically. First, the most ancient Jewish and Christian sources point to the mountain, not Mount Ararat."

Sociologist and Ararat climber B. J. Corbin from Maryland offers a dissenting view: "In 1990, at the base of Mount Ararat, I questioned a lot of the local people and I asked them, 'Where is Noah's Ark?' They all pointed to the ice cap of Mount Ararat—about 80 percent pointed towards the West and the others to the East. To me this really verifies that the locals do believe that the ark is on Ararat in Turkey."

"The second biggest reason I believe it's on Judi," says Dr. Willis, "is that Bishop Epiphanius of Salamis said in the fourth century A.D. that visitors could see the ark ruins at Mount Cudi, meaning Al-Judi."

"Is Mount Ararat the right mountain, or is it another mountain," asks Dr. Elfred Lee, illustrator and lifetime ark researcher-expeditioner. "Some bring to mind Al-Judi—but I spent a long time studying this particular passage in the Koran at the Islamic Center in Washington, D.C., with the curator there.

"The curator told me that the term 'Al-Judi' could also be pronounced, 'Al-Cudi' and he pointed out this is possibly where the Kurdish people get their name—the Cudi people. But the real point is that Al-Judi/Al-Cudi is one of the peaks in the cluster of peaks forming the Mount Ararat summit—not another mountain 200 miles away," Dr. Lee explains. "Islamic scholars believe Al-Judi refers to Ararat."

"The third very important reason that it's Judi, is that the ancient Jewish commentaries known as the Targums reveal that there had to be two peaks at the mountain of Noah," explains Dr. Willis, "and at Mount Judi, there are two peaks."

Dr. Don Shockey, leader of the FIBER Foundation ark expeditions to Mount Ararat says, "Mount Judi does not fit the biblical account. When the ark came to rest on the mountains of Ararat, it was seventy-four days before the water receded enough for the next highest peak to come into view. The receding rate of the floodwaters fits Greater and Lesser Ararat and does not fit the geography that's there at the Mount Judi site."

Dr. Willis also contends that a European geologist in 1954 found rotten wood on Mount Judi that dated extremely old. Dr. Willis would not provide the name of the geologist or any test results on the wood. If wood was found, it probably was the remains of ancient monasteries that were known to have been built on Mount Judi.

AKYAYLA DAGI

Meanwhile, the alternative site that has received the most news media attention and much scientific study is the Durupinar site south of Mount Ararat on Akyayla Dagi (High White Plain) slightly to the west of an escarpment called Yigityatagi.

Ron Wyatt was the first American since 1960 to visit the site in 1977 and again in 1979. In 1984 he enlisted the help of David Fasold, a marine salvage specialist. Both are utterly convinced it is the authentic ark of Noah, but Fasold, who has written a book titled *The Ark of Noah* explaining his theories, no longer identifies with Wyatt, who, he claims, often makes unsubstantiated statements.

ASTONISHING CLAIMS BY WYATT

The claims by self-proclaimed biblical archaeologist Ron Wyatt are nothing short of astonishing. A few of Wyatt's alleged "finds" include:[3]

- The true site of the crucifixion.
- The ark of the covenant in a cave beneath this alleged crucifixion site.
- The true site of the Israelites' Red Sea crossing with a marker "built by King Solomon" as a memorial.
- Chariot wheels from Pharaoh's drowned army.
- The actual rock Moses struck to release water.
- Noah's grave.
- Noah's house with inscriptions about the Flood.
- Noah's wife's grave. He claims he dug her up

and found $75 million worth of gold in her grave—unfortunately later stolen by another.

The bottom line seems to be that no hard evidence exists to prove any of his claims. When contacted during the preparation of this book, he refused to cooperate by supplying any evidence supporting his claims, whether relating to the alleged ark site or any of his other finds. Supporters of his also could not offer any impartial scientific evidence for his many findings. Later in this chapter we will present the conclusions of scientists concerning some of his ark site claims made at public forums and on television.

FASOLD THEORY

Even though he has distanced himself from Wyatt, David Fasold does hold some similar opinions about the Durupinar location known to most in the English-speaking world as the Wyatt-Fasold site.

"I realize," says Fasold, "that it's a bitter pill for some people to swallow that the ark is not on Mount Ararat, but sooner or later, I think they'll come around to realizing that this 'Wyatt-Fasold site' seventeen miles south of Ararat is the true site of the remains of Noah's ark."

Samuel Windsor of the Bronson and Windsor Naval Architectural and Engineering firm in Seattle agrees with Fasold and told the Turkish government that, "If it's not Noah's ark, then it was another large vessel with a large crew that survived, swept in on the same cataclysmic event that brought Noah's vessel to a halt in the same area. Of these two options, reasonable logic dictates that these remains are those of the ark of Noah. The chance that it is a geological freak of nature and a natural formation is absurd, and a thesis that no marine engineer is willing to entertain."[4]

Says Fasold, "The first time anyone outside of ark hunters became aware of the correct location was in the September 5th, 1960, issue of *Life* magazine. Now, the people who investigated this site in 1960 quickly wrote it off as a freak of nature, probably because it was on the 'wrong' mountain and it didn't fit the biblical description of a rectangular ark—but I see things differently."

FREAK OF NATURE?

Well, just what did the group find at the site in 1960? That summer, the Turkish government authorized an expedition by the Archaeological Research Foundation of Washington, D.C. The team was headed by George Vandeman and included Dr. Brandenberger, Captain Durupinar, and Captain Sevket Kurtis.

After days of excavation at the site nothing was found but dirt. Finally, out of frustration and desperation, Captain Durupinar blasted a hole in the east side of the "mud wall" with dynamite. The result was the same: nothing was uncovered but dirt, stones, and clay.

Captain Durupinar concluded that, although the original hopes had run high that this was the remains of the ark of Noah, they were forced to concede the formation looked to be nothing more than a natural phenomenon resembling a ship.

Over the next thirteen years, the formation in the Tendurek foothills gradually slipped from the forefront of investigative archaeological "Noah's ark" excavation endeavors, yet historical research continued that would eventually inspire still more controversial conclusions.

In 1973 the formation at Tendurek again resurfaced in the "Arkaeological" community and was again identified as the ark of Noah. Again expeditions were made to the Tendurek hills to investigate the object.

Geologist Clifford Burdick of Tucson, Arizona, gave a convincing argument upon his return from the site in 1973 in favor of the natural phenomenon theory when he said, "The object is nothing more than a clay push-up in what some think is an old lava flow. Apparently, the extrusion widens a few feet below the surface along the center part of the formation, thus giving the whole thing the outline of a 'ship.' Although in an aerial view the formation may look quite shiplike, it does not take a geologist on the site long to dismiss the notion that the strange phenomenon is an actual ship. It is indeed a very strange phenomenon, a remarkable freak of nature."

Again in 1974 the "Tendurek Ark" theory was put to rest. There it remained until 1977 when Wyatt visited the site.

For the next ten years Wyatt, convinced that the Tendurek site was in fact the mud-encased remains of Noah's ark, worked tirelessly to convince the world of that fact. So successful was Wyatt's promotion, based upon his "conclusive artifacts" said to be found at the site, that in 1986 the Turkish government decided to promote tourism by advertising to the world that the boat-shaped object at Tendurek was in fact the actual remains of the legendary Noah's ark. The site was declared a national park, a road was built to the location for the benefit of drawing tourists, and a tourist viewing building was built on the hill overlooking the area.

"Ancient literature explains how the ark was made out of reeds and how early pilgrims could go to the site—it was easily accessible. It wasn't up on the snows of Ararat, but at a much lower elevation," says Fasold, citing one of the 217 nonbiblical accounts of the Flood. He continues as follows:

> [T]he epic of Gilgamesh . . . describes the boat as a "lifesaver" and as a "ship of reeds." So my premise is that most ark hunters are not only searching on the wrong mountain, they're also looking for the wrong type of boat—a wooden boat rather than a reed boat. The hull of the reed boat would be completely gone by now. So, all we can see is about 10 percent of the very lower portion of the remains above the hull.
>
> The best evidence we've found so far that this is not a natural formation is evidence of a man-made structure within the outlines of this boat form. In 1985 we found thirteen longitudinal lines and nine transverse lines of metal, along with the remains of metal fittings spaced 20 to 30 inches apart. A total of about 5,400 iron fittings were found within this boat shape. Some of the iron fittings were scanned by an electron microscope at Los Alamos National Laboratory and found to contain 93.84 percent man-made iron.

The following year, we brought in a subsurface interface radar and some technical equipment that wasn't available in the 1960s and took pictures of the man-made structure that's 3½ feet under the ground.

There are other indicators that this is the site of Noah's ark. Just 14 miles from the site we find a field that's just loaded with what appears to be ancient drogue stones ten times larger than anything we've ever seen before. These stones each weigh about 11,000 pounds and take a 3½-inch diameter rope and are probably the stones mentioned in the epic of Gilgamesh. There's a lot also mentioned in the Koran. It says, "In the name of Allah, it will cast anchor."

These twelve enormous anchor drogue stones are not really anchors. The flat surface of the stone is used trailing through the water to keep the stern in what they call "irons." This confirms that the ark landed at a lower elevation.

EXAMINING THE SCIENTIFIC EVIDENCE

Is there any scientific evidence to substantiate Fasold's or Wyatt's claims? What did Fasold mean by the "scientific equipment" he used that wasn't available in the 1960s? And if it isn't the ark that they found, could it be some other type of formation used by humans in the past? What has been discovered about the site after several scientific studies?

The size of the formation conforms somewhat to the biblical dimensions of 300 cubits long by 50 cubits wide and 30 cubits high, according to Bill Crouse, editor of the *Ararat Report*. The formation is approximately 530 feet long by 160 feet wide. Wyatt argues that this is a perfect match since Moses would have used the longer Egyptian cubit of 20.6 inches.

Almost all biblical commentators and reference works state that the cubit used by the Hebrews was approximately 18 inches. Wyatt could be right on this one, though, since Moses was indeed educated in Egypt. However, it should be pointed out that the Egyptians had two different standards: a royal cubit of 20.6 inches and a shorter, common cubit of around 18 inches.

"Assuming Wyatt is correct that the cubit was 20.6 inches, that would make the width of the ark 86 feet," says Crouse. The formation, however, is close to 160 feet in width! Wyatt believes this discrepancy is due to a splaying (widening) effect as the ark decayed and slid down the mountain. He says the ark landed about two miles higher than its present location.

"To this we must say: How could the width almost double with the length staying the same? And if the ark had straight sides originally—as Wyatt's model reveals—how do we explain the almost perfectly symmetrical almond shape that we see in the early photos? The formation does not look like a ship nearly so much as it did when first photographed because of rapid erosion of the soft clay over the years," says Crouse.

San Diego professor of geology, Dr. John Morris, has studied the formation on a couple of occasions and has concluded,

The more we study it, the more we conclude that it's not an archaeological structure. It's a rare geologic formation, but it is geologic in nature.

I've collected rock samples from every place on that site and got every rock type there—more than 100 pounds in my laboratory—and it's all rock.

Rock samples in the formation have been chemically analyzed and studied under microscope. The rock types are rather exotic and the suite of rocks present represent an ophiolite belt, extremely rare on the earth's surface. These dark, crystalline rocks are the type normally found on the ocean floor. The several rock types give evidence of hydrothermal activity on the ocean floor, and are highly altered. There is nothing present which must be attributed to human construction.[5]

"The so-called Wyatt-Fasold formation is caused when mud or avalanche material comes down a slope and goes around a stable area and as it goes around, it forms this streamlined shape," Dr. Morris explains. "There's nothing there that gives any hint of any man-made artifacts or petrified wood. As much as I wish I could say it was Noah's ark, I have to tell you, it's just a rock formation."

Dr. Don Shockey, a New Mexico–based ark expeditioner and chairman of the FIBER Education Foundation who has been to the Wyatt-Fasold site, says, "I can take you to seven or eight very identical formations in the same area around Mount Ararat. In fact, the proponents of this formation never even talk about the little formation—dubbed Noah's rowboat—on the southeast side of their alleged Noah's ark."

Dr. John Baumgardner, a geophysicist at the prestigious Los Alamos National Laboratory in New Mexico, was an ardent proponent of the Wyatt-Fasold theory and made appearances on "The 700

Club" and "Good Morning America" television shows to say that the formation was probably the remains of the ark. Both Fasold and Wyatt frequently quote Dr. Baumgardner as part of their supportive evidence regarding the formation. However, Dr. Baumgartner provided a different story for this book.

> Initially, I had a moderate amount of optimism about the Wyatt-Fasold site containing the remains of Noah's ark. This optimism was based on the shape of the site, its amazing symmetry, its location in the mountains of Ararat, and its length—approximately 300 cubits as stated in Genesis.
>
> In addition, I was giving some credence to a technique that David Fasold was using which I later determined to be a form of dowsing without any scientific basis. It was this technique that was responsible for producing the patterns of lines that Fasold has shown, which he believes indicates a pattern of metal under the ground. I have since determined that this method does not have any scientific basis and cannot be reproduced by other types of well understood geophysical methods.

Dr. Baumgardner and his team conducted additional on-site geophysical work in 1987 and 1988 and ruled out the possibility that the formation is any type of an archaeological remains.

> In 1987 we did a systemic radar survey at the site as well as some seismograph work. In 1988 we drilled four core-holes into the site to sample the subsurface material and, based on these investigations, I've concluded that it's only a natural formation. There's a large ridge of basement rock that runs the length of the site that

appears to be responsible for its stability as well as its unusual shape. This was initially thought to indicate the ark's top deck. Finally, it's located in the midst of a large mudslide, and the mud flowing around this obstacle is what has produced the boatlike shape.

AUTHENTICITY OF ARTIFACTS DISPUTED

But what about the other artifact findings reported by either Wyatt or Fasold at the site? Did Fasold find 5,400 man-made iron fittings? Did Wyatt find petrified wood from the ark at the site? Did Wyatt and Fasold find anchor stones from the ark? What about the numerous other alleged ark- and Noah-related finds reported by Wyatt?

Regarding the iron fittings, Dr. Baumgardner says,

> There have been claims made that rock samples taken from the site are iron fittings used to help hold the boat together. One such sample—the other half of a piece Fasold publicly displays as an iron fitting—I've had analyzed in our lab at Los Alamos. The composition is unusual as it's almost pure iron oxide. But there's absolutely nothing about this sample that would suggest it has anything to do with human activity or that it's man-made.

"IRON LINES" UNVERIFIED

According to Fasold, he conducted metal-detecting surveys using a "molecular frequency generator/discriminator that mapped out 'iron lines' that represent the longitudinal and crossbeams of the ark." Dr. Andrew A. Snelling, an Australian geologist, points out that the molecular frequency generator is a dowsing technique similar to witching for water using a forked stick.

"It's a technique that has no scientific explanation and I do not believe that those results are reliable," Dr. Baumgardner explains. "They cannot be reproduced by any other geophysical method."

So the iron lines on diagrams of the boat shape and the lines of plastic tape in photographs of the Wyatt-Fasold site are only an interpretation based on "results" from a pseudo-scientific instrument. "They [the lines] have not been reproduced or verified by any reputable scientific survey technique, including standard metal-detection equipment," says Dr. Snelling. "This includes the highly sophisticated types of magnetometer used by mining companies."[6]

The pattern of iron lines that were located by the metal-detecting surveys was said to be duplicated and verified by other subsurface techniques including ground-penetrating radar scans conducted by Fasold and Wyatt. These radar scans allegedly showed an internal structure typical of a boat framework. Wyatt claims that Tom Fenner of Geophysical Survey Systems, Inc., in New Hampshire looked at the 1986 radar scans and concluded that the formation is "a man-made boat."

However, geophysicist Tom Fenner tells a different story. He says that neither he nor his company believes the formation is man-made. "In 1987 I performed an extensive ground-penetrating radar study in an attempt to characterize any shallow subsurface features in the boat-shaped formation at the site. A great deal of effort was put into repeating the radar measurements acquired in 1986 by Wyatt and Fasold. After numerous attempts over a period of one and a half days, we were unable to duplicate their radar records in any way. I was never convinced the site was the remains of Noah's ark. In fact, the more time I spent on the site, the more skeptical I became."[7]

PETRIFIED WOOD QUESTIONABLE

Wyatt continues to show untrained people samples of what he claims is petrified wood from the site. "There are trainloads and boatloads of petrified wood out there and it is all in the boat structure," he claims. Furthermore, the prized exhibit Wyatt shows to visitors, photographs of which are regularly displayed, is a sample of "petrified wood identified as pecky cypress—removed from inside the 'hull' in the presence of the governor of Ağri."[8]

No trained scientist of the many who have visited the site has ever seen any sign of these "trainloads" of petrified wood. Turkish geologist Dr. Salih Byraktutan has collected one or two small fragments of semi-petrified wood which in his opinion have flowed onto the site within the mud from elsewhere. He confirms that none of the regular rock types of the area are petrified wood. "Not one of the other scientists—including geologists familiar with petrified wood—has ever once seen any," Dr. Snelling explains.

"There is absolutely nothing that would suggest these rock samples are petrified wood," confirms Dr.

Baumgardner. "There's certainly no tree ring structure."

Dr. Shockey, ark expeditioner and cultural anthropologist, went a step further. He actually clandestinely tested a chip off the "petrified wood exhibit" Wyatt shows at his speaking engagements and in his media interviews. The lab test results: "This is a sedimentary rock that has undergone metamorphism. It consisted of three distinct sedimentary layers."[9]

DROGUE STONES, NOAH'S ANCHORS?

Both Wyatt and Fasold, to fortify their Noah's ark argument, place a lot of faith in a number of large rock slabs found across the valley—some within sight of the boat formation. These so-called drogue stones are alleged by Wyatt and Fasold to be used for steering or anchoring vessels. Their proximity to the site suggests that they could well have been giant anchor stones used by Noah to steer the ark and keep it facing the wind. The stones have carefully made holes, and these would have been where ropes were attached. Furthermore, some of these rocks have eight crosses carved on them, one being larger than all the others, representing an iconographic depiction of Noah, his wife, his three sons, and their wives.

"If these were anchor stones, the holes were carved too near the edges of the rocks," says Dr. Snelling. "Because of their sheer weight, the rock around the holes would have too easily broken off.

There is no sign of any wear of the rock surface around the top side of these holes, which one would expect if ropes had been tied through them to drag these heavy stones around in the water for up to a year.

According to Dr. Snelling, "the number of crosses carved on these stones range from three to twenty, and the number eight is conveniently overplayed to build a connection to Noah and his family. Furthermore, many of these publicized stones are found in an ancient cemetery for Armenians, and similar stones and their crosses have to do with earlier Armenian inhabitants," explains Dr. Snelling.

Larry Crews, a researcher of ancient Anatolia who has done extensive research around the Ararat area says, "As you travel around the area, you see that there are literally hundreds if not thousands of large and small stones carved with crosses. They choose a few of these and called them anchor drogue stones. The Armenians, realizing their pagan roots, Christianized them by putting crosses on them. Those who have examined these stelae report that there is evidence of an earlier defacement. Also, we find that the material these rocks are made out of is merely the same type of rocks that we find all around the mountain. There is no evidence of these anchor stones coming from any faraway site."

Dr. Abraham Terian of Andrews University, a recognized authority on classical Armenian studies, says the crosses carved on the stones are known as Armenian *Khatchkars.* He believes the crosses were probably carved in the period between when the Armenian nation was converted to Christianity (A.D.

301) and when the Armenian language was first put down in written form in A.D. 406.

Originally, these stones were probably pre-Christian Armenian stelae containing pagan inscriptions, he indicates. It is known that the holes in such stones had occultic significance, possibly representing the "eye of the dragon."[10] So these stones are Noah's anchor stones only to those who want them to be. Again, the onus is on Wyatt and his colleagues to produce definitive evidence that these are not stelae quarried by Armenians from basalt in the region.

FRAUDULENT CLAIMS

As if to add credence to his claims of Turkish government support for the site, Wyatt's video says that an "eight-lane multimillion-dollar highway is near completion which leads to the site." The pictures shown are of the highway into neighboring Iran, and not the one-lane trail of dirt, rock, and mud that tortuously winds its way to the site. There is no eight-lane highway to the site or close to it.[11]

POSSIBLE MONGOL FORT

Another historian and researcher in this area has an intriguing explanation for the formation at the Wyatt-Fasold site. Dr. Ron Charles, a historian of ancient cultures and a leader of archaeological expeditions to several parts of the world, says,

> I've been to the Wyatt-Fasold site three different times.
> I've discovered that proponents of this site use just one
> portion of it to say that a reed boat would fit in there

without any problems. When I actually looked at it, it seemed to me that they were only using part of the formation rather than examining all of it and I believe you can't justify it without examining the entire structure.

After examining the site, I have come to the conclusion that it is a natural formation on top of which a Mongol reconnaissance fort was built by the Mongol conqueror Tamerlane in the latter part of the 1300s. He went through this area and this particular type of construction was typical for Tamerlane.

At the time of Tamerlane's conquest, the foothills of Tendurek were part of the conquered territory of Armenia/Kurdistan; with the valley that lies north of the little village of Uzengili and south of Aghri Dagh being the main caravan route from Persia to Anatolia and on into Europe and Syria. So if Tamerlane was consistent in his conquest tactics, then on the foothills that overlooked the main east-west caravan route that connected Persia to Anatolia at least one, probably as many as seven reconnaissance base–storage camps were built by Tamerlane as he moved forward conquering the area.

He would take 240 of his handpicked soldiers into an area to be conquered and build these forts. He would use existing geological formations such as lava flows, earthquake fissures, riverbeds, or creekbeds. They were always facing north and south on a caravan route.

Then, on top of these natural formations, he would reinforce them with hand-laid stones and cover it all with mud. They would use these as a temporary reconnaissance fortification, an observation point, and as a storage facility.

Looking at the formation in its full composition, the part being referred to as the ark by Wyatt and Fasold is the upper tier of the fort, with the lower portion being a tier of equal length to the right. The lower end of both tiers would have been the supply entrance, while the entrance at the other end would have been for pedestrians.

The upper tier has a high point for observation, along with two alignment stones that were always a part of Tamerlane's forts. Also, the upper tier would have been the officer's quarters, while the lower tier would have been quarters for the mercenary army.

I am convinced that this site is something other than the ark of Noah, and it sure fits the pattern for one of Tamerlane's forts.

Now back to the same question we asked in the beginning of this chapter: Are there valid alternative locations where Noah's ark could have come to rest after the Flood? Certainly the scientists and other experts who have studied the Mount Judi and Durupinar sites make it very clear that the remains of Noah's ark are not there.

In the case of the Durupinar-Wyatt-Fasold site, Dr. Morris may have best summed it up when he said, "A Noah's ark visitors' center had been constructed nearby and a road sign directing travelers off the main road had been erected. However, perhaps due to the fact that European tour groups taken to the site have by and large been offended that someone would try to pass off a rock as Noah's ark, as of November 1989, the sign had been removed, the visitors' center was not operating, and sheep were grazing on the 'ark' as they had before all the excitement."[12]

The Durupinar-Wyatt-Fasold site being the remains of Noah's ark received a severe blow when David Fasold made the following disclosure to Peter

Pockley in the Australian *Sun-Herald* on November 6, 1994:

> David Fasold, a marine salvage expert from San Diego, California, was so convinced that the structure was the fabled Ark that he went broke in spending $250,000 (U.S.) to finance twelve expeditions to the site over seven years.
>
> His 331-page book published in 1988, *The Ark of Noah,* became widely quoted around the world by literal interpreters of the Old Testament stories as providing "scientific" evidence for the truth of the Bible. . . .
>
> Mr. Fasold, fifty-five, visited Sydney for final filming of an ABC-TV "Four Corners" report on the search for the Ark. The film, screened last month, showed Mr. Fasold and Professor Ian Plimer, forty-eight, head of earth sciences at Melbourne University, looking in vain for evidence on a hillside twenty-five kilometers from Mount Ararat in eastern Turkey.
>
> It was not until he went to Turkey with Professor Plimer in September that real doubts about the "Ark structure" arose in his mind. He had been convinced by the dimensions of the structure (300 cubits long and 44,100 square feet in area) being close to those quoted in the Bible, but Fasold now thinks this is what made the ancients believe it was the Ark.
>
> He [Fasold] said, "I believe this may be the oldest running hoax in history. I think we have found what the ancients said was the Ark, but this structure is not Noah's Ark."
>
> Professor Plimer's on-the-spot study caused him to change his mind as to the geological nature of the structure. . . .
>
> Examining the site for three days in September, he showed that the structure was "a large block of cooked-up basalt interleaved with limestone which had slipped down the mountainside in a mud slide and twisted around in the process."

"Our drilling showed nothing beneath the surface but rock and mud. All around it is nothing but mud. There is no evidence of wooden beams or metal rivets as claimed by the Ark believers," said Professor Plimer.

Meanwhile, the search for Noah's ark moves back to Mount Ararat with three of the most amazing eyewitness ark sighting accounts to unfold this century —one as recent as 1989!

Notes

[1] Ronald E. Wyatt, *Discovered: Noah's Ark!* (Nashville: World Bible Society, 1989), pp. 2–3.

[2] Ibid., p. 2.

[3] Andrew A. Snelling, *Creation Ex Nihilo Bulletin* (Sunnybanks, Australia: Creation-Science Foundation, no date given), p. 1.

[4] Letter dated November 20, 1990, from David Fasold to Bill Crouse, editor of the *Ararat Report.*

[5] John Morris, "The Boat-Shaped Formation," *Ararat Report 26* (September–October 1990), pp. 3–4. Published by Christian Information Ministries, Richardson, TX.

[6] Snelling, *Creation Ex Nihilo Bulletin,* 14, no. 4, p. 29.

[7] Ibid., pp. 29–30.

[8] Ibid., p. 31.

[9] Letter to Dr. Don Shockey from Thomas Servilla, Director of Universal Petrographic, Geologic and Geochemical Consultants, Inc., November 24, 1992.

[10] Snelling, *Creation Ex Nihilo,* pp. 33–34.

[11] Ibid., p. 35.

[12] Morris, "The Boat-Shaped Formation," p. 4.

14

THREE MODERN-DAY ARK EYEWITNESSES

People see only what they are prepared to see.

Ralph Waldo Emerson, 1863

MODERN EYEWITNESSES OF THE ARK ON MOUNT Ararat cover the human spectrum—young, old, rich, poor, and everyone from firm believers in God, to apathetic agnostics, to atheists. Their stories have many similarities even though their sightings may have been many years apart.

The eyewitnesses have never met, but many of their experiences are so similar that at times you feel that they must have seen the ark together. For some, locating the ark was a true paradox: What they found was not necessarily what they were looking for. . . .

Maybe it's ironic, or perhaps fitting, that those in recent years who have seen the ark are the most average of people—humble individuals who have no exalted point to prove, no book to sell, no doctrine to foist upon the world. Just simple people, like many in the Bible.

We chose three modern-day eyewitness accounts to examine in this chapter. All are men—two were soldiers stationed in the Middle East who just happened to become friends with some of the local people. The third man accidentally stumbled on the ark after a near-fatal fall on the slopes of the mountain. All three cases are unique because all of the eyewitnesses are still alive and all three had close ground encounters with the ark. In each fascinating account, the explorer's experience of seeing the ark was very moving, intriguing, and highly personal.

ED DAVIS

In 1943 a young serviceman named Ed Davis was stationed in Northern Iran and became friends with a young Kurdish man. In his military position, Davis did some significant favors for his friend, and in return, the man's Kurdish family adopted Davis and gave him their most valuable "possession"—the rare experience of a visit to Noah's ark.

When they asked Davis if he would like to see the ark, he wasn't even aware that the ark was on Mount Ararat or what agreeing to see it would entail. It was the adventure of his life, and now, in his late eighties, Davis still speaks about seeing the ark with awe and wonder. Here is the story in his own words:

> I was Master Sergeant in charge of construction in the Army Engineer's Special Service Group in northern Iran

in 1943. I was hauling rock from a rock quarry. I had a crew of men building, and this boy was driving for me, and one day when the atmosphere was just right, we saw Mount Ararat.

He smiled and said, "Yes, that's where my folks live —where the ark was and my dad knew where the ark was."

I said, "Boy, I sure would like to see that." He said that when his dad comes to visit, he'd bring him over and introduce him.

One day, his dad came to see him. He brought him over to introduce him to us. His name was Abas.

At that particular time you couldn't see the ark. When it got where you could see it, he would come back and get me.

A couple of months later, Abas came back. He said, "We can see it, let's go."

There were six or eight of us who went up, and I've never been so cold or so wet or so tired in all my life. If I'd known it was going to be that bad, I don't know that I would've even gone.

As we went up the mountain, we stopped at Jacob's Well. It was a tradition there before traveling on to make a prayer on a small stone and place it on a large pile of other stones that folks before you had laid down.

We left Jacob's Well and traveled a distance, and we crossed from the main trail to what they call the back door. There are easier routes, but this was the shortest. The climb up went on for a few days and we were all roped together. They gave us two staffs and a long rope with a noose tied in it. Also, we were all roped together. I was fifth in the line.

Two Kurds walked behind me at all times. I guess they were like my bodyguards. Abas had lost two sons before they tied themselves together, and he was real careful now.

I could tell this group of climbers had made this trip many times. They knew exactly where they were going even in the dark. I felt more than a little strange being the only American on the trail.

I didn't have any really special equipment other than my G.I. issue. The Kurds and Abas had good equipment. They acquired it from raids or it was found on the mountains. All of the climbers were given an aviator-type goggle by Abas. We wore them most of the time.

Abas gave me a piece of shiny metal that we could signal with. I never once had a chance to use mine. There wasn't enough sun for it to work. Abas also gave each of us a hand-operated flashlight we used in the caves. They never yelled or used loud voices at any time. I was given a small whistle to blow if I needed to get their attention.

We slept in four to six caves on the way up and ate out of one big stew pot. I don't know what was in it. Meat and vegetables and stuff. There were pictographs on the cave walls and Abas knew what they meant.

They kept everybody roped together for safety and even when nature calls, you didn't go off alone. There were always two or three together no matter where you went.

There wasn't any good weather on the trip. It was all bad—wind and rain. You could be walking along and go around a corner and bam—it would be completely different weather. We walked in snow, ice, and rain with rocks rolling all around us. That's one of the reasons why we had to use staffs. There are so many dangers. We all got skinned up falling, slipping, and sliding.

They said they never bring a body down when someone gets killed on the mountain. You can see bones and stuff sticking out of the ice. They leave people that die up there. I don't know why.

Abas was the caretaker of the ark just like his father and grandfather were before him, all the way clear back to Noah. Abas told me he hated anyone that went up exploring and searching for the ark. He said everyone wants to get a piece, chop it up, and carry it off. They made sure that the ark wasn't molested.

When the ark broke in two, they found some lamps and some pots and tools, hammers, wedges, and other things. The pots were about 2½-feet high. The workmanship on the tools, the metal, was quite primitive. And Abas will tell you right quick that they didn't take those things out of the ark. They came out when the ark broke up.

Abas and his family have found what looked like the pantry or kitchen area in the front of the ark. Here they have found everything from beans, honeycombs, nuts and shells, to dried fish bones. I saw some of the things in Abas' home—pottery vessels that were about seven or eight inches long, kind of like the shape of a boat and opened in the middle. They said I could look but I couldn't touch them. They told me they even found some honey in one of the jars and sent it to Switzerland to be tested and it was pure honey.

Abas described a small opening or door that opened to the outside of the ark. I don't recall his telling me where it was, but he called it by the same name they use for toilet hole. He said the people on the ark used it to dump and remove the animal waste into the water. I wish I had asked him more about it, but I didn't at the time.

Abas described to me the method Noah used to water the animals. They used animal stomachs sewn together. Abas says there are many, many of these on board the ark. They are still there. I didn't see any of these because they have never carried them down off the mountain.

When we walked from Doomsday Point to the spot where we viewed the ark, there was whispered talking. There was a reverence and awe. You could feel like someone was watching your every step, every minute.

The first time I saw the ark, I was on a ledge above it, and it looked like a big blue rock. As we got closer, I saw it wasn't a rock at all. It was the end of the ark that had broken off. It was big and had different levels to it. Different decks, I guess you'd say. The only word I can think of to describe what it was like to see the ark is "awesome." We saw the ark in snow but both pieces were in water too.

Looking at it, you felt like someone was standing behind you or watching you. You didn't dare move hardly. I don't know how to explain the feeling except to say there was a mighty power present.

I was very disappointed that I couldn't walk and explore inside this biblical treasure. I had an overwhelming desire to touch it, something I can't explain.

I have a picture of the village and camp that Abas gave me. I wish he had given me a photo of the ark, but he never showed me one or offered one even though he told me where two are located. I wish I could go back and visit just one more time.

They say there's a curse on the ark. Some people got stuck in it one time and they died right away with a lung infection or fungus in their lungs. Anyway, that's what they told me.

Seeing the ark made a big difference in my life. I joined the church. I never thought I'd see the ark when I was growing up. I never thought about it at all. When I did see it though, it made me begin to think about the future, and I sure don't want to die and go to hell.

The people with me were very proud of the ark. You could see it in their faces. It was a big honor.

There's no question in my mind what I saw on that mountain. I saw Noah's ark. I won't argue with nobody if they disagree, but I know I saw Noah's ark.

Dr. Paul Meier, co-founder of the Minirth-Meier New Life Clinics and author of forty books on human behavior, reports thus on his analysis of Ed Davis's testimony:

I analyzed several hours of Ed Davis's audio and video interviews. I found him to be a very normal, well-rounded personality. He was concerned about others and he did not brag about himself. Usually when people are confabulating or making up stories they talk excessively about themselves. He didn't do that. He was very reverent. He respected the Muslim faith of his Kurdish friends and guides. He's also intelligent.

He knew that his friend Abas had lost two sons in previous treks, which is something only someone who has actually been on the mountain would know specifically—that many people have died from all the dangerous crevasses and rock slides and glaciers in that area.

He based his descriptions of the ark totally on his own experience rather than on what he had read in the Bible. At times it seemed like the interviewer was planting words or remembrances in his mind and Ed would say, "No, that's not how I saw it." He gave very clear details.

A grateful father of two Kurdish soldiers took him up there in gratitude for something he had done that he didn't brag about—in fact, he won't even talk about it. Ed knew the customs of the Kurdish people very well. He knew the towns. He knew about Jacob's Well and the buildings around it in the Ahora Gorge. He knew about the religious practices of the Kurds. He knew about the glaciers, the rock slides, the walking sticks, and being tied together on the climb, which is very necessary. He talked about the ledge, the cliff wall where the ark was sticking out of the ice.

The reason why this is important is that I have personal knowledge of some secret U.S. Government reconnaissance photos that the government has taken of the ark above the Ahora Gorge on the northeast corner of Mount Ararat. This is exactly where Ed describes that he went, and his description of what he saw is what I have personally known to be true from those reconnaissance photos.

I firmly believe that Ed Davis is telling the truth.

Dr. Meier wasn't the only expert who carefully examined the Ed Davis account. Larry Williams of San Diego, an internationally known commodity trading advisor, author of two books, and publisher of the *Treasure Hunter Confidential* newsletter, also decided to check out Davis's story.

I publish a newsletter for treasure hunters and archaeologists throughout the world. I've investigated archaeological sites throughout North America and Europe and when I heard the Ed Davis story, I was fascinated, but I've found that you simply can't trust a lot of stories. So, I decided to personally investigate not only the story, but Ed Davis himself.

To investigate most stories, archaeologists try to investigate the secondary data, but I think you can use high technology to investigate stories, and there's no better way to do this than with a polygraph or lie detector test.

I asked Ed Davis if he would be willing to take a polygraph test to find out if this guy was telling the truth or not. To do that, I went to Albuquerque, New Mexico, and found the most competent polygraph expert not only in Albuquerque, but in the entire state of New Mexico, with fifteen years of experience on the New York City police force.

This man was aware of the Ed Davis story and he frankly didn't believe it. He told me, "Larry, I'll talk to this guy for an hour or so and I'll literally eat him up and spit him out of here. Give me an hour and I guarantee I'll break this man."

After two intense hours with Ed, the polygraph expert came out and said, "Larry, I can't tell you what mountain Ed was on or where the boat is, or even whether or not it was Noah's ark, but I can tell you this —he's not lying and he did see a boat on that mountain."

ED BEHLING

In 1973 another American soldier became an unlikely eyewitness of the ark. Ed Behling was in the Air Force assigned to a defense installation at Diaberker, about 100 miles southwest of Mount Ararat. He became friends with a Turkish soldier, a Kurdish man named Mustafa. Behling is now a family therapist in Colorado.

This is his own story from articles and two appearances on the "Prophecy in the News" television show.

His name was Mustafa and he was in the army at that time . . . and I probably never would have met him. However, I wanted to see how the people operated, who the people were, what feelings they had since this was a rare experience for me to be in a foreign country.

I met Mustafa and I told him how privileged he was to live in a country where all these artifacts of the Bible existed. He said he had a great-uncle who had been to the ark, and he'd ask him to take us to see it. Mustafa had never seen it before either.

It was the last weekend of May when we took off to go see the ark. It was exciting. I asked him if I could take a camera. He said, "I would prefer you not take a camera because Ararat is close to the Russian border, and you're American, I'm Turkish, and it's not going to look good. It would mean trouble if we were stopped by soldiers." I didn't have a very good camera at that time anyway, so that was fine with me.

We got our gear together and took off to see his

uncle. Three to four hours later, we were at this old tent, this old camp of three shepherds plus Mustafa's great-uncle. He was like the master shepherd. He looked like he had been dead three years and just didn't know enough to drop over.

His uncle seemed rather reluctant to take us up there. Locals are very suspicious of outsiders. "I convinced him you're okay," Mustafa said. Mustafa made it possible for me to go up there and if it wasn't for him, they wouldn't have taken me up there at all.

I had the impression that most of the shepherds around the mountain know where the ark is located—at least the older ones do anyway.

It's amazing so many groups have gone to the mountain in recent years looking for the ark of Noah, and none of them have been able to find it. All of their guides seem to be taking them off into another part of the mountain. Some of the younger men might want to take them to it. But the older ones won't allow it and you better believe that those young men won't go against the ruling of the older men. Nobody goes near that ark without the elders' permission.

We got up early. Basically, my night was spent battling the cold; it was chilly that night. I had no idea how high we were because I really wasn't paying attention to specifics.

[Mustafa's great-uncle] took us right up the side of the mountain. We were going around rocks and above cliffs and below cliffs—it was like a trail. There was a lot of snow on the mountain at this time, but it wasn't that uncomfortable. It was hard snow; it wasn't very slippery. He was like a guide; he knew exactly where he was going.

I was incredibly worn out. I half hoped they'd decide to go back down. Suddenly, Mustafa turned to me and motioned.

I looked over the side of a ledge and 50 feet below us was a gigantic black structure. It was so large and awesome I was overwhelmed . . . completely amazed by its size.

The snow had melted quite a bit off the ark so there wasn't very much on top, and there was nothing on the sides.

The front end of the ark is broken off, with a gaping hole. It is hard to give you a mental picture of just how wide and how tall it is. I saw no doors at all, nothing that looked manufactured. I have no idea how something that large came to rest that high on Mount Ararat. I can't explain it. It was kind of eerie, especially when I looked down over the cliff and saw the ark. I didn't have any direct sun any time I was there, so the gaping hole that I saw was dark. The whole ark was black.

I don't know how long it was; but looking into the mouth where it was broken off on the edge of the shelf, I saw it was basically square. The walls were straight up and down on each side and the base, which I couldn't see because of the angle, looked fairly flat.

From where I was standing, you could tell the roof sloped very gradually, maybe a 10-degree slope, 15-degree slope to it. Then it had a wide spot in the center of it that went the length of it. Now this was maybe 10 feet wide—like a catwalk. It was about 10 to 15 inches high with a roof over it. I guess they walked on that or maybe it was used for windows, but that's the way it looked to me.

Basically, it was a big box that was very long. I could only see 150 to 200 feet of it and then it tapered off into the snow. I noticed from where I was standing that the front was chopped off or broken off or something. How much of the front was broken off, I had no idea, but it was broken off. The Ark was 40 to 50 feet high and about 60 feet wide. The walls must have been 18 inches thick.

After we looked at it a little bit, Mustafa's uncle motioned for us to come on. We couldn't jump down on it because it was too far to jump. We didn't have any ropes or anything. I kind of wanted to walk on it, but I never got a chance. But we walked down below it. There was about a 100-foot cliff—the shelf that it was on, a big table.

When I was up there, the clouds were low on the mountain. We could see at the maximum maybe 100 or 200 yards because of the fog around us. It was so dark and overcast late in the afternoon that we left the next morning. We spent the night underneath it [the ledge] and went back down the mountain.

Dr. Meier analyzed Ed Behling's account, and this is what he had to say:

Ed Behling is a therapist in Colorado who, at the age of twenty-three, was in the Air Force in the Middle East and made friends with a Kurdish soldier by the name of Mustafa. Like Ed Davis, Ed Behling was befriended by local people which led to his encounter with the ark.

They had been friends for about five months when Mustafa took Ed to see his great-uncle who was a sage on Mount Ararat.

The people have great respect for these sages, and you don't do anything without their permission. I was there and I talked to the Kurdish people and analyzed what their personalities were like. Ed describes their customs and behavior very accurately.

Ed's trip to the ark after he went to where the sage was, which was about halfway up the mountain, took one day. Now, the things that make his testimony credible are that Ed had good eye contact with his interviewer. He did not seem dramatic. He did not brag about himself. He seemed to have a well-rounded personality.

In general, usually therapists are quite honest so I tended to believe his story about the ark and especially since his description fits the U.S. reconnaissance photos of the ark above the Ahora Gorge. The only thing that made me question Ed's story slightly is that he said he made it up [the mountain] in one day.

Now, with good weather, that can be done, and I know that my own team made it down in half a day because we were being chased down by Kurds with guns! Usually, a team will take several days to get up and several days to get back down. But it made me question him somewhat—although he did say that it was one day from the location of the sage.

Another questionable aspect is that Ed didn't know where he was. He thought it was on the northwest corner [of Mount Ararat], and we know that it is more towards the northeast corner.

His description of the customs, the climate, and the ark being near the Ahora Gorge is in agreement with what we know from secret U.S. reconnaissance photos. His description was accurate enough. His personality traits and body language were satisfactory to me. . . . I believe Ed was telling the truth.

AHMET ALI ARSLAN

Fate played a big part in the eyewitness account of Dr. Ahmet Ali Arslan. Dr. Arslan is the Washington Bureau Chief for *Turkiye,* a major Turkish newspaper, and a former broadcaster for the Voice of America radio network. Also, he is an advisor and senior researcher for the International Science and Technology Institute in Washington, D.C. But he knows Mount Ararat like few other people.

My family is from Aralik at the base of Mount Ararat toward the Soviet side. That's where I grew up. I've gone up on the mountain maybe fifty times—including expeditions with Fernand Navarra, Don Shockey, and the late James Irwin.

I was accompanying a scientific group [the 1989

Shockey expedition] in exploring a site on the Ahora Gorge side of the mountain, a very treacherous place, covered with crevasses.

Because I was a Turkish national, only I was allowed to investigate certain sections of the mountain. I was sent off to check out a particular site identified by satellite as one that could possibly be the location of the ark.

As I was nearing that site, the ice and snow I was standing on began to give away. I ended up sliding a couple hundred feet down the slope. Fortunately for me, I did not fall into a crevasse.

When I regained my footing, I noticed about 100 to 200 feet away what appeared to be a building-type structure—definitely made of wood. It was something that shouldn't be there—just a few thousand feet below the summit.

It almost looked like kind of a captain's cabin. You could look in and see beams and things like that. I immediately took my camera and shot three pictures— one wide-angle, one regular, and one close-up. In the pictures you can see flat beams and such, in what appears to definitely be a man-made structure.

My belief is that what I saw and what is in the photographs I took was without question Noah's ark.

The photographs taken by Dr. Arslan while on Don Shockey's 1989 FIBER Foundation expedition will be discussed further in the next chapter along with 1990 photographs taken of the same site from helicopter and by U.S. and foreign satellites.

So far we have recounted a number of twentieth-century civilian and military aerial sightings of Noah's ark. We've also presented the modern eye-witness accounts of Ed Davis, Ed Behling, and

Ahmet Ali Arslan. But is there one single factor that all these accounts have in common that would help us solve the Noah's ark mystery? Is there something to help us actually find the ark for the world to see?

The answer is yes. The one single factor common to all these accounts is the ark's location on Mount Ararat. All reliable sightings have been on the north side of Mount Ararat above the Ahora Gorge. Furthermore, satellite imagery also helps pinpoint the area where the ark could be located. The question is, why do the military and CIA keep these photos top secret?

15

COMPELLING NEW SCIENTIFIC EVIDENCE

The lot of critics is to be remembered by
what they failed to understand.

George Moore (1852–1933)

In 1985 I decided to become the team
physician for an expedition to Mount Ararat
to search for Noah's ark with Jim Irwin and
his team. But before I put my life in danger I
wanted to be sure that the ark was up there
so I talked to a close friend who is a former
reconnaissance pilot for the Strategic Air
Command in Omaha, Nebraska. He told me
that right now at the Strategic Air Command
there are secret documents—including
photographs—confirming the existence and
location of Noah's ark. In fact, the
photographs are even labeled "Noah's Ark"
and match the description of the ark given in
the Bible. The ark is buried in ice but,
periodically, the glacier melts enough for the
ark to be revealed and it looks like it's
sticking out of a lake.

The classified secret reconnaissance
photos were seen by my close friend and by

several close friends of Jim Irwin. They clearly reveal that the ark is above the Ahora Gorge on the northeast corner of Mount Ararat facing Russia at, or a little below, the 16,000-foot level.

When Jim Irwin went to the moon he took a Turkish flag with him—partially so that he could ask the Turkish authorities for a favor when he got back. He asked them if he could go and find Noah's ark on Mount Ararat and they gave him permission.

Jim went to Turkey faithfully year after year. Each year, however, the authorities would give him permission, but when he went near the site on the northeast corner of Mount Ararat, the Turkish soldiers would turn him away and say, "No, you can't go any further." They used different excuses each time, such as, "This is too close to the Russian border and it's going to create tension with the Russians."

Tragically, he never actually got to the site on the northeast corner of Ararat, and two weeks before he died, in 1991, Jim told a very close friend of mine that a general and several other senior officials in the United States Air Force had given him up-to-date information on the reconnaissance photos confirming the ark's location. So, Jim knew for a fact where the ark is and desperately wanted to go there but was always prevented from doing so.

Dr. Paul Meier, Medical Officer,
1985 Ark-Ararat Expedition

The search for Noah's ark is rapidly reaching a climax as eyewitnesses, aerial observers, military reconnaissance pilots, and spy satellites have pin-pointed a specific location above the Ahora Gorge.

Our mystery would be solved if the U.S. Central Intelligence Agency and Defense Department would release their reconnaissance photos and spy satellite imagery of Mount Ararat. The obvious question is, why won't they?

COVER-UP

Seeking answers to these questions, we hired Dr. Ray Smith, a top government relations consultant who has in the past been highly successful in obtaining cooperation from the Defense Department, CIA, and Secret Service for television and film producers. For example, he received nothing short of miraculous cooperation from these agencies for movies such as *Patriot Games, Top Gun, The Hunt for Red October, A Few Good Men, For the Boys, In the Line of Fire,* and many others.

Dr. Smith was supplied with seven solidly documented military/CIA-related sightings of the ark on Mount Ararat. Our request to government agencies —communicated through Dr. Smith and our own personal visits to high-level Defense Department officials—was threefold: (1) to gain access to their Mount Ararat/Noah's ark files and search for evidence establishing the fact that the ark is still on Ararat, (2) to obtain permission to use old and current photographs or footage of the ark taken by military or intelligence personnel, and (3) to gain use of Defense/CIA high-resolution aerial/satellite photos and radar-penetrating imagery of the ark on Ararat.

To Dr. Smith's surprise, the Pentagon, Defense Department, various service branches of the military, and the CIA quickly denied even having any information or photos of the ark in their files. Typical was the Department of the Air Force response stating, "We checked with the offices most likely to have the information you requested and none was found." Talk about being stonewalled by a government agency! The CIA response probably reflects it the best:

> I have made an informal inquiry of the appropriate offices in the Agency about the availability of such materials. They have informed me that there are no current records bearing directly on the subject of your inquiry. Further, they advise that any systematic review of general Agency records for such material would be a daunting task requiring many man-years of work and in all likelihood unproductive.
>
> Peter Earnest, Chief, Media Relations

This was a most interesting denial by the CIA since we provided the agency with the exact Mount Ararat coordinates to pinpoint the satellite photos and radar-penetrating imagery. In addition, we gave them the name of a former high-level CIA official who was conducting a formal investigation of Noah's ark on Mount Ararat.

Back to the same pressing question—why won't U.S. intelligence services and military agencies release these materials if they don't have any impact on national security?

Although no one in the Department of Defense would publicly answer this question, retired USAF fighter pilot Captain Gregor Schwinghammer made this observation: "The government probably does have surveillance photos and satellite imagery of Noah's ark on Mount Ararat. They won't declassify or release these pictures, however, because it would disclose just how good our spy technology is and the fact that we have spied on a friendly nation—Turkey —while monitoring military activities in the former Soviet Union."

It seems puzzling that any agency of the U.S. government that happened to have information concerning the existence of Noah's ark would withhold even a sanitized version of that information. If there is some reason for doing so, then the government should at least be willing to provide a general explanation for such sensitivity.

From our understanding of government intelligence practices, there are three reasons for not acknowledging or providing this information to us: (1) the delicate nature of our intelligence-gathering methods, (2) the classified technical capabilities of our spy equipment, and (3) a possible agreement made with a foreign government. All three of these reasons, however, become less important with the passing of years.

INTELLIGENCE INVESTIGATION

Since the U.S. government will not cooperate with our search for Noah's ark on Mount Ararat and provide copies of clear photos of the ark that we know exist, we decided to conduct our own intelligence investigation. We acquired the satellite imagery of Mount Ararat from two foreign governments, France and the former Soviet Union. We also uncovered some significant military and CIA ark accounts—some of which were related to us on the condition that we not use the informants' real names.

One incident still classified as "top secret" that occurred around 1980 involved U.S. military personnel from various branches who made an on-the-ground survey of the ark on Mount Ararat. Their original objective was to check out reports of objects foreign to the terrain that might have military implications.

Members of this secret military expedition boarded the vessel, measured it, and took both black-and-white photographs and color slides. They did not remove any major pieces or harm the ship. Their report on the location and description of the ark is consistent with sightings described by Ed Davis and George Hagopian as well as the Shockey FIBER expedition sightings and photographs.

The following CIA-related account is quoted directly from a confidential Air Force colonel's memorandum dated August 4, 1978. The document relates to a couple who were stationed at Maxwell Air Force base but working for the CIA:

> Betty Plum [all names in this account have been changed], who worked in the CIA headquarters for Mr. Roland Rhodes from 1973 to 1974, saw a file in her office labeled *Noah's Ark, Eyes Only—Mr. Roland Rhodes*. Betty described Mr. Rhodes, chairman of the Visual Requirements Committee, as a Christian gentleman who probably would not be inclined to

suppress any concrete evidence of Noah's ark. However, both Betty and her husband, Leonard Plum (the CIA advisor to the Air War College), said that it wouldn't do any good to contact Mr. Rhodes about this file.

Betty at first thought the title "Noah's Ark" was a code name and stated that to Mr. Rhodes. He told her that it was not a code name and that she was not to open the file. Betty said that she "was a good girl and never looked in that file; it was the only file that I couldn't see." Betty has no reason to believe that the file contained a photo, but it could have. Furthermore, there is no reason to believe that the file contained direct evidence of the ark. It could have contained only sensitive information that was illegally obtained from another government.

In an earlier confidential memorandum dated June 24, 1975, the same Air Force colonel cites an Air Force account of U-2 photos of the ark:

About five or six years ago, Lieutenant Colonel Walter Hunter saw two photos of what allegedly was Noah's Ark. These photos (either 5″ × 7″ or 8″ × 11″) were in the possession of "two guys" who were standing in Base Operations at Beale Air Force Base in California.

An object in the photos which looked like a boat was enclosed in a glacier on an unrecognizable mountain. Lt. Col. Hunter did not know who took the photos or where they were taken but felt that they probably were taken from a U-2 aircraft. He thought they may have been taken in November but did not say why. He also recalled that the photos were oblique shots.

In further describing the photo(s), he said, "It looked like a glacier with an object buried in it—obviously underneath ice. The photo had red caliper marks on it which were used in determining its length of 450 feet. The first photo was a pan shot of a large glacier."

Lt. Col. Hunter described this experience in Base

Operations as a "passing thing," lasting no more than ten minutes while he filed his flight plan.

After reviewing these two memos we concluded that both the U.S. Air Force and the CIA had more than a passive interest in Noah's ark, despite their official denials and "know nothing" policy expressed to the public.

An even more interesting CIA-related report comes from retired USAF Colonel Walter T. Brown of Phoenix, Arizona. In 1974 he was summoned to CIA headquarters in Virginia and debriefed about Noah's ark by the special assistant to CIA Director William Colby. They wanted to know everything Colonel Brown could possibly tell them about Noah's ark. No piece of information was considered trivial. Colonel Brown suspects that as a result of the meeting, a later top-secret photography mission to Mount Ararat was conducted by the U.S. Air Force. Al Shappell, a military reconnaissance photographer (whose account was given in an earlier chapter), participated in the mission.

The next break in exposing military/CIA involvement in the reconnaissance of Noah's ark came in 1988 when inventor-satellite analyst George Stephen met Dr. Don Shockey of the FIBER Foundation expedition group. Stephen was developing top-secret high-tech equipment for a government contractor that would aid the military and the CIA in enhancing satellite imagery as well as improve the interpretation of imagery from radar-penetration satellites.

Although Stephen said he couldn't show Dr.

Shockey the imagery or the processing equipment, he did tell him that the military satellite imagery revealed a large, wooden, rectangular structure under the Ararat snow and ice. It was at an elevation of about 15,800 feet with an additional large portion of the structure at about the 14,900-foot level. According to the satellite data, the location was above the Ahora Gorge and not only matched the eyewitness sightings but was, in fact, where Dr. Ahmct Ali Arslan (1989) and the Shockey FIBER Foundation expedition had photographed the structure from helicopters in 1990.

Stephen did not go public with the information until the television show "Unsolved Mysteries" featured an investigative report on Noah's ark in 1992. On the program, Stephen confirmed what he knew but refused to be identified, allow his face to be shown, demonstrate the processing equipment, or show the imagery. Frankly, many thought the reason for the secrecy was that Stephen had no evidence for his claims. When asked to do the same interview for the television special related to this book, Stephen first agreed and then declined, telling us that his employers had forbidden him to proceed with the interview.

It was later learned from other sources, and confirmed by Stephen, that he had been severely reprimanded for doing the "Unsolved Mysteries" interview. His use of the military/CIA satellite imagery and the secret, high-tech equipment he was developing had not been authorized.

From several other sources we were able to confirm and learn more about the secret satellite imagery that Stephen was using and the capability of the processing-enhancing equipment. Both the Russians and the United States have microwave radar-penetrating satellites. However, these satellites do not penetrate very far below the surface—as will be discussed later when we examine the use of the Russian ALMAZ, radar-penetrating satellite imagery in the search for Noah's ark.

From what experts are willing to say off the record, Stephen has apparently made a significant breakthrough. His processing equipment will identify structures buried up to 600 feet under water, ice, or snow. The ark was 60 feet under the ice when he discovered it. In 1990, when Shockey's expedition flew over the site, the ark was 28 feet under the ice, with a portion partially exposed. The upper piece of the ark is reportedly 200 feet long.

Military and scientific analysts can determine the atomic elements composing an object using a combination of satellite infrared and radar imagery high-tech processing equipment. They can conclude whether it is organic or inorganic and whether or not it's a man-made object. The technicians involved performed a spectrographic atomic analysis where each element gives off a different level of energy. The analysts were able to determine quite easily that the structure under the ice on Ararat is made of wood.

Since the U.S. government won't cooperate in providing photographic, infrared, or radar-penetrating satellite imagery, we approached the French SPOT Corporation to obtain photographic imagery and we approached the Russians for radar-penetrating imagery as well as their spy satellite photos.

We already knew that the Russian imagery was very good from a 1984 interview with Dr. Bulent Atalay in the *Washington Post*. Dr. Atalay, the son of a Turkish general who served as a military attache to Washington, relates this story regarding the Russian surveillance of astronaut James Irwin:

> Turkish officers and their Russian counterparts have protocol meetings at the border to talk about the weather and small things. In this instance, they told the Russians that the American astronaut was going on the mountain for an expedition. There was nothing more to it. Nothing clandestine. The Russian officers laughed and they produced a photograph they had taken from a satellite and said, "There he is." They had identified him up there. So from time to time on the mountain I'd look up and wave to the satellites.

In our search for the exact location of the ark, we turned first to the Russian ALMAZ Radar Remote Sensing Satellite. Launched in 1987, the Russians claim "no other remote sensing satellite can offer around-the-clock, year-round coverage of the earth's surface—regardless of cloud cover or illumination conditions—with continuous, high-quality, high-resolution imagery."

In reviewing their portfolio of radar images we saw unusual land surfaces, winding rivers, and mineral deposits that were crystal-clear but geographically totally covered with dense jungle foliage. Even more impressive was seeing images of the trails of submerged U.S. submarines. We were entering the world of high-tech spy and commercial satellite applications.

This sounded exactly like what was needed to pinpoint the ark under the glacial ice of Ararat—particularly when Bill Wirin, the ALMAZ Radar Applications Director, told us that ALMAZ, orbiting at 300 kilometers above the earth, "will reveal something that's 45 feet in size. ALMAZ does this by differentiating between ice and snow and the geological features of the mountain. It can reveal sharp edges which might indicate the location of Noah's ark. An expert analyst viewing these images can detect unusual surfaces or structures beneath the ice and snow which give a hint that an object is there."

Since this was the best satellite spy radar imagery commercially available from any government, we gave the Russians the Mount Ararat summit coordinates and requested that the imagery be shot in September of 1992—generally the month of greatest ice meltback on Ararat. As often happens, however, something was confused in the English-to-Russian translation, and the Russians shot the wrong coordinates, completely missing Mount Ararat. "No problem," they said, and resubmitted the order to direct the satellite to shoot the correct coordinates.

Just when we were expecting to receive our ALMAZ imagery, the following message arrived from Moscow: "I am sorry to inform you that ALMAZ 1 de-orbited on October 17, 1992, at 07:28 Moscow time. It is difficult to predict when a successor radar satellite will be launched by the Russians. They did not capture Mount Ararat. I am very sorry this order was never completed."

We, too, became the victims of the "missing photos syndrome" due to an ironic twist of fate . . . or are the old legends true that God and the angels protect the ark from outsiders?

SPY PHOTOS

Next, the Russians offered us their best declassified spy photographs from their DD-5 Digital Satellite, which takes pictures from 280 kilometers above the earth. This is the first time any government has offered black-and-white photographs with the ability to capture images down to 2 meters in resolution.

"That's an object 6 feet in size," says Wirin, the Russians' representative, whose office is in Palm Springs, California. "The imagery is even better than this resolution. However, they 'dumbed' it up to 2 meters from what we were told was the ability to read license plates."

As a selling point for these spy photos, they showed us photographs taken of the U.S. Pentagon in which the type of cars could be identified in the parking lot, and employee picnic tables were noted in the inner quad area. We did not pursue this imagery of Ararat due to the expensive cost.

U.S. radar spy satellites can detect objects down to basketball-size from 1,000 kilometers. Photographic satellites operated by the United States are so good that David Hafemeister, a physicist at California Polytechnic University says, "We sometimes read the other guy's mail before he does." During the Iranian hostage crisis in 1980, [satellite] photos were of such high quality that specialists claimed they could identify individual Ayatollahs by the shape of their beards."[1]

SATELLITE IMAGERY

We finally turned to French SPOT satellite imagery to definitively locate and measure the size of Noah's ark on Mount Ararat.

"The SPOT satellites orbit at an altitude of over 500 hundred miles and acquire the most detailed imagery that's available commercially in the world," says Clark Nelson, SPOT Applications director, who probably was not aware of the Russians coming on the market with their DD-5 2-meter resolution imagery.

"We acquire both black-and-white and color imagery from every particular point on the earth at about 10:30 in the morning local time. The black-and-white has a 10-meter ground resolution—about half the size of a tennis court. The multi-spectral imagery has 20-meter resolution and includes infrared bands which are used for vegetation, productivity studies, and other geographic information. The imagery can be used to explore Mount Ararat and could possibly even find Noah's ark."

SPOT imagery has been used for a wide variety of applications. Some of the more exotic applications include overlay databases with the ability, for example, to pick out all of the hamburger fast-food or pizza restaurants in a large city. You could make your dining selections by satellite.

"SPOT satellite data was used quite a bit during the Persian Gulf War for a variety of things—particularly for flight briefings and target objectives before they flew," SPOT applications technician Sheila Pelczarski explains. "Also, SPOT was used to monitor the Kuwaiti oil fires set by Saddam Hussein. You could actually see the flames from the oil wells from over 500 miles above the earth. Military analysts monitored bombing damage successes against such targets as small bridge spans in the Gulf War."

The SPOT imagery containing the Mount Ararat data was retrieved in September of 1989, the same year Dr. Arslan clicked his photo of the ark after his near-fatal fall and the same year the Shockey FIBER Foundation took still photos of the location from a helicopter. We took the SPOT imagery to Mike Holman, a physicist, computer scientist, and satellite imagery analyst, to determine if the ark seen by the eyewitnesses could be confirmed by satellite. He reported,

> I put the SPOT Ararat imagery on computer, where I could detect objects down to 32 feet in size. I examined an "S"-shaped area above Ahora Gorge where photographs taken from a helicopter show a rectangular object extending out of the snow on a rocky ledge. Military satellite information says there is a wooden object at this location.
>
> This "S"-shaped crevasse is about 1,500 feet long and 90 feet wide. In the middle of this crevasse, I saw a defined object approximately 80 feet wide with 90 feet of the length extending out of the snow over a rocky ledge.
>
> It should be noted that the SPOT satellite image and the helicopter photo show the object aligned in the same direction over the ledge; they are the same size in

terms of width to length and they show that it is definitely not just a part of the surrounding terrain.

I'm not here to tell you this is Noah's ark or a broken portion of it. But, in my opinion, both the satellite imagery and the helicopter photo enhancement confirm that this object is not part of the natural terrain. According to military satellite information, it is an organic, fibrous object made of wood.

HELICOPTER PHOTOGRAPHS

Exactly what did the 1989 and 1990 Shockey-Baugh expeditions see and photograph from their helicopter? Carl Baugh, author and museum curator from Dallas, Texas, explains their aerial discovery.

In late August of 1990, our team did eleven separate helicopter expeditions around Mount Ararat. We were especially interested in the northeast slope facing Russia. As we flew at approximately 15,000 feet, and approximately 150 feet from the surface of the glacier, I personally saw a huge beam of laminated wood protruding out of the ice and snow.

The beam was variant in color and it had an indenture near the top with extensions at the top and the bottom. It was approximately 4 feet thick, and about 12 feet of it extended out of the ice and snow.

This was in the Abich Glacier area on the northeast face of Mount Ararat. The geographic location of this wood sighting matches precisely the area of our advance satellite information.

Our advanced satellite information identified this specific Abich Glacier area as the primary artifact location. Then, 800 to 1,200 feet below the primary location were secondary fragments of the same object under the ice and snow. It was in this 800-foot-square area that I saw the beam of laminated wood.

Our advance satellite information identified

spectographic lines of a wooden object under 60 feet of ice and snow . . . and at the time we flew there, it was under 28 feet of ice and snow.

The satellite information identified a crevice, a cliff that extended, and a wooden object under the ice and snow extending in a north and south direction.

This structure we photographed appears to have a bargelike shape to the end, a deck, a superstructure in the middle, and it continues back into the icebank.

It is of special interest to note that there appears to be a platform with an incline leading up to the deck of whatever this vessel might be. Eyewitness accounts in previous decades identified that configuration at the end of this bargelike vessel as a series of steps extending to a platform, all built into the vessel itself. This matches the specific identification in our photograph. It is our opinion that we have located portions of the ark of Noah.

We also took the Shockey-Baugh helicopter photograph to Mike Holman for computer enhancement and analysis to determine if Carl Baugh's conclusions were valid. Was it Noah's ark?

"As I enhanced the computer image of this object it became apparent that the object was rectangular in shape," says Holman, "and that the object extends over a ledge. I could clearly see the outline of the object with even an icicle hanging over what appears to be a catwalk area. It's not my job or expertise to confirm that it's Noah's ark, but in my opinion, this is clearly a man-made object."

CONCLUSIVE PROOF

To summarize the findings so far: When enhanced by computer and compared to SPOT satellite data, the

Shockey-Baugh helicopter photo gives strong proof that a large wooden ship is located near the Abich Glacier above Ahora Gorge—exactly where eyewitnesses have placed it. In other words, space technology has scientifically confirmed the existence and location of Noah's ark on Mount Ararat.

Furthermore, it's known that the ark is no longer intact but has broken into two to four pieces. The first piece has been identified by ark expeditioner and photo analyst Ray Anderson as being locked in the ice high up in the fishhook area of the eastern plateau of the Ararat summit. Neither SPOT nor military satellite data were able to confirm this Anderson sighting.

The Shockey-Baugh FIBER expeditions placed two pieces of the ark above the Ahora Gorge. The highest portion is at 15,800 feet while the lower portion is at 14,900 feet. Also, some artifacts appear to be scattered between the two sites. Both SPOT and military satellite data confirm these sites.

Dr. Don Shockey's group is so convinced of the evidence for their particular ark location that in 1993 they entered into a contract for a forty-nine-year lease on Mount Ararat with the assistance of Turkish President Turgut Ozal. The lease calls for a joint venture between Majesty Ventures (Shockey's group) and Kolan Tourism of Turkey to build resorts, hotels, ski lifts, helicopter sightseeing tours, and a clinic/hospital at the base of Ararat.

The Creation Evidences Museum, founded by Carl Baugh, and the FIBER Archaeological Foundation, which is headed by Dr. Shockey, will oversee the academic sponsorship of projects relating to research on Mount Ararat. The organization also plans to build a Noah's Ark Museum at the base of Mount Ararat.

Some experts believe an additional portion of the ark is located below the Shockey-Baugh site on the treacherous upper edge of the Ahora Gorge. They say the broken portion of the ark protrudes from the glacial ice and is clearly visible when the weather permits. Several years ago, it was here that the late astronaut James Irwin and a Dutch National Television crew took an amazing photograph.

Jan van den Bosch, executive producer for Dutch National Television, describes what they saw that day in 1986:

> We were in a plane with Jim Irwin flying around the Ararat mountain on an afternoon at the end of August. Our excitement was really great when we noticed that the snow cap had melted more than ever before.
>
> Nearly at the end of the trip, we saw an object high up in the Ahora Gorge that looked like the ark of Noah. In fact, it was a boat-shaped object, and so we went for a closer look. We did see an object sticking out of the snow cap.
>
> Our cameraman took all the pictures he could, but our time of flying was running out. We had to go back to our base. Some of us were really convinced this could well be the ark of Noah. It was as big as a soccer field, and part of it was sticking out of the mountain. So, on that very last expedition on that afternoon we think we saw Noah's ark.
>
> When the pictures were developed and Jim Irwin studied them, he said, "I want to be sure that this is really the ark of Noah and for that reason I want to do a ground expedition and do a better survey of the

object." That never happened because we weren't able to get permission from the Turkish authorities.

Colonel Irwin didn't want to announce any startling discovery until he could mount a successful ground expedition to film at the site. Unfortunately, Irwin died of a heart attack in 1991 before he could return to Mount Ararat.

His quest to explore space and his incredible accomplishments in that frontier will be remembered for many generations to come. Maybe Irwin's personal, spiritual quest to find Noah's ark has been fulfilled as well. Dutch National Television included the historic photo taken during the flight in a 1987 documentary on Noah's ark. Unfortunately, however, the vital SPOT satellite imagery that could possibly confirm or reject the Irwin photo and sighting was not available for those years.

The photograph has created some controversy among Irwin family members, including Irwin's widow, who says she had never seen the photograph before it appeared on television. The authors have learned that because of Irwin's top secret security clearance, he often had special knowledge about the ark from secret military files, and had even seen photographs of the ark taken during U.S. reconnaissance operations.

Although some of his expedition associates and family members may not have seen the photograph described here and shown in the photo section of this book, the authors received an unusual confirmation regarding the photograph in October of 1994.

According to Murray Fisher—a close friend of

Col. Irwin's as well as his publicist during a national tour to promote his book—Irwin and his mother visited the Fishers in Orlando, Florida, in 1989 or 1990. During the visit, Col. Irwin showed them a photograph that he believed was of Noah's ark.

"It was the exact same photo or one extremely similar to the one you have in your book's photo section," says Fisher. However, Mrs. Fisher recalls that Irwin said the photograph came from government files.

Could it possibly be that the controversial photograph was actually from U.S. government files? Is it possible that the story of Dutch National Television taking it on one of Irwin's expeditions was a cover for Dutch TV releasing it in their news documentary —a show that was never intended for viewing outside of Holland? The real answers surrounding the source of the photograph may never be known.

JUDGING THE EVIDENCE

Is the ark on Mount Ararat? All of the evidence is now before you. You've read about the numerous sightings throughout history, the eyewitness accounts and their analysis by Dr. Meier and a recognized polygraph expert, and read the findings of scientists and experts in a number of other fields. You've seen and read about the satellite and photographic imagery—some of which clearly reveals a great ship frozen under the ice and snows of Mount Ararat. Is it Noah's ark?

Inside the great ship, cages and pens have reportedly been examined by Napoleon's party and the atheistic English scientists. The interior and exterior of the ark have also been measured and photographed by the czar's expedition, the Turkish earthquake expedition—and possibly by U.S. scientific organizations unwilling to divulge their findings. Wood samples have been recovered by many and tested at labs around the world, and artifacts have been seen and examined by scores of people over the past 5,000 years.

Reports and photographs from pilots of many nations over several decades have been discussed, along with the accounts of people from all walks of life who have seen the photographs.

The evidence is overwhelming, and yet so much of it has mysteriously disappeared that it makes the existence of the ark suspect in some people's eyes.

Press reports, speeches, and ancient to modern secular and religious books on Noah's ark have been presented in these pages. What conclusions can we draw from all of this? We asked Dr. Tim LaHaye, coauthor of *The Ark on Ararat,* to give us his final thoughts on the matter:

> You can look at all of the stories that come out of that community of nations around Mount Ararat and they all seem to have one central thought that surfaces—the story of Noah. All of the evidence leads us to the fact that the great ship that has been sighted by so many on Mount Ararat *has* to be the ark of Noah.

THE ULTIMATE LEAP OF FAITH

The man called Noah demonstrated faith in epic proportions—a valuable lesson in courage to all of us today. Just think about what Noah went through during his long lifetime: He spent more than a hundred years building the ark—enduring the jeers and laughter of those who refused to believe that God was actually going to judge the world in a catastrophic way. Noah believed and clung to the truth during that entire time in spite of the fact that he had no hard evidence to show the critics—skeptics who, ironically, have a lot in common with the ones of today.

Noah spent 120 years faithfully constructing and stocking the enormous ark in spite of the fact that not one person outside his immediate family came to believe he was telling the truth. Not one person was converted or turned from his wicked ways. Some scholars even claim that Noah had another son who refused to believe and was lost. Just think of the courage Noah required to stand alone and tackle such an awesome project in the face of such incredible adversity.

When the door of the ark was sealed shut, his convictions were further tested. Noah and his family had to spend another seven days with a ship full of restless animals without any overt sign of the imminent destruction about to take place and silence the cruel laughter of the doomed people outside. He had nothing to cling to but his faith.

No one inside or outside the ark could conceive of the enormity of the calamity that was to come—not even Noah. This is more than just a story about a worldwide Flood and a mysterious 5,000-year-old shipwreck under the ice near the top of a mountain in Turkey. This is the story of an extraordinary man of conviction and faith who faced and overcame incredible odds to accomplish the seemingly impossible task God had given him.

Noah took what could be called the "ultimate leap of faith," and his courage is a message as powerful today as it was when his ship "docked" on a radically changed earth. Noah's life and his 5,000-year-old ship anchored in ice serve as a powerful testimony that God always keeps His word.

There's more to the incredible discovery of Noah's ark than the remains of the great ship on Mount Ararat. There's the personal discovery of those timeless lessons of courage and faith for us all.

Notes

[1]Stanley N. Wellborn and Robert A. Kittle, "Can Eyes and Ears in Space Monitor an Arms Deal?" *U.S. News and World Report*, November 25, 1985, p. 41.

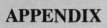

APPENDIX

THE SEARCH FOR
ARK ARTIFACTS/PHOTOS

One of the most puzzling aspects of the Noah's ark mystery is the amount of evidence that has disappeared over the last century.

"How there could be so much evidence and so little proof defies reason," say Dr. Tim LaHaye and Dr. John Morris in their book, *The Ark on Ararat.* "It almost seems that by design, the proof is kept from the hands of those who would make it public."

Everyone loses things from time to time, but the amount of "missing" ark evidence including photographs, artifacts, and wood samples has become phenomenal. For example, when ten people recall seeing the same photo of the ark, which then turns up missing, no one is too surprised, as this has occurred several times. However, when you multiply that one photo by about fifty people seeing it, you can't help but wonder what's happening in regard to photos of Noah's ark.

Where are the photographs taken by George Greene, Prince Nouri, and the explorers of the czar's expedition? What about the evidence from the Turkish geological mission? Where are the *Stars and Stripes* articles and pictures, or the articles about the deathbed confession of the British scientist? Where are the photos and other evidence seen at the Smithsonian Institution? What about the secret U.S. reconnaissance photos?

Does anyone have copies of these startling photographs or access to them? Will they ever surface again? The new evidence we have recently uncovered is astounding, but the mystery behind the missing evidence continues.

NOAH'S ARK–ARARAT EXPEDITION GROUPS

The following individuals and/or groups conduct research expeditions to Mount Ararat:

Chuck Aaron
27W430 North Avenue
West Chicago, IL 60185

Dr. Ahmet Ali Arslan
9430 Cloverdale Court
Burke, VA 22015

Carl Baugh
Creation Evidence Museum
P. O. Box 309
Glen Rose, TX 76043

Richard Bright
19506 Leaning Timbers Drive
Humble, TX 77346

Tom Hayek
43600 Cactus Valley Road
Hemet, CA 92544

John McIntosh
P. O. Box 1729
Crestline, CA 92325

Dr. John Morris
Institute for Creation Research
10946 Woodside Ave., North
Santee, CA 92071

Dr. Don Shockey
Albuquerque, NM

ALTERNATIVE ARK SITES

David Fasold
14781 Pomerado Road #234
Poway, CA 92064

Dr. Charles Willis
2490 W. Fir Street
Fresno, CA 93711

ARK RESEARCH CENTERS

David W. Balsiger
Writeway Research International
P. O. Box 1987
Loveland, CO 80539-1987

Bill Crouse
Christian Information Ministries
2050 N. Collins Blvd. #100
Richardson, TX 75080

BIBLIOGRAPHY

Bailey, Lloyd R. *Noah—The Person and the Story in History and Tradition.* Columbia, SC: University of South Carolina Press, 1989.

———. *Where Is Noah's Ark?* Nashville: Abingdon, 1978.

Balsiger, David W., and Charles E. Sellier, *In Search of Noah's Ark.* Los Angeles: Sun Classic Books, 1976.

Balsiger, David W., and Fernand Navarra. *Noah's Ark: I Touched It.* Plainfield: NJ: Logos International, 1974.

Baring-Gould, S. *Legends of the Patriarchs and Prophets.* New York: Hurst and Co., n.d.

Baugh, Carl E. *Panorama of Creation.* Oklahoma City, OK: Southwest Radio Church, 1989, rev. 1992.

Bell, Gertrude, L. *Amurath to Amurath.* 2d ed. London: Macmillan and Co., 1924.

Berlitz, Charles. *Doomsday 1999 A.D.* Garden City, NY: Doubleday and Co., 1981. See chapter 10.

———. *The Lost Ship of Noah.* New York: G. P. Putnam's Sons, 1987.

Bright, Richard C. *The Ark, A Reality?* Guilderland, NY: Ranger Associates, Inc., 1989.

Brown, Walter T. *In the Beginning.* Phoenix: Center for Scientific Creation, 1989.

Bryce, James. *Armenia and Mount Ararat.* London: Macmillan and Co., 1878.

———. *Transcaucasia and Ararat,* 4th ed. London: Macmillan, 1877.

Budge, E. A. Wallis. *The Babylonian Story of the Deluge.* London: 1920.

Bueler, William. *Mountains of the World: A Handbook for Climbers and Hikers.* Seattle: The Mountaineers, 1970. See pages 205–208.

Burdick, Clifford L. "Geological Reconnaissance of the Anatolia and the Ararat Area." In *The Geological, Glaciological and Botanical Reports Taken During the 1964 and 1966 Expeditions to Eastern Turkey and Mount Ararat.* Edited by Lawrence Hewitt. New York: The Archaeological Research Foundation, 1967.

Burney, Charles, and David Lang. *The Peoples of the Hills.* New York: Praeger, 1972. (History of Armenia)

Cassuto, Umberto. *A Commentary on Genesis.* Jerusalem: Magnes Press, 1961.

Chantre, Madame B. *A Travers L'Armenie Russe.* Paris: Librairie Hachetteet, c. 1893. (French)

Coan, Frederick B. *Yesterdays in Persia and Kurdistan.* Claremont, CA: Saunders Studio Press, 1939. See chapter XVL.

Crouse, Bill. *Ararat Report.* Richardson, TX: Christian Information Ministries, 1986–. (Newsletter)

Cummings, Violet M. *Has Anybody Really Seen Noah's Ark?* San Diego: Creation-Life Publishers, 1982.

———. *Noah's Ark: Fact or Fable?* San Diego: Creation-Science Research Center, 1972.

———. *Full Circle: From the Twin Peaks of Karada to Noah's Ark.* Published by the author, no date.

Dillow, Joseph C. *The Waters Above: Earth's Pre-Flood Vapor Canopy,* Chicago: Moody Press, 1981.

Dundes, Alan, ed. *The Flood Myth.* Los Angeles: University of California Press, 1988.

Fasold, David. *The Ark of Noah.* New York: Wynwood Press, 1988.

Filby, Frederick A. *The Flood Reconsidered.* Grand Rapids: Zondervan, 1970.

Freely, John. *The Companion Guide to Turkey.* Englewood Cliffs, NJ: Prentice-Hall, Inc., 1984. See chapter 26.

Gaster, Theodore. *Myth, Legend, and Custom in the Old Testament.* New York: Harper and Row, 1969.

Ham, Ken, Andrew Snelling, and Carl Wieland. *The Answer Book.* El Cajon, CA: Master Books, 1990.

Harthausen, Baron Von. *Transcaucasia.* London: Chapman and Hall, 1854.

Heidel, Alexander. *The Gilgamesh Epic and Old Testament Parallels.* Chicago: University of Chicago Press, 1949.

————. *The Babylonian Genesis.* Chicago: University of Chicago Press, 1942.

Humberd, R. I. *Noah's Ark.* 5th ed. Flora, IN: R. I. Humberd, n.d.

Irwin, James B. *More Than an Ark on Ararat.* Nashville: Broadman Press, 1985.

Kalisch, M. M. *Historical and Critical Commentary on the Old Testament: Genesis.* London: Longman, Brown, Green, Longmans, and Roberts, 1858.

Kang, C. H., and Ethel R. Nelson. *The Discovery of Genesis.* St. Louis: Concordia Publishing House, 1979.

Katz, Robert. *The Spoils of Ararat.* Boston: Houghton Mifflin Co., 1978.

Kolosimo, Peter. *Timeless Earth.* New York: Bantam Books, 1968. See pages 140–150.

LaHaye, Tim, and John Morris. *The Ark on Ararat*. Nashville: Thomas Nelson, Inc., 1976.

Lambert, W. G., and A. R. Millard. *Atra-hasis: The Babylonian Story of the Flood*. New York: Clarendon Press, 1969.

Lang, David. *Armenia: Cradle of Civilization*. London: Allen and Unwin, 1970.

Lewis, Jack P. *A Study of the Interpretation of Noah and the Flood in Jewish and Christian Literature*. Leiden, the Netherlands: E. J. Brill, 1968.

Lynch, H. F. B. *Armenia: Travels and Studies*. 2 vols. London: Longmans, Green and Co., 1901. See vol. 1, chapters XI-XIII.

McLean, G. S., Roger Oakland, and Larry McLean. *The Early Earth*. Eston, Canada: Full Gospel Bible Institute, 1987.

———. *The Evidence for Creation,* Eston, Canada: Full Gospel Bible Institute, 1989.

Meyer, Nathan M. *Noah's Ark Pitched and Parked*. Winona Lake, IN: BMH Books, 1977.

Montgomery, John Warwick. *The Quest for Noah's Ark*. 2d ed. Minneapolis: Dimension Books, 1974.

Morris, John D. *Adventure on Ararat*. San Diego: Institute for Creation Research, 1973.

———. *Noah's Ark and the Lost World*. El Cajon, CA: Master Books, 1988.

———. *Noah's Ark and the Ararat Adventure*. Colorado Springs: Master Books, 1994.

Morris, Henry, Jr. *The Genesis Record.* Grand Rapids: Baker Book House, 1976.

Navarra, Fernand, and David W. Balsiger. *Noah's Ark: I Touched It.* Plainfield, NJ: Logos International, 1974.

Navarra, Fernand. *The Forbidden Mountain.* London: Macdonald and Co., 1956.

Nelson, Bryon C. *The Deluge Story in Stone.* Grand Rapids: Baker Book House, 1931, 1968.

Noorbergen, Rene. *The Ark File.* London: New English Library, 1974.

Ousley, Sir W. *Travels in Persia 1810–1812.* Vol III. London: Rodwell and Bartin, 1823.

Parrot, Andre. *The Flood and Noah's Ark.* London: SCM Press, 1955.

Parrot, J. J. Friedrich. *Journey to Ararat.* London: Longman, Brown, Green, and Longmans, 1845.

Patton, Donald Wesley. *The Biblical Flood and the Ice Epoch.* Seattle: Pacific Meridian Publishing Co., 1966.

Petrosyan, Gavrill. *Armenia.* Moscow, Russia: Novosti Press Agency, 1981.

Piotrovsky, Boris. *The Ancient Civilization of Urartu.* New York: Cowles, 1969.

Porter, Sir Robert Ker. *Travels in Georgia, Persia, Armenia, Ancient Babylonia, during the years 1817, 1818, 1819, and 1820.* 2 vols. London: Longman, Hurst, Rees, Orme, and Brown, 1821–1822.

Rehwinkel, Alfred M. *The Flood*. St. Louis: Concordia Publishing House, 1951.

Rich, Claudius James. *Narrative of a Residence in Koordistan*. London: James Duncan, 1836.

Rutstein, Harry, and Joanne Kroll. *In the Footsteps of Marco Polo: A Twentieth Century Odyssey*. New York: Viking Press, 1980. See pages 50–65.

Segraves, Kelly L. *Search for Noah's Ark*. San Diego: Beta Books, 1975.

Shockey, Don. *The Painful Mountain*. Fresno, CA: Pioneer Publishing Co., 1986.

Smith, A. J., and G. F. Fletchall. *The Reported Discovery of Noah's Ark*. Rev. ed. Published by authors, 1944.

Smith, A. J. *On the Mountains of Ararat in Quest for Noah's Ark*. Apollo, PA: West, 1950.

Southwest Radio Church, ed. *In Search of Noah's Ark*. Oklahoma City: Southwest Radio Church, 1983.

Stark, Freya. *Riding the Tigris*. New York: Harcourt, Brace and Co., 1959.

Thomsen, Paul. *The Mystery of the Ark*. Brentwood, TN: Wolgemuth and Hyatt, 1991.

Wells, Carveth. *Kapoot: The Narrative of a Journey from Leningrad to Mount Ararat in Search of Noah's Ark*. New York: Robert M. McBride & Co., 1934.

Wenham, Gordon J. *Word Biblical Commentary:*

Genesis 1:15. Vol. 1. Waco, TX: Word Books, 1987.

Whitcomb, John C., Jr. *The World That Perished.* Rev. ed. Grand Rapids: Baker Books, 1988.

Whitcomb, John C., Jr., and Henry Morris. *The Genesis Flood.* Phillipsburg, NJ: Presbyterian and Reformed Publishing Co., 1961.

Wigram, W. A., and T. A. Edgar Wigram. *The Cradle of Mankind.* London: 1914.

Wright, Thomas, ed. *Early Travels in Palestine.* London: 1848.

Wyatt, Ron. *Noah's Ark Found.* Published by the author, 1980.

INDEX